Airframe Album
Second 2 Edition

The Hawker Sea Fury

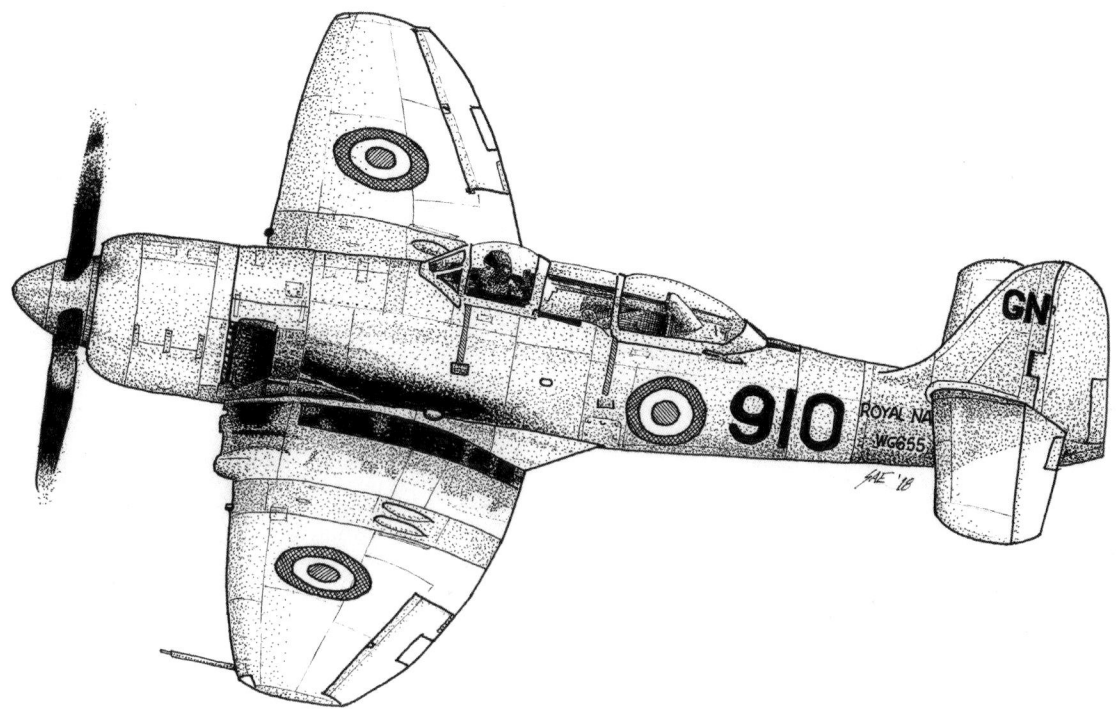

Sections

1. **Technical Description**
   Detailed coverage of the construction and equipment

2. **Evolution – Prototype, Production and Projected Variants**
   3D-isometerics illustrating differences between variants

3. **Camouflage & Markings**
   Colour side profiles, notes and photographs

4. **Kit Builds**
   Steve A. Evans builds the multi-medium T Mk 20 from AMG and the new Airfix FB Mk 11, both in 1/48th scale

5. **Survivors**
   An updated list of those airframes that survive today

   Appendices
   I   Kit List
   II Accessory List
   III Decal List
   IV Bibliography

Sea Fury Information

Airframe Album No.2 – Second Edition
The Hawker Sea Fury
A Detailed Guide to the Fleet Air Arm's Last Piston-engined Fighter
by Richard A. Franks

First published in 2018 by
Valiant Wings Publishing Ltd
8 West Grove, Bedford, MK40 4BT, UK
+44 (0)1234 273434
valiant-wings@btconnect.com
www.valiant-wings.co.uk

© Richard A. Franks 2013 & 2018
© Richard J. Caruana – Colour Profiles
© Jacek Jackiewicz – Isometric Lineart
© Seweryn Fleischer – Cover Art
© Steve A. Evans – Model Builds
© Crown Copyright used with the permission of Her Majesty's Stationary Office (HMSO)

The right of Richard A. Franks to be identified as the author of this work has been asserted in accordance with sections 77 and 78 of the Copyright Designs and Patents Act, 1988.

The 'Airframe Album' brand, along with the concept of the series, are the copyright of Richard A. Franks as defined by the Copyright Designs and Patents Act, 1988 and are used by Valiant Wings Publishing Ltd by agreement with the copyright holder.

All rights reserved. No part of this publication may be reproduced or transmitted in any form or by any means, electronic or mechanical, including photocopy, recording, or any other information storage and retrieval system, without permission in writing from the publishers.

ISBN: 978-0-9957773-3-0

Acknowledgements

The author would like to give a special word of thanks to the staff of the FAA Museum, RNAS Yeovilton and the Department of Records and Information Services, RAF Museum for their invaluable help with historical material and to Luc Boerman, Kev Darling, Jim Grant, Jamie Haggo, Nigel Perry, Przemyslaw Skulski & George Papadimitriou for supplying photographs. Special thanks must also go to Richard J. Caruana, Jacek Jackiewicz and Seweryn Fleischer for their superb artwork and to Steve A. Evans for his superb builds.

Note

There are many different ways of writing aircraft designations, however for consistency throughout this title we have used one style for the pre-1948 period (e.g. Mk X) and another for the post-1948 period when the FAA adopted the Arabic system of numbering (e.g. FB Mk 11) that is still in use today.

Cover

The cover artwork depicts Sea Fury FB.11s TG118 '108' and WG569 '135' of No.870 Squadron, Royal Canadian Navy, 1952. This artwork was specially commissioned for this title
© Seweryn Fleischer 2018.

Hawker Aircraft advertising 1946–47

below: Bristol advertising 1951

Sea Fury
Glossary

A&AEE	Aeroplane & Armament Experimental Establishment
ASI	Air Speed Indicator
CAG	Carrier Air Group
Capt.	Captain
Cdr	Commander
CO	Commanding Officer
CofG	Centre of Gravity
CPO	Chief Petty Officer
DTD	Director of Technical Development
FAA	Fleet Air Arm
F Mk	Fighter Mark
FB Mk	Fighter-bomber Mark
Flt	Flight
FRU	Fleet Requirements Unit
ft	Foot
GGS	Gyro Gun Sight
GP	General Purpose
HMS	His/Her Majesty's Ship
HMAS	His/Her Majesty's Australian Ship
HMCS	His/Her Majesty's Canadian Ship
HQ	Headquarters
IFF	Identification Friend or Foe
in	Inch
lb	Pound
Lt	Lieutenant
Mk	Mark
MLD	Marine Luchtvaartdienst (Royal Netherlands Naval Air Service)
Mod	Modification
mph	Miles Per Hour
MU	Maintenance Unit (RAF)
NAS	Naval Air Squadron
No.	Number
PO	Petty Officer
R3636	(Radio) Receiver Type 3636
RAE	Royal Aircraft Establishment
RAF	Royal Air Force
RAN	Royal Australian Navy
RCN	Royal Canadian Navy
RN	Royal Navy
RNAS	Royal Naval Air Station
RNAY	Royal Naval Aircraft Yard
RNethN	Royal Netherlands Navy
RNVR	Royal Navy Volunteer Reserve
RP	Rocket Projectile
SOC	Struck Off Charge
T Mk	Trainer Mark
TOC	Taken On Charge
T.R.	(Radio) Transmitter/Receiver
Sqn	Squadron
UK	United Kingdom

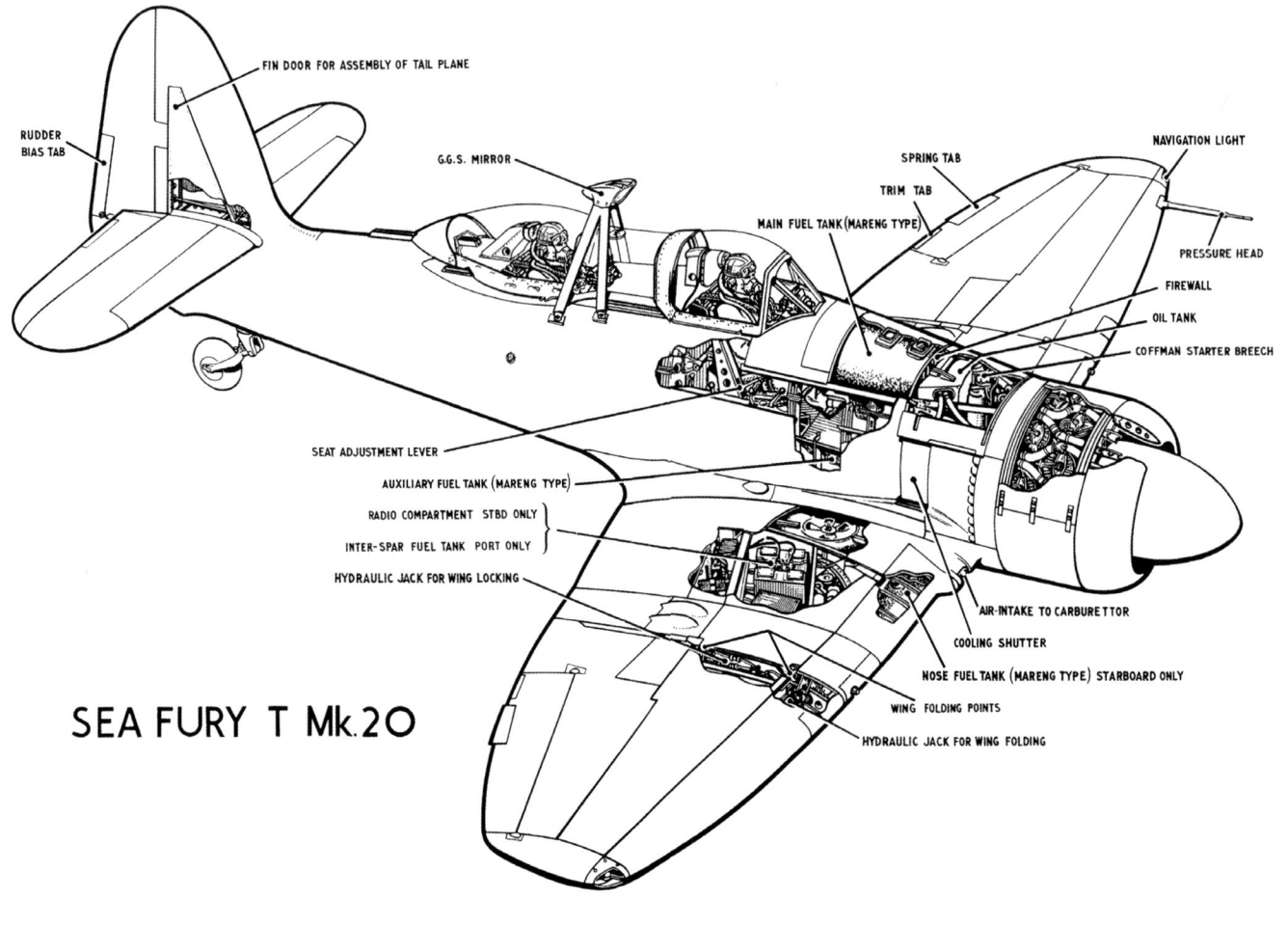

Cutaway drawing of the T.20 from the Flight Manual (©Crown Copyright)

Preface

The story of the Sea Fury goes back to 1942 when Sidney Camm, Chief Designer at Hawker, was developing a lightweight replacement for the Hawker Tempest. The overall design owes a lot to the Focke-Wulf Fw 190, as an A-3 version had landed in error at RAF Pembrey flown by Oblt. Arnim Faber on the 23rd June 1943, and it was the detailed study of this machine that led to the release of Specification F.6/42 for a high-performance fighter. Camm's design evolved from this and a new Specification (F.2/43) was later written around it. The new fighter basically reduced the span of the Tempest by removing the centre section and joining each mainplane directly under the fuselage. Named the Fury, two Rolls-Royce Griffon-powered examples was ordered to F.2/43, but only one (LA610) was ever built. This machine first flew on the 27th November 1944 with a Griffon 85 and a six-blade contra-rotating propeller but no further development of this type was undertaken. LA610 was then fitted with a Centaurus XV radial engine and from this came the development of the Sea Fury to meet Royal Navy Specification N.7/43 for a carrier-based interceptor. LA610 continued development work when, in 1946, it was fitted with a Sabre VII engine and Rotol five-blade propeller and in this form it became the fastest Hawker piston-engined fighter when it reached a speed of 485mph.

Development of the Sea Fury, as already mentioned, dates back to Specification N.7/43, however in early 1944 this requirement was revised as N.22/43 and it was in April 1944 when both the RAF (Fury) and RN (Sea Fury) were still interested in the design that contracts were placed for 200 F.2/43 Furies for the RAF and 200 N.22/43 Sea Furies for the RN. Development and production of the RAF Fury remained with Hawker, but the Sea Fury became the responsibility of Boulton-Paul at Wolverhampton. The first true Sea Fury was SR661, which first flew on the 21st February 1945 and although it had an arrestor hook it retained non-folding wings. This was followed by SR666, powered by a Centaurus XV engine it was fully navalised, including folding wings. SR661 undertook carrier deck suitability trials at A&AEE Boscombe Down from May 1945, but the development trials were still under way when Japan surrendered in August 1945. The end of the war saw the RAF no longer interested in a piston-engined fighter, wishing to develop jet aircraft, so with the cessation of hostilities the RAF cancelled its order for 200 Furies. The Royal Navy also reduced its order by half and with the loss of the RAF Fury order at Hawker all production of the remaining 100 Sea Furies reverted to Hawker, with Boulton-Paul having their ordered cancelled completely.

The first Sea Fury variant to see service was the Mk X, which first flew in September 1946 and was a fully equipped carrier fighter with folding wings. Deck trials began on HMS Victorious during the winter of 1946-1947 with TF898 and the Mk X was approved for carrier operations in the Spring of 1947. In 1948 the Royal Navy adopted the Arabic numbering system, so the Mk X was now designated the Mk 10. The Mk 10 equipped five squadrons and was followed by the fighter-bomber Mk 11 (FB Mk 11). Six hundred and fifteen FB Mk 11s were eventually delivered to the Royal Navy and the type remained in frontline service until replaced by the Sea Hawk in 1953. Development of a two-seat trainer version was not initially considered and it was not until Iraq placed an order for four such machines that RN interest was roused in the type. The first prototype machine was VB818, which was ordered in June 1948 against Specification N.19/47 written around it. In the end the RN took over the first two two-seaters from the Iraqi order and these were subsequently followed by production orders for 87 additional machines. On top of this three were supplied to Burma, two to Cuba and five for Pakistan (designated T Mk 61). In excess of 12 machines were

HMAS Sydney leaving Sasebo, Japan on the 27th January 1952 with Nos.805, 808 & 817 Squadrons Sea Furies on deck – identified are VW623/108-K, WE677/139-K, WE673/135-K and VX761/131-K
(©via J. Grant)

A very atmospheric in-flight image of a Sea Fury in the initial scheme, sadly the identity of this machine is unknown *(©Author's collection via K. Darling)*

later modified for target-towing duties (TT Mk 20) and operated for the Luftwaffe by *Deutsche Luftfahrt Beratungsdienst*. It was these machines that were to see the longest service, remaining in use until retired in 1970.

Abroad

The Sea Fury was also to see service abroad, in Australian, Canada and The Netherlands, as well as land-based only by Pakistan, Burma, Iraq, West Germany and in clandestine operations in Cuba – the type also saw very limited use by Egypt and Morocco.

The Royal Australian Navy (RAN) was allocated Sea Furies diverted from RN contracts and these were assigned to Nos.805, 808 and 850 Squadrons. The first squadron to have the type was No.805 at Eglinton on the 28th August 1948, where they trained before going on board HMAS Sydney on the 8th February 1949 and arriving in Australia on the 25th May 1946. The squadron served in Korea and finally disbanded on the 26th March 1958. No.808 formed at St. Merryn on the 25th April 1950 and went on HMAS Sydney on the 29th August. It too saw action in Korea, plus service on HMAS Vengeance before disbanding on the 5th October 1954. No.850 formed at Nowra on the 12th January 1953 before serving on HMAS Vengeance and Sydney plus deployments to Japan and Hong Kong before it disbanded on the 3rd August 1954. The only other RAN units to operate the Sea Fury include No.723 Squadron, which offered aircraft for communications, fleet requirements, air-sea rescue and training and existed from 7th April 1952 to 25th October 1956. No.725 also undertook the same work with the Sea Fury from 13th January 1958 before relinquishing the type in May 1959. The final unit to use the type for these roles was No.724, which did so until as late as October 1962, although the Sea Fury was officially retired by the RAN in March 1958.

Dutch Sea Furies in the production hall at Langley *(©via L. Boerman)*

The Royal Canadian Navy (RCN) took the Sea Fury on charge in Canada at Rockcliffe on the 23rd June 1948 and the squadrons that used the type were Nos.803 and 883. No.803 initially received (on loan) thirteen F Mk Xs at Eglinton in Northern Ireland in August 1947 to train the air- and ground-crews prior to going on board HMCS Warrior, while No.883 Squadron received their machines at their base at Datrmouth at some time after September 1948. RCN FB Mk 11 Sea Furies were ferried to Canada on HMCS Magnificent, having first arrived at Eglinton before being put aboard the carrier for shipment to Canada, where they arrived in June. Nos 803 and 883 Squadrons were renumbered 870 and 871 on the 1st May 1951, then in 1952 the RCN adopted the USN system of squadron identification so No.870 and 871 Squadrons were redesignated VF-870 and VF-871, the 'V' standing for fixed-wing and 'F' for fighter. Neither RCN units took an active part in the Korean War and VF-870 disbanded on the 30th March 1954, with VF-871 following suit in August 1956. The Sea Fury was also operated by the RCN fixed-wing training unit, VT-40, and the last flight of an RCN Sea Fury was WG565 being ferried into storage in Alberta on the 3rd April 1957. In all, the RCN operated sixty-four Sea Furies.

The Netherlands ordered the Sea Fury F Mk 50, which was an export version of the F Mk X fitted with different radio and other equipment specified by the Dutch Military. The initial order of ten machines, placed on the 21st October 1946, were coded 10-1 to 10-10 and were acquired for operation by the *Marine Luchtvaartdienst* (MLD – Royal Netherlands Naval Air Services). Delivered from Hawker during April and May 1948 they were initially operated by the *Opleiding Gevechtsvlieger* (OGV or Fighter Pilots School), although later, and briefly, they were also used by No.4 Squadron. In the interim the remaining nine aircraft (10-1 had crashed) were upgraded as fighter-bombers and as such were redesignated the FB Mk 60 and between May and June 1950 a further twelve were diverted from an RN order and delivered directly from Hawker (coded 10-11 to 10-22). Licence production of the type was agreed with the Fokker Company and this resulted in a further twenty-five FB Mk 60s (6-23 to 6-47), although 6-23 and 6-24 may have been made from sets of parts supplied by Hawker? The first unit to operate the type was No.860, which formed at Valkenburg on the 15th July 1950. The type was re-marked in the 1950s with the move from the 10- and 6-prefixed codes being changed to 'J', the reason being that J stood for *Jachtvliegtuig* (fighter). No.860 Squadron disbanded on the 15th June 1956, and all their aircraft were passed to No.4 Squadron for training purposes until they too were retired in 1957.

Pakistan declared independence from the UK on the 14th August 1947 and the new nation received its first Fury in March 1949, this being the F.2/43 prototype NX802. This was followed by three separate orders, 50 in 1950 (designated the FB Mk 60), 24 in 1951 and 13

This shot of the deck of HMS Theseus shows the Sea Furies of No.898 Squadron during the Korea War. Of note is the UN identification stripes on these machines, comprising black/white/black stripes, instead of the usual black/white/black/white/black (©Crown Copyright/FAA)

in 1951-52, plus a further five more ex-RN examples in 1953-54. Trainers were also acquired, with four new T Mk 61s being supplied by Hawker and one being taken from an Iraqi contract. The type replaced the Tempest in PAF service and was operated by Nos.5 and 9 Squadrons from 1950 and No.14 Squadron from 1951. The type remained in service with Nos.5 & 9 Squadrons until replaced by the F-86 in 1955, and with No.14 Squadron in 1960 by the F-104

Iraq placed an order for 30 single-seat fighters and four two-seat trainers on the 4th December 1946. It should be noted that until this point no two-seat versions existed and no RN interest in the type was forthcoming, so once such a machine was requested by Iraq it stimulated RN interest and the first four two-seaters was actually taken over by the Royal Navy. In the end Iraq

The MLD machine 6•34 coming in to land at Luqa, Malta GC. Note the flaps are down but the hook is up and the pilot has raised his seat to the maximum to give him a view over the nose (©Author's collection)

F Mk X, TF946 in the initial scheme applied to the type. Going by the hangar in the background we would guess this is during its time with No.767 Sqn at Henstridge – Jan-May 1952 *(©Author's collection via K. Darling)*

MLD operated FB Mk 11 6•16 in flight

(©Author's collection via K. Darling)

VX672, again either with No.736 or 738 Squadron at Culdrose, is seen here fitted with RATOG under the fuselage

(©Author's collection via K. Darling)

VX653 served with Nos. 736, 738 and 811 Squadrons ending up with Airwork on FRU duties as seen here. It later went as gate guard at Lossiemouth and is extant today as G-BUCM

(©Author's collection via K. Darling)

FB Mk 11 WG603 was operated by No.738 Squadron from RNAS Culdrose in 1951-2. It made a wheels-up landing at Benson in May 1955 and was SOC the next month as a result
(©Author's collection via K. Darling)

VX652 was operated by No.738 Squadron and is seen here at their Culdrose base. The aircraft is obviously involved in gunnery training as it is carrying R.P.s with 60lb concrete heads (©Author's collection via K. Darling)

A line-up of FB Mk 11s operated by No.825 Squadron, seen at Kuala Lumpur in 1954 (©British Official/Authors Collection)

Two Sea Fury FB Mk 11s from Nos.805 and 809 Squadrons with a pilot conferring with two RAAF personnel are seen at Pearce in February 1952 (©via J. Grant)

RAN-operated WZ645 operated off HMAS Sydney with No.805 Squadron but is seen here when based at Nowra with the squadron in the mid-1950s *(©Author's collection via K. Darling)*

received only two two-seaters, as the other one went to Pakistan. The thirty single-seat fighters were delivered during 1947-48, with all the naval equipment such as tail hooks and catapult attachments removed. The type also had no wing-fold, and it was known under various designations, such as the FB Mk 60, the ISS (Iraqi Single Seater) and the Hawker Baghdad or Baghdad Fury. Another fifteen new-built aircraft were ordered on the 21st July 1951, and these were followed, on the 7th March 1953, by a further ten refurbished ex-RN FB Mk 11s and three T Mk 20s. In Iraq the Furies equipped Nos.1, 4 and 7 Squadrons of the Iraqi Air Force, and it is thought that they may have been used against the Kurds in Northern Iraq. The type remained in frontline service until the early 1960s, when it was withdrawn and replaced by the Hawker Hunter.

Burma placed an order for eighteen FB Mk 11s and three T Mk 20s in 1957-58 and these were all ex-RN aircraft that had been purchased back by Hawker, refurbished and delivered to Burma in 1958. At some stage three of the FB Mk 11s were fitted with target-towing hooks but no winches, and were designated TT Mk 11

Production

- Fury Prototype – LA610, to Spec. F.2/43, originally ordered as a Tempest Mk II, later fitted/tested Griffon, Centaurus XV and Sabre engines
- Fury Prototypes – NX798 & NX802, ordered 22/03/43 to Spec. F.2/43
- Fury Prototypes – VP207 & VP213, ordered 27/02/46 to Spec. F.2/43
- Sea Fury Prototypes – SR661 & SR666, ordered 22/02/44 to Spec. N.22/43
- Sea Fury F MK X – VB857, ordered 22/03/44 to Spec. N.22/43
- Sea Fury Mk X (Later Mk 10) – 300 ordered from Boulton-Paul 28/04/44 to Spec. N.22/43 – Serial Numbers TF212 to 248, TF263 to 305, TF320 to 367, TF383 to 413, TF427 to 459, TF472 to 515, TF530 to 576 & TF591 to 607 – All cancelled
- Fury Mk I (Sabre-powered) – 200 ordered 28/04/44 from Hawker to Spec. F.2/43 – Serial Numbers TF620-667, TF681 to 720, TF735 to 768, TF781 to 793, TF798 to 824 & TF839 to 876 – All cancelled
- Sea Fury F Mk X (later F Mk 10)- 50 ordered 28/08/44 from Hawker to Spec. N.22/43 – Serial Numbers TF895 to 928 & TF940 to 955
- Sea Fury FB Mk 11 – 150 ordered 28-08044 from Hawker to Spec. N.22.43 – Serial Numbers TF956 to 973, TF985 to 999, TG113 to 160, TG176 to 202 and TG217 to 258 – 50 built, all from TG130 cancelled
- Sea Fury FB Mk 11 – 35 ordered 23/10/46 – Serial Numbers VR918 to 952
- Sea Fury FB Mk 11 – 20 ordered 19/12/47 – Serial Numbers VW224 to 243
- Sea Fury FB Mk 11 – 128 ordered 19/12/47 – Serial Numbers VW541 to 590, VW621 to 670 and VW691 to 718
- Sea Fury FB Mk 11 – 136 ordered 5/07/48 – Serial Numbers VX608 to 643, VX650 to 699, VX707 to 731 & VX740 to 764
- Sea Fury FB Mk 11 – 97 ordered 15/09/49 – Serial Numbers WE673 to 694, WE708 and 742 & WE767 to 806
- Sea Fury FB Mk 11 – 24 ordered 5/07/48 – Serial Numbers WF590 to 595 & WF610 to 627
- Sea Fury FB Mk 11 – 37 ordered 18/08/50 – Serial Numbers WG564 to 575, WG590 to 604 & WG621 to 630
- Sea Fury FB Mk 11 – 26 ordered 18/08/50 – Serial Numbers WH581 to 594 & WH612 to 623
- Sea Fury FB Mk 11 – 54 ordered 18/08/50 – Serial Numbers WJ221 to 248 & WJ276 to 301
- Sea Fury FB Mk 11 – 24 ordered 02/01/51 – Serial Numbers WM472 to 495
- Sea Fury FB Mk 11 – 14 ordered 06/02/51 – Serial Numbers WN474 to 487
- Sea Fury FB Mk 11 – 30 ordered 16/10/51 – Serial Numbers WZ627 to 656
- Sea Fury FB Mk 50 – 10 built for The Netherlands (similar to F Mk X) plus another 22 (similar to FB Mk 11)
- Sea Fury F Mk 60 – 92 built (some state 93), similar to FB Mk 11 for Pakistan Navy
- Sea Fury T 20 prototype – Ordered 23/06/48 to Spec. N.19/47, serial number VB818
- Sea Fury T Mk 20 – 27 ordered 27/08/47 – Serial Numbers VW750 to 776 but these numbers not used, built as VX280 to 292 & VX297 to 310
- Sea Fury T Mk 20 – 27 ordered 15/04/48 – Serial Numbers VX280 to 292 & VX297 to 310
- Sea Fury T Mk 20 – 21 ordered 21/08/48 – Serial Numbers VZ345 to 355 & VZ363 to 372
- Sea Fury T Mk 20 – 7 ordered 15/09/49 – Serial Numbers WE820 to 826
- Sea Fury T Mk 20 – 5 ordered 18/08/50 – Serial Numbers WG652 to 656
- Sea Fury T Mk 20 – 3 for Burma, 2 for Cuba
- Sea Fury T Mk 61 – 5 built for Pakistan, similar to T Mk 20
- Sea Fury TT Mk 20 – 12+ modified T Mk 20s for target-towing for Deutsche Luftfahrt Beratungsdienst

Sea Fury
Introduction

or FB Mk 11(TT). All of the Sea Furies were used for internal security and counter-insurgency operations before being replaced by the Lockheed Shooting Star in 1968.

Cuba's Batista government ordered fifteen FB Mk 11s and two T Mk 20s in 1957, with them arriving by sea in 1958. It is thought some may have been re-assembled before Fidel Castro overthrew the Batista government and seized power that year. The new Cuban Air Force had twelve operational Sea Furies listed by November 1959, although various purges by the new government meant by 1960 there were only six qualified pilots left. When the CIA-backed Democratic Revolutionary Front supported by the paramilitary group Brigade 2506 attempted to invade Cuba on the 17th April 1961 the Sea Furies flew operations over the landing point (*Playa Girón* – Bay of Pigs), shooting down B-26 Invaders and an A-4 Skyhawk, although two machines were destroyed on the ground and one aircraft crashed into the bay (flown by Carlos Ulloa Arauz) leaving just three operational. With the

Being taken below deck, this FB Mk 11 of No.804 Squadron on HMS Glory has Korea War recognition stripes and is fitted with drop tanks plus rocket rails (*©British Official/FAA*)

sinking of the supply ship Houston and a lack of support from the US forces off-shore, the invasion failed and soon after this Castro received MiG-15s from Russia which became Cuba's new frontline fighters, resulting in all remaining Sea Furies being grounded and withdrawn. Today a restored Sea Fury can be seen as part of the small Museum Girón commemorating those lost in the invasion.

Egypt received the Fury prototype F.2/43 NX798, which was refurbished by Hawker and given a new Centaurus XVIII engine. Hawkers took it to Egypt in April-May 1948 where it was shown to the Egyptian Air Force who placed an order for twelve aircraft. Delivery of these aircraft was delayed due to the British arms embargo in place during the 1948 Arab-Israeli war, so the first two Sea Furies to reach Egypt came from Iraq. It was not until 1950-51 that the twelve aircraft ordered from Hawker were finally delivered. Little is known of their subsequent operational service, although it is reported that one was destroyed on the ground during the Suez Crisis in 1956. It is unlikely they remained in use for long, as Meteor and Vampire jet fighters were supplied in late 1949 and by 1955 Egypt was acquiring all its military aircraft from Russia.

Morocco never actually ordered the Fury directly, instead it received four aircraft as gifts from Iraq. The first two arrived on the 4th February 1961, followed by the other two in late 1961. Little is known of their subsequent service use and it is believed at least one still remains in the country?

West Germany was the last country to order the Sea Fury because by late 1950s the new Luftwaffe needed target-towing aircraft, and asked the private firm *Deutsche Luftfahrt Beratungsdeinst*, to provide this service. As a result ten aircraft were ordered in 1958 from Hawker and these were all delivered during 1960. A further six more were ordered in 1962 and a single machine was also acquired from The Netherlands. Designated the TT Mk 20, with a target-towing winch fitted on the starboard mid-fuselage side and operated by the crew member in the back seat, they served throughout the 1960s, and were only finally retired in 1970.

Specification

Engine	• Fury I – Napier Sabre VII
	• Fury – Bristol Centaurus XV air-cooled radial
	• Sea Fury F Mk X and FB Mk 11 – Bristol Centaurus XVIII air-cooled radial
Span	• 38ft 4 3/4in, [folded] 18ft 2in
Wing Area	• 279.96sq ft
Length	• Fury prototype NX798 (Centaurus XII) – 34ft 6in
	• Fury LA610 (Griffon) – 35ft 6in
	• Fury LA610 (Sabre) & Fury I (Sabre) – 34ft 8in
	• Sea Fury F Mk X prototype SR666 (Centaurus XV) – 34ft 7in
	• Sea Fury F Mk X, FB Mk 11 & T Mk 20 – 34ft 7in
Height, on ground	• Five-blade propeller, one blade vertically downwards – 13ft 7in
	• Five-blade propeller, one blade vertically upwards – 13ft 10.5in
All Up Weight	• Fury NX798 – 11,930lb
	• Fury I (Sabre) – 12,120lb
	• Fury (Centaurus VXV) – 11,675lb
	• Sea Fury F Mk X – 12,030lb
	• Sea Fury FB Mk 11 – 12,350lb
	• Sea Fury T Mk 20 – 11,930lb
Take Off	• Maximum weight (FB Mk 11) – 14,650lb
Maximum Speed	• Fury I – 422mph @ Sea Level, 480mph @ 20,000ft, 446mph @30,000ft
	• Fury (Centaurus XV) – 375mph @ Sea Level, 454mph @ 25,000ft, 448mph @ 30,000ft
	• Sea Fury F Mk X – 367mph @ Sea Level, 440mph @ 21,000ft, 433mph @30,000ft
	• Sea Fury FB Mk 11 – 380mph @ Sea Level, 460mph @ 18,000ft, 415mph @ 30,000ft
	• Sea Fury T Mk 20 – 445mph @ 18,000ft
Service Ceiling	• Sea Fury F Mk X – 36,180ft
	• Sea Fury FB Mk 11 – 37,800ft
	• Sea Fury T Mk 20 – 35,600ft
Armament	• Sea Fury F Mk X & FB Mk 11 – 4x 20mm Hispano Mk 5* cannon with 580 rpg
	• Sea Fury T Mk 20 – 2x 20mm Hispano Mk 5* cannon with 580 rpg
Ordnance	• Sea Fury FB Mk 11 – Max of 2,000lb of bombs or twelve 3in. rocket projectiles (only four [two per side] carried if 180lb warheads fitted). Could also carry reserve (drop) fuel or Napalm tanks (one under each wing)

Note: Please note that as the Sea Fury was built and tested using Imperial measurements we have refrained from offering Metric conversions in the above data

Technical Description

What follows is an extensive selection of images and diagrams that will help you understand the physical nature of the Hawker Sea Fury.

Group 1 – Fuselage
1 – Cockpit Interior
2 – Canopy
3 – Main & Aft Fuselage
4 – Fuel, Hydraulic, Oil & Oxygen systems

Group 2 – Undercarriage
1 – Main
2 – Tailwheel & Arrestor hook
3 – Pneumatic system

Group 3 – Tail
1 – Tailplanes
2 – Vertical Fin & Rudder

Group 4 – Wings
1 – Wings
2 – Undercarriage Bays

Group 5 – Engine
1 – Engine, Cowling & Propeller

Group 6 – Weaponry
1 – Armament
2 – Ordnance
3 – Sighting
4 – Drop tanks

Group 7 – Electrical
1 – Radio
2 – Miscellaneous

Group 8 – Miscellaneous
1 – Access Panels
2 – Equipment

All photos © the author unless otherwise noted

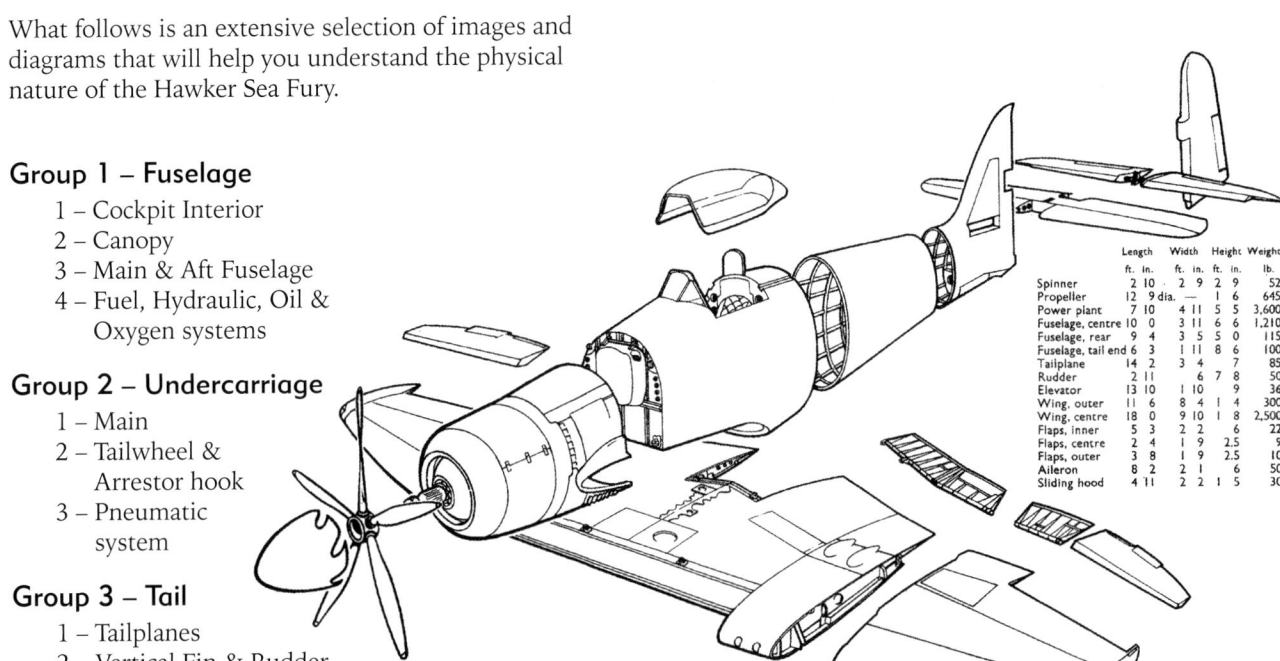

	Length		Width		Height		Weight
	ft.	in.	ft.	in.	ft.	in.	lb.
Spinner	2	10	2	9	2	9	52
Propeller	12	9 dia.	—		1	6	645
Power plant	7	10	4	11	5	5	3,600
Fuselage, centre	10	0	3	11	6	6	1,210
Fuselage, rear	9	4	3	5	5	0	115
Fuselage, tail end	6	3	1	11	8	6	100
Tailplane	14	2	3	4		7	85
Rudder	2	11		6	7	8	50
Elevator	13	10	1	10		9	36
Wing, outer	11	6	8	4	1	4	300
Wing, centre	18	0	9	10	1	8	2,500
Flaps, inner	5	3	2	2			22
Flaps, centre	2	4	1	9		2.5	9
Flaps, outer	3	8	1	9		2.5	10
Aileron	8	2	2	1		6	50
Sliding hood	4	11	2	2	1	5	30

Major components diagram from the FB Mk 11 manual (©Crown Copyright)

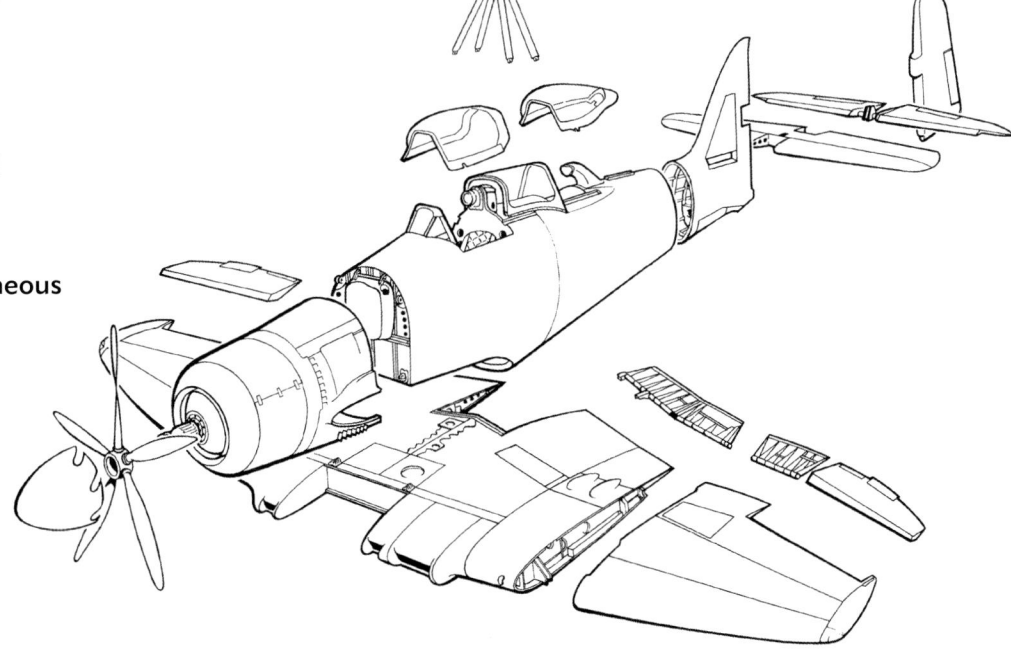

Major components diagram from the T Mk 20 manual (©Crown Copyright)

Group 1 – Side 1
Fuselage
14 Cockpit Interior

This is the main diagram of the instrument panel etc. from the Mk 10 & 11 Pilot's Notes
(©Crown Copyright)

Key
1. Undercarriage position indicator
2. Throttle and RPM controls friction knob
3. RI compass indicator
4. Ignition switches
5. Undercarriage position indicator switch
6. Supercharger warning light
7. Contacting altimeter switch
8. Flaps position indicator
9. RPM control lever
10. Contacting altimeter
11. Throttle lever
12. Gyro gunsight selector dimmer control
13. Ventilating louvre
14. Undercarriage warning light
15. GGS master switch
16. GGS skid indicator
17. Cine camera master switch
18. Cloudy/sunny selector switch
19. Gyro gunsight
20. Emergency lamp
21. Cockpit lamps dimmer switch
22. Guns/RP selector switch
23. GGS skid indicator
24. Cockpit lamps master switch
25. Emergency lamp switch
26. Windscreen de-icing pump
27. U/V lamps dimmer switch
28. Generator failure warning light

29. Sliding canopy control
30. Engine cooling shutters control
31. Oxygen regulator
32. Boost gauge
33. Oil temperature gauge
34. Canopy jettison control
35. Engine speed indicator
36. Triple pressure gauge
37. Cylinder temperature gauge
38. Oil pressure gauge
39. Spare bulbs for GGS
40. P.11 compass
41. Parking brake lever
42. Press-to-speak switch
43. Firing button
44. Starter re-indexing control

This photograph shows the instrument panel etc. of the airworthy FB Mk 11 operated by the RNHF – you can see where the GGS has been replaced with modern radio equipment
(©Crown Copyright via J. Haggo)

Group 1 – Side 2
Fuselage
Cockpit Interior

Port side console from the Mk 10 & 11 Pilot's Notes
(©Crown Copyright)

Key

45. IFF control unit
46. IFF selector unit
47. RATOG jettison push button
48. Flare door warning light
49. Flare doors operating switch
50. Camera container master switch
51. Fusing switch
52. Pairs/salvo switch
53. RP/bombs selector switch
54. Canopy locking control
55. Port/starboard selector switches
56. Single/salvo switch
57. S.C. jettison push button
58. RATOG master switch
59. Supercharger gear change control
60. Cockpit (port) lamps dimmer switch
61. Fuel cut-off control
62. RATOG firing button
63. Flaps selector lever
64. Arrestor hook indicator light
65. Arrestor hook training switch
66. Arrestor hook control
67. Undercarriage control lever safety catch
68. Sanitary bottle
69. Undercarriage control lever
70. Elevator trimming handwheel
71. Rudder trimming handwheel
72. Hydraulic hand pump
73 Bomb rack jettison control

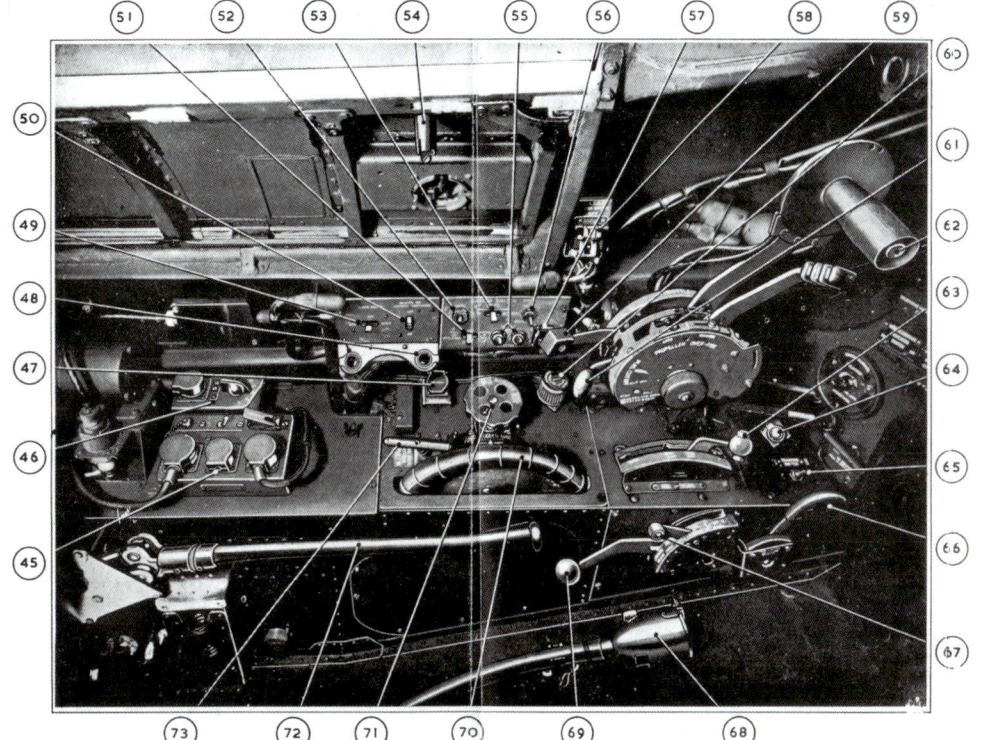

The top LH corner of the instrument panel and side console of the RNHF FB Mk 11 *(@Crown Copyright via J. Haggo)*

A close-up of the top RH corner of the instrument panel and side console in the RNHF FB Mk 11 *(©Crown Copyright via J. Haggo)*

Group 1 – Side 3
Fuselage
16 Cockpit Interior

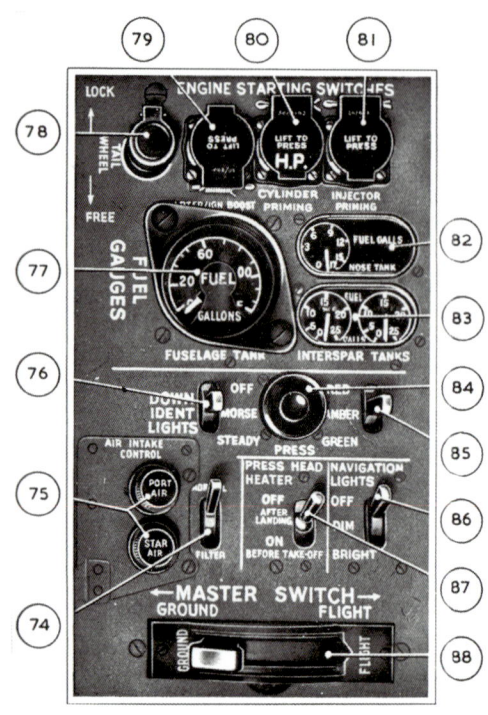

Panel on the Starboard Shelf from the Mk 10 & 11 Pilot's Notes
(©Crown Copyright)

Key
74. Air intake filter control
75. Air intake filter control warning lights
76. Downward identification lights signalling switch
77. Main tank fuel gauge
78. Fuel level warning light
79. Cartridge starter and booster-coil push button
80. Cylinder priming push button
81. Injector priming push button
82. Nose tank fuel gauge
83. Inter-spar tanks fuel gauge
84. Downward identification lights signalling push button
85. Downward identification lights colour selector switch
86. Navigation lights switch
87. Pressure-head heater switch
88. Ground/flight switch

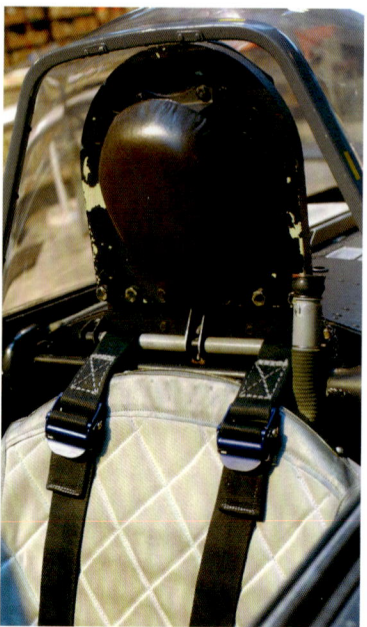

A useful image showing the head armour plate, headrest and upper seat harness attachment points on the FB Mk 11 seat (©Crown Copyright via J. Haggo)

Starboard side console from the Mk 10 & 11 Pilot's Notes
(©Crown Copyright)

Key
89. Locking pin for emergency hydraulic selector lever
90. Flaps emergency selector lever
91. Undercarriage emergency selector lever
92. Main fuel cock
93. Drop tank jettison control
94. Drop tank selector lever
95. 'Window' launcher override control unit
96. Mixer box
97. 'Window' launcher speed control unit
98. Safety harness locking control
99. VHF control unit
100. ZBX control unit
101. IFF auxiliary control unit
102. Watch holder
103. Clock holder
104. Oil dilution circuit breaker
105. Fuel pump circuit breaker
106. Fuel pump ammeter test push button
107. Fuel pump ammeter test socket
108. Ignition booster-coil test push button
109. Air intake heat control
110. Wing folding control lever
111. Wing folding control safety lever
112. Oxygen pipe
113. Map case
114. Chartboard container
115. See Panel on Starboard Shelf diagram
116. Tailwheel locking control
117. Cockpit heating control
118. Signal pistol stowage
119. Fuel tank air pressure gauge

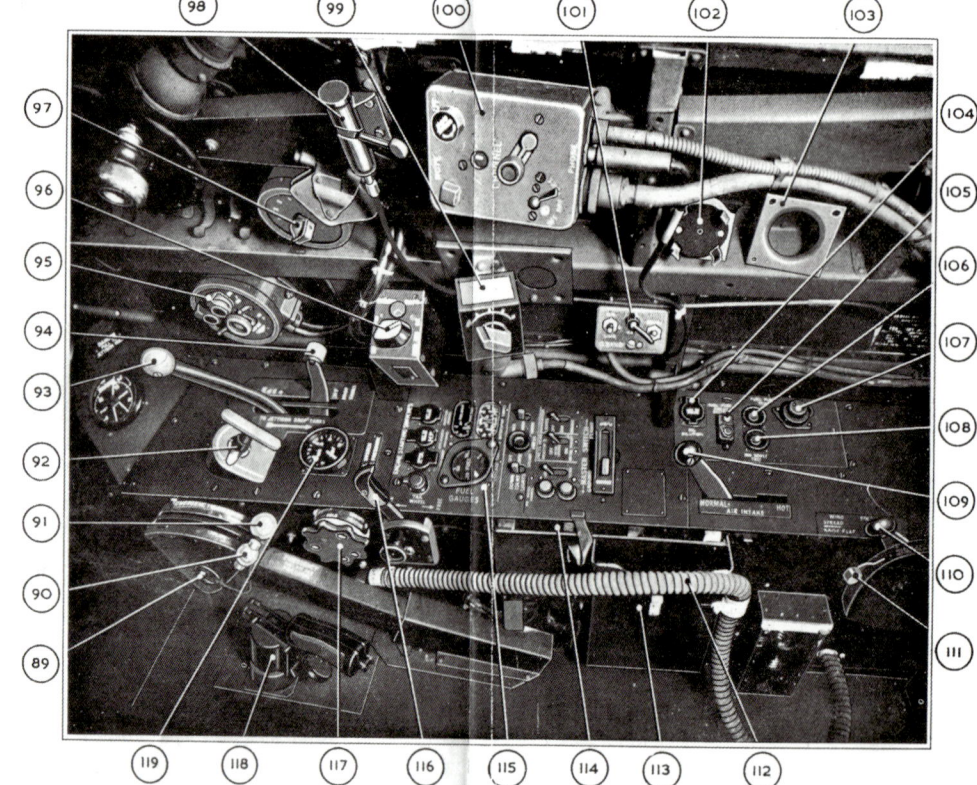

Group 1 – Side 4
Fuselage
Cockpit Interior

Controls and instruments – front cockpit (©Crown Copyright)

Note: The illustration shows the differences between the Sea Fury FB Mk 11 cockpit and the front cockpit of the T Mk 20

Key
1. Stowage for amber screens
2. Red cockpit lamp, moved to face aft
3. External stores switch panel redesigned
4. Firing aperture for signal pistol
5. Switch for muting wireless
6. Cockpit air-conditioning ventilator (replacing Punkah louvre)
7. Contacting altimeter switch moved from the port cockpit shelf to the port instrument panel
8. Signal pistol cartridge stowage
9. Channel selector control box replacing VHF control until
10. IFF control unit moved from port cockpit shelf to port decking
11. IFF selector unit moved from port cockpit shelf to port decking
12. Bomb rack jettison control moved aft
13. Hydraulic hand pump moved from the side of the cockpit shelf to the top of the shelf

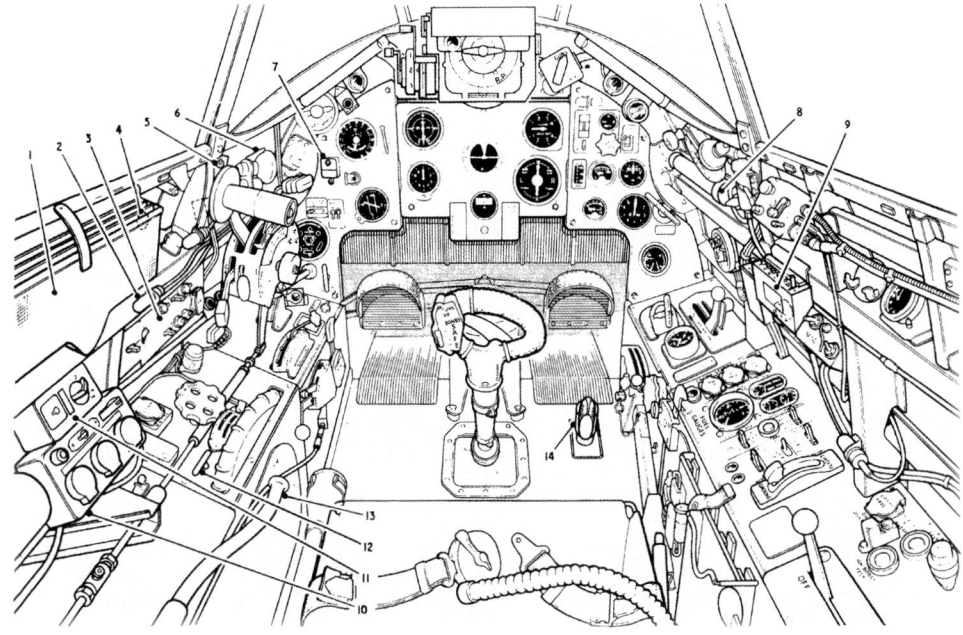

Controls and instruments – rear cockpit T Mk 20 (©Crown Copyright)

Key
1. Dimmer switch for cockpit port lamps
2. Propeller speed control
3. Red cockpit lamps
4. Throttle control
5. Friction adjuster
6. Ignition switches
7. Flap position indicator
8. Dimmer switch for red cockpit lamps
9. Switch for muting wireless
10. Press-to-speak switch
11. Red lamps master switch
12. Gyro gunsight
13. U/V cockpit lamps
14. Dimmer switch for U/V lamps
15. Power failure warning lamp
16. Oxygen regulator
17. Oil Pressure gauge
18. Hood winding handle
19. Pilot's harness control
20. Footstep control (push forward and down to operate)
21. Elevator trim hand wheel (operation in natural sense)
22. Flap control lever
23. Pilot's sanitary tube
24. Undercarriage control lever
25. Undercarriage safety catch
26. Undercarriage indicator switch
27. Distant-reading compass indicator
28. Undercarriage warning light
29. Supercharger warning light
30. Oil temperature indicator
31. Boost gauge
32. Engine cylinder temperature gauge
33. Engine speed indicator
34. Warning lamp, fuel level
35. Warning lamp, hook
36. Intercommunication emergency switch
37. Front hood jettison control
38. Rear hood jettison control
39. Mic-Tel socket

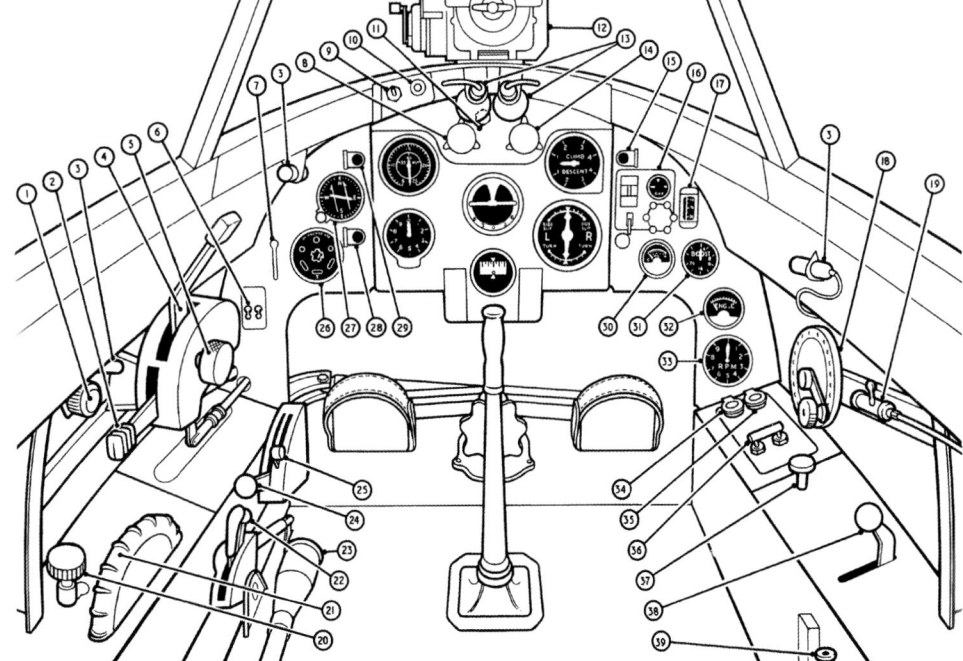

Fuselage
Cockpit Interior

A look down onto the starboard side console in the RNHF FB Mk 11 (©Crown Copyright via J. Haggo)

A look down into the floor area of the cockpit inside the FB Mk 11 being restored by TFC

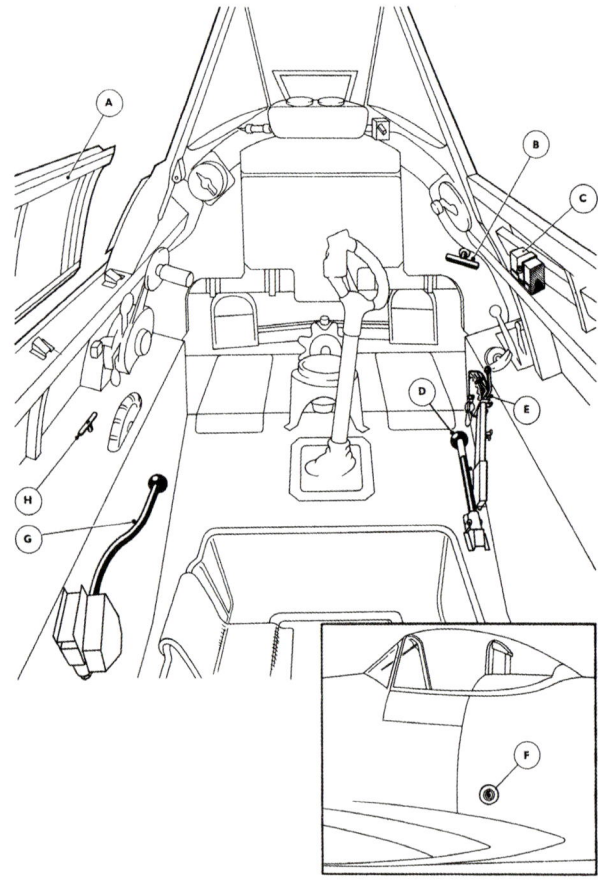

Emergency exits and equipment for the F Mk X and FB Mk 11 (©Crown Copyright)

Key
A. Emergency exit panel
B. Pilot's jettison toggle for sliding hood & emergency exit panel
C. Pilot's first aid pack
D. Undercarriage release lever (Pre. Mod. N.30)
E. Undercarriage & flaps emergency lowering controls (Mod N.30)
F. External jettison toggle for sliding hood & emergency exit panel
G. Hydraulic hand pump
H. Universal carrier jettison toggle

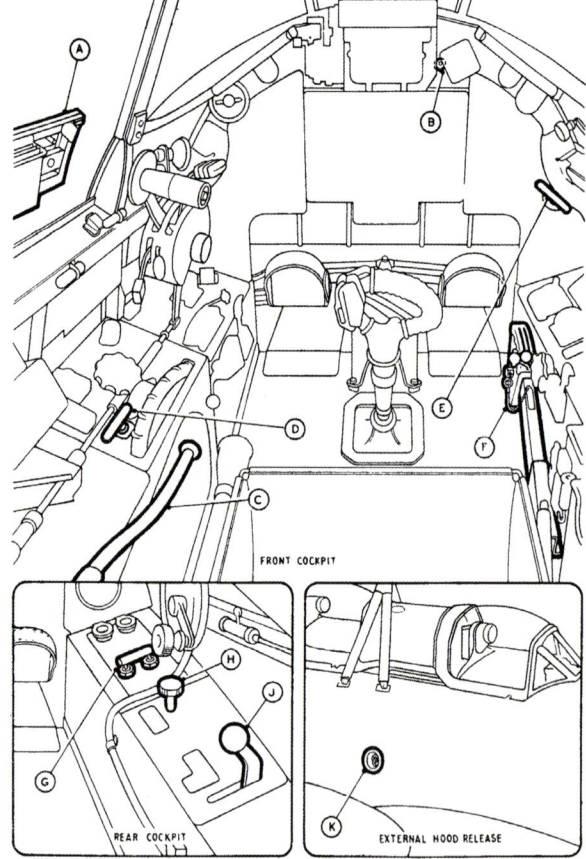

Emergency exits and equipment for the T Mk 20 (©Crown Copyright)

Key
A. Jettison panel
B. Emergency lighting master switch
C. Hydraulic hand pump
D. Universal carrier and external stores jettison control
E. Front hood jettison control (front cockpit)
F. Undercarriage and flaps emergency lowering controls
G. Emergency intercommunication switches
H. Front hood jettison control (rear cockpit)
J. Rear hood jettison control
K. External hood-release rings

Group 1 – Side 6
Fuselage
Cockpit Interior

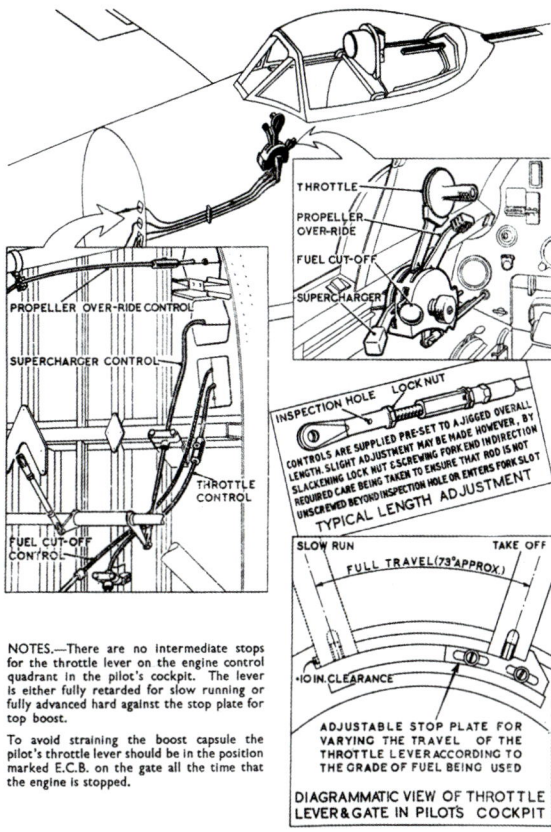

The engine controls, applicable to all Sea Fury versions
(©Crown Copyright)

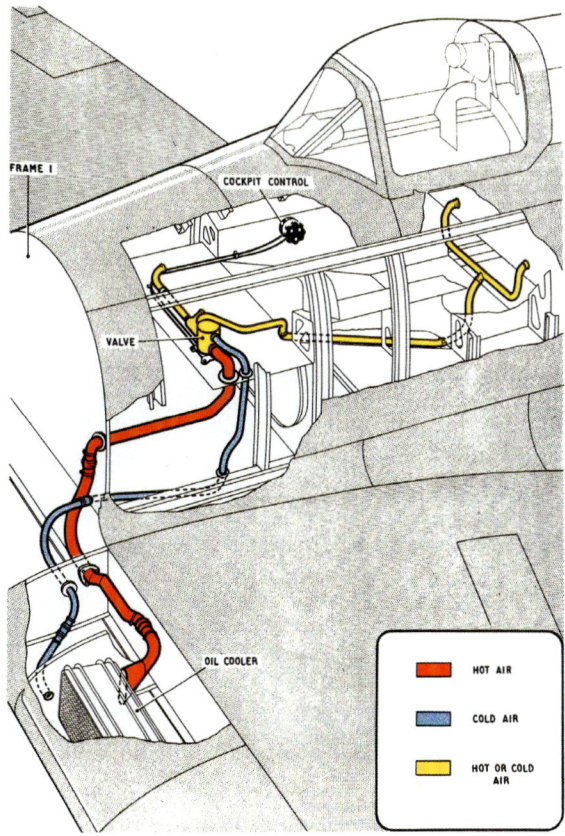

Cockpit air conditioning unit for both single- and twin-seat versions
(©Crown Copyright)

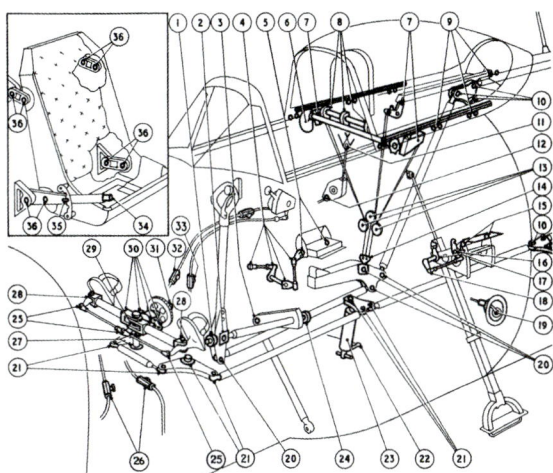

Showing all the various lubrication points within the cockpit area of the F MK X and FB Mk 11, this diagram helps to show the general layout of controls, canopy rails and access step etc. *(©Crown Copyright)*

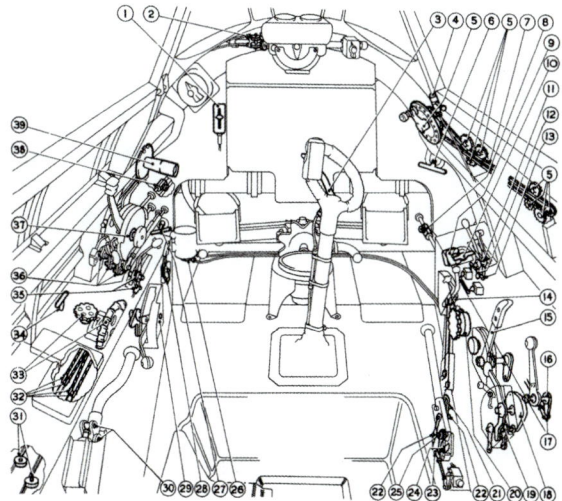

This lubrication diagram for the F Mk X/FB Mk 11 highlights such items as the flap indicator (1), brake lever (3), Sutton harness control lever (4), the operating handle and sprockets of the sliding hood (5), the tailwheel lock control (15), the undercarriage control lever (21-26). Coffman starter control (27), hydraulic hand pump (30) and tail trim and rudder bias control (33) *(©Crown Copyright)*

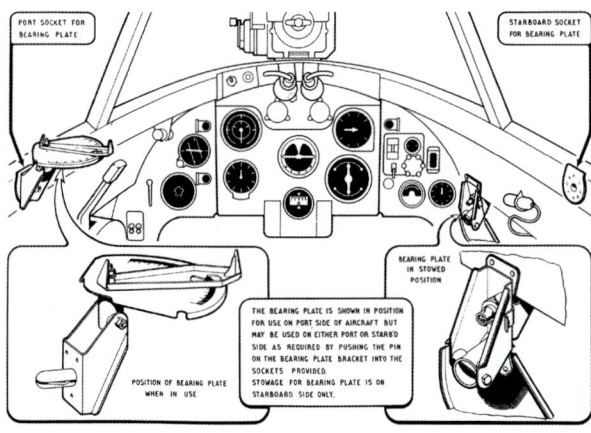

The T Mk 20, as a trainer, had this fitment for a Navigation Bearing Plate installed in the front cockpit for astro-navigation *(©Crown Copyright)*

Group 1 – Side 7
Fuselage
Canopy

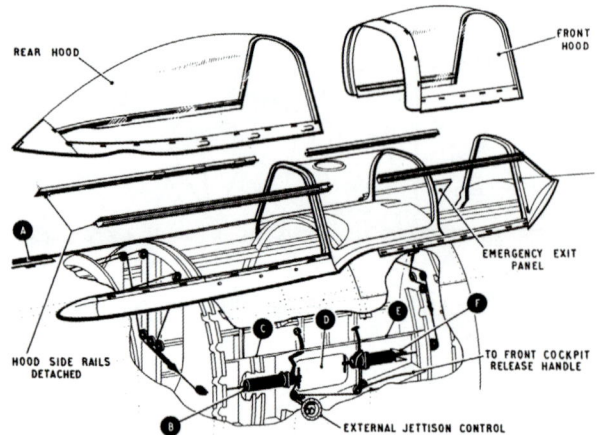

This diagram shows the canopy system fitted to the two-seat versions (©Crown Copyright)

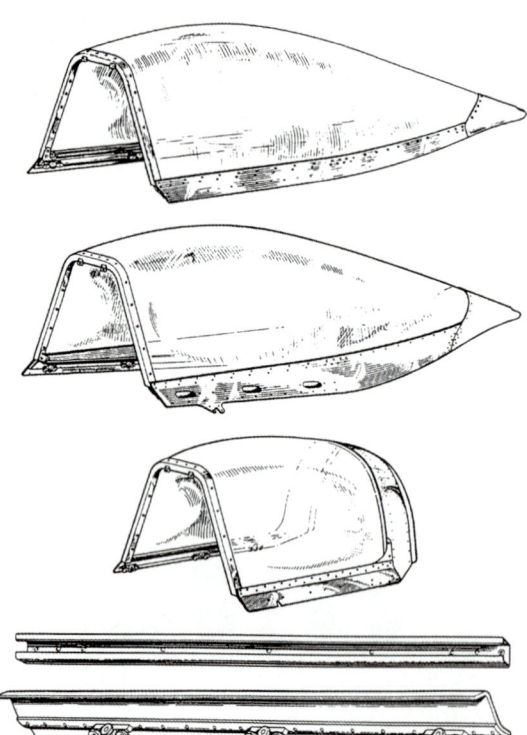

This diagram from the parts manual shows the three styles of canopy used on the Sea Fury, the top one is the standard version for the single-seat variants, the middle one is the rear canopy of the two-seat trainer and the bottom one is the front canopy of the two-seater. The two rails at the bottom are the single-seat/front or two-seater (upper) and two-seat/rear (lower) versions (©Crown Copyright)

Both single- and twin-seat versions had this emergency canopy jettison toggle switch under perspex on the port fuselage below the canopy

left: This photograph of the T Mk 20 airworthy with TFC at Duxford clearly shows the revised (truncated) front sliding section, the fixed mid-section and the revised framework of the rear section (©Nigel Perry)

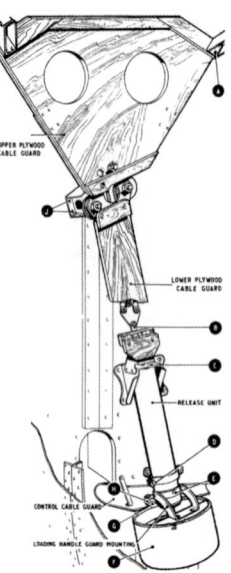

The operating system for the canopy mechanism on the single-seat versions (©Crown Copyright)

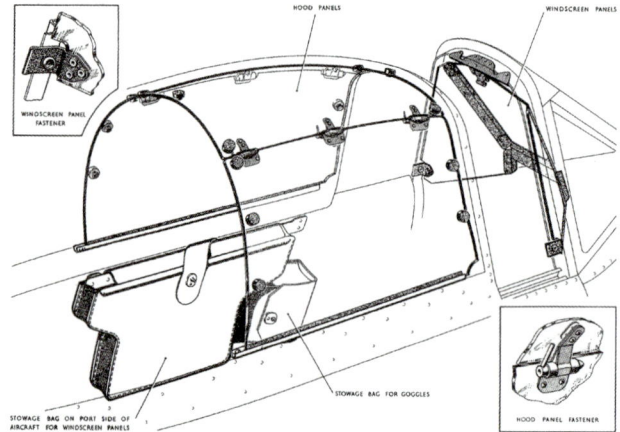

For instrument flying practice, in both single- and twin-seat versions, these screens could be attached inside the canopy and windscreen (©Crown Copyright)

This shot of the fuselage side on the FB Mk 11 on display in Australia clearly shows the canopy/windscreen and the relation between them and the release toggle. The port in the wing root is for an oblique tactical camera, there is another on the other side (P. Skulski)

Group 1 – Side 8
Fuselage
Main & Aft Fuselage

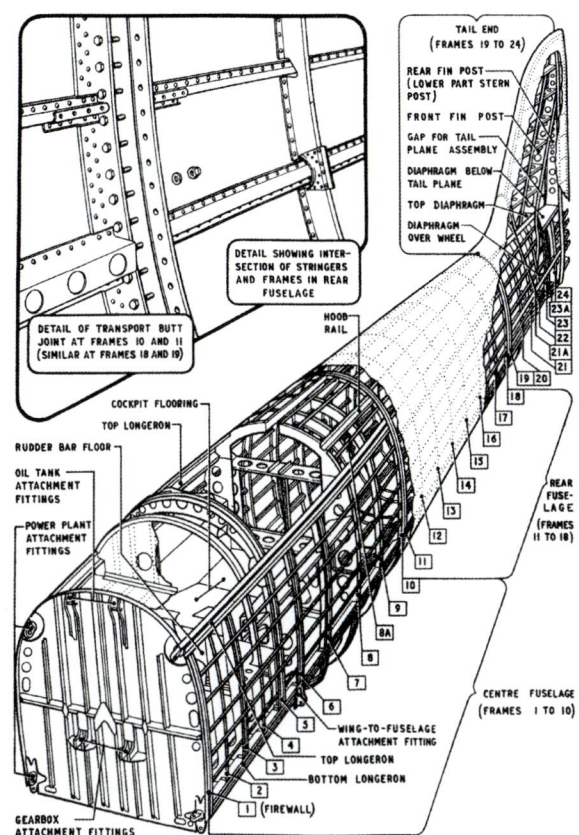

This diagrams shows the fuselage construction of the single-seat versions. There is another transit joint at frames 18 & 19
(©Crown Copyright)

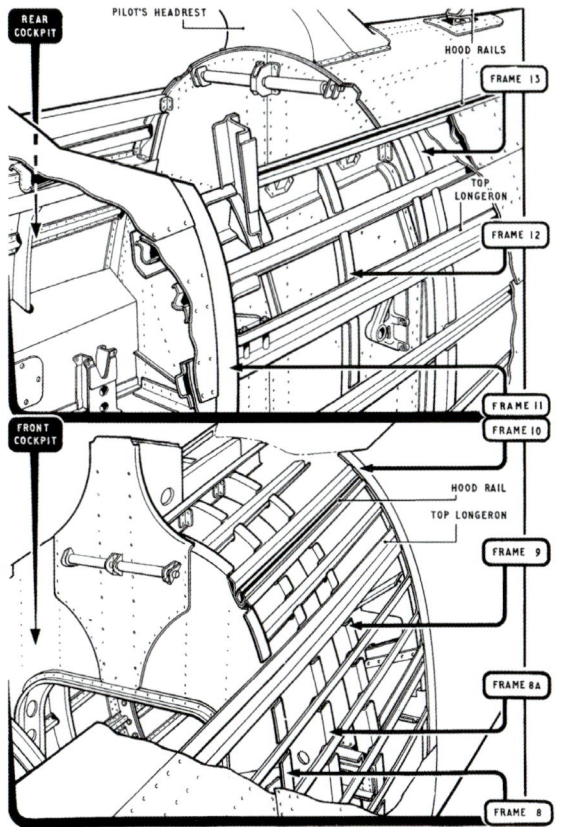

In this diagram you can see the changes made to create the two cockpits in the trainer versions (©Crown Copyright)

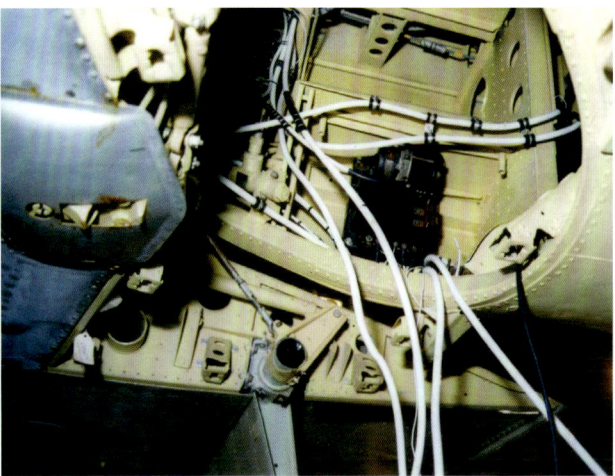

Due to the monocoque construction you can't access the rear fuselage via the cockpit, so to do this you need to remove the ventral access panel directly under and slightly aft of the cockpit in the fuselage underside as seen here – the flap linkage visible gives you a better idea of the location

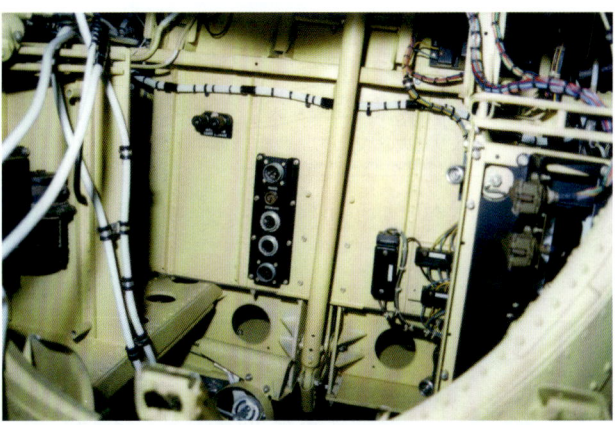

If you look directly up inside the fuselage underside access hatch you will see this, the underside of the cockpit 'tub' – the tube you can see in the middle is the control column linkage, the bottom of the image is forward

This shot gives you a good idea of the whole wing root area, with the prominent aft wing pick-up point clearly visible. You can also see the hole for the retractable footstep in the aft wing root area, plus the crew access hand-holds and canopy jettison toggle. The large hole above the aft wing root fairing is for an oblique camera when fitted (©George Papadimitriou)

Fuselage Systems

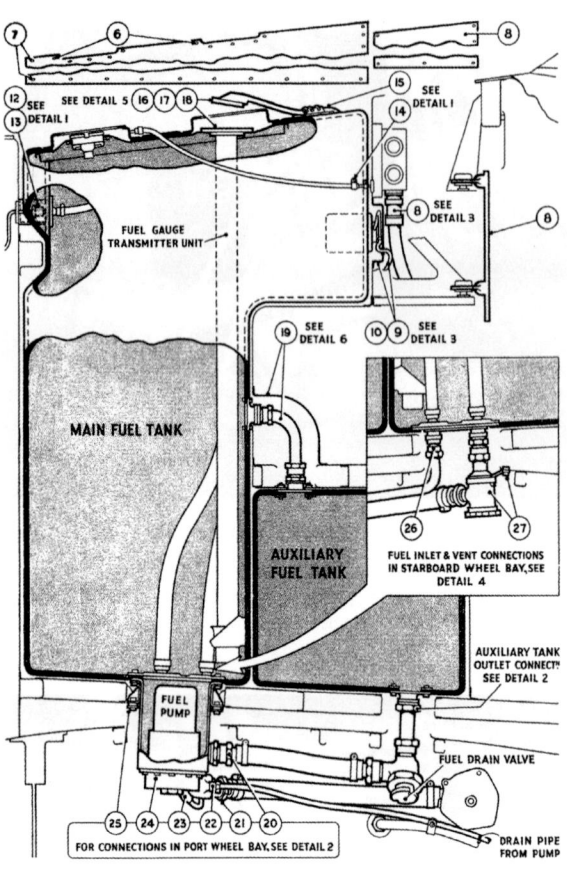

This diagram shows the main and auxiliary fuel tanks fitted to the single-seat versions *(©Crown Copyright)*

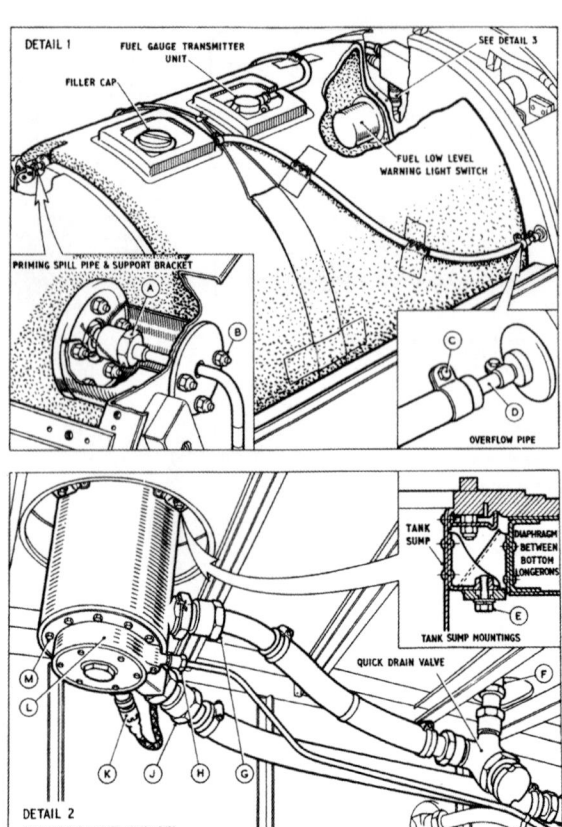

This more detailed diagram of the main fuel tank shows all the various equipment attached to it, as well as the sump unit in the port wheel well *(©Crown Copyright)*

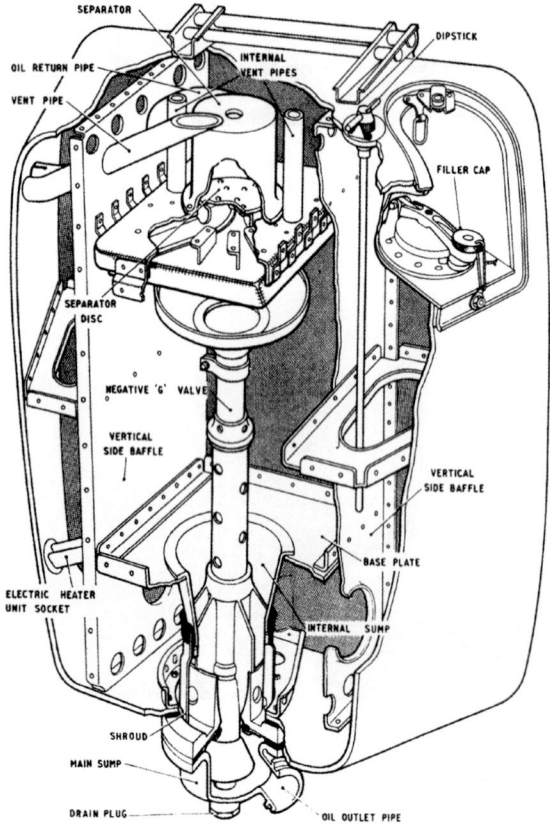

This cutaway shows the construction of the oil tank *(©Crown Copyright)*

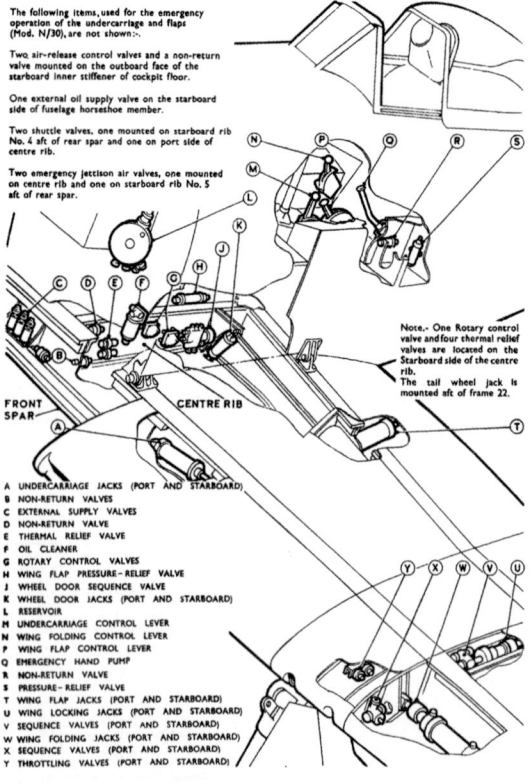

The hydraulic system, this remained the same for both single- and two-seat versions, the only change with the latter being the extension of a duplicate set of controls into the rear cockpit *(©Crown Copyright)*

Group 1 – Side 10
Fuselage
Systems

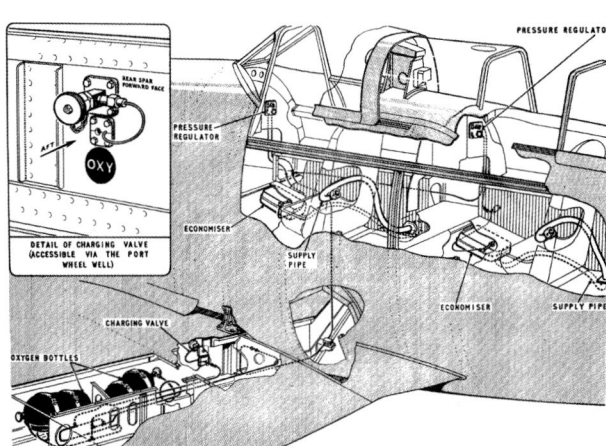

The oxygen equipment for the two-seat versions, the single-seat versions were the same, just using the same forward cockpit installation (*©Crown Copyright*)

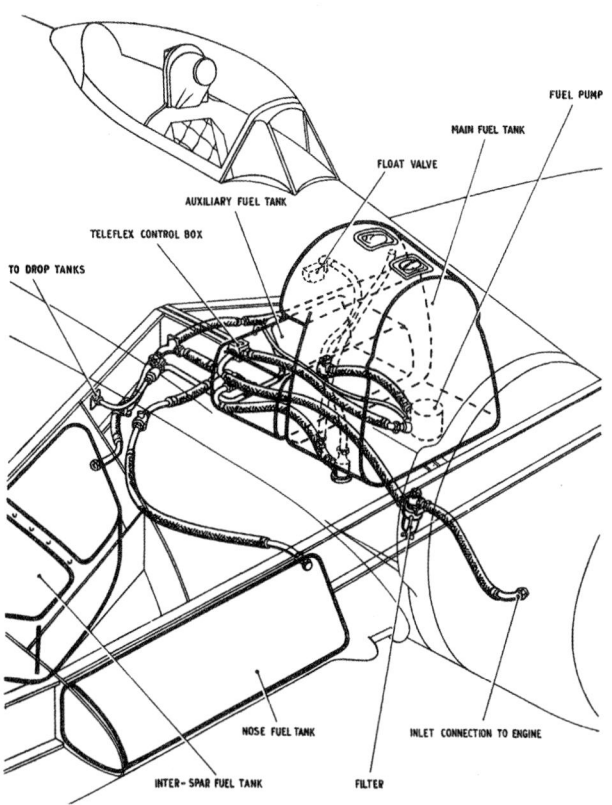

This diagram shows the full fuel tank installation along with all associated pipework (*©Crown Copyright*)

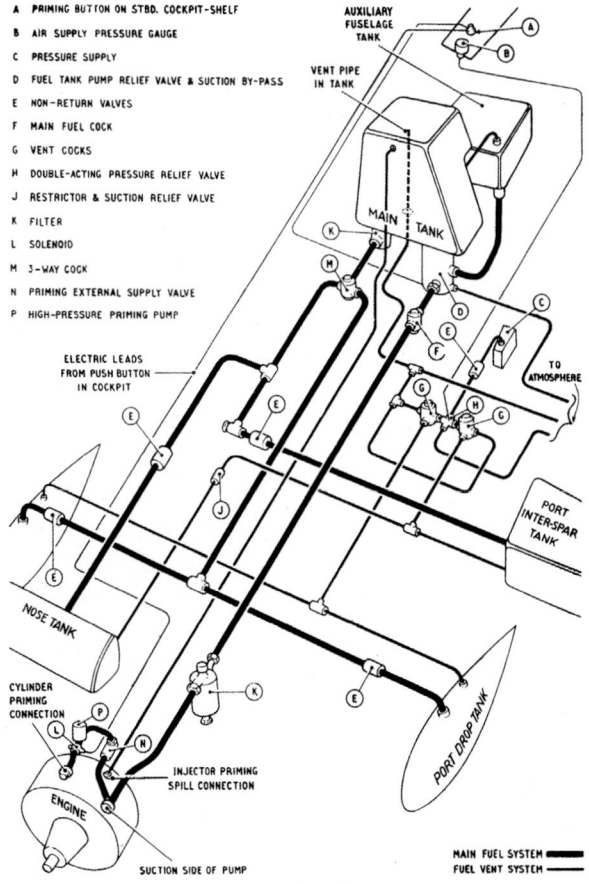

With the two-seat versions the main and auxiliary tanks were moved aft behind the rear cockpit, this diagram shows their location as well as the 'nose' (wing leading edge) and inter-spar tanks which are also found on the single-seat versions (*©Crown Copyright*)

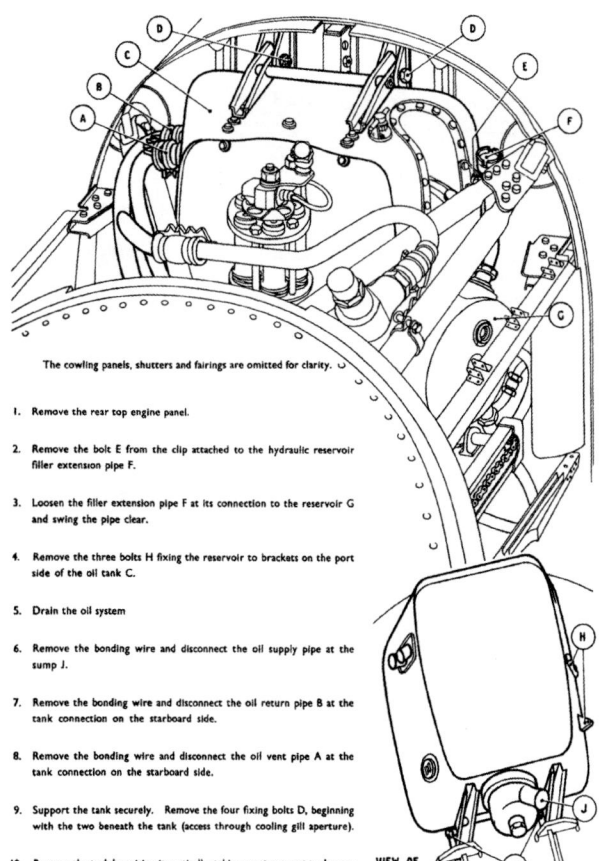

The oil tank is forward of the main tank and aft of the engine firewall and it remained in this location even when the main tank was moved aft on the two-seaters
(*©Crown Copyright*)

Group 2 – Side 1
Undercarriage
Main Undercarriage

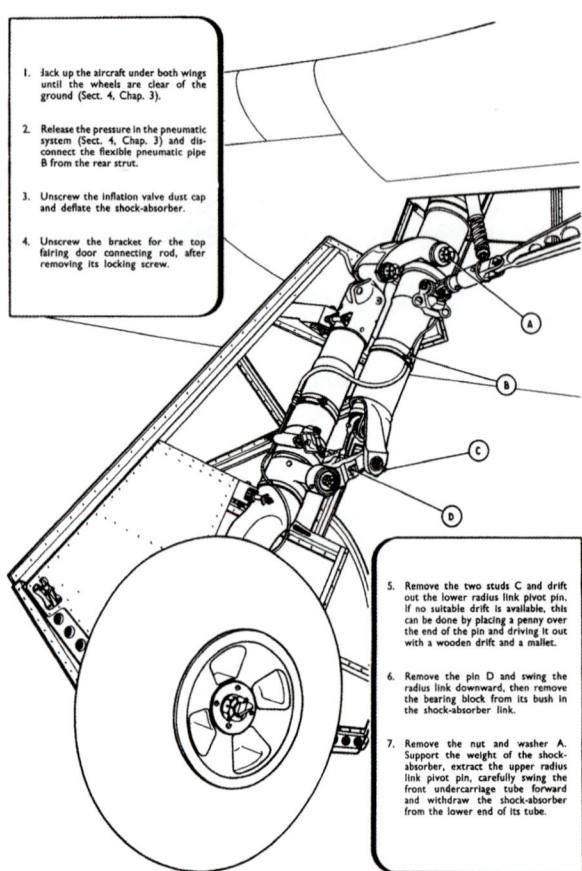

A useful diagram showing the main oleo, wheel and doors as used on all versions of the Sea Fury *(©Crown Copyright)*

This is the outer face of the port u/c door and as you can see it had a blister mid-way up *(©Crown Copyright via J. Haggo)*

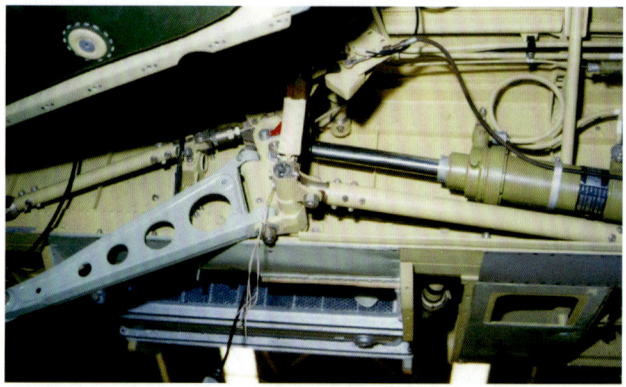

The main oleo leg is retracted via this hydraulic ram and cast linkage arm at the front of each wheel well

Overall view of the port u/c unit in the RNHF airworthy FB Mk 11, which is seen fitted with modern tyres with radial tread

(©Crown Copyright via J. Haggo)

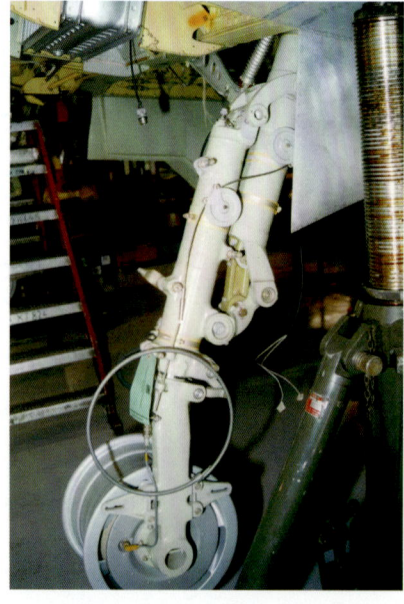

Here you can see the port oleo, viewed from the outside with the doors not fitted, of the example being restored by TFC. Note the pulley runs and the brake line going into the drum

Again the TFC FB.11, this shot shows the port oleo from the inside, but with the main door now attached and the wheel off exposing the spindle

Group 2 – Side 2
Undercarriage
Main Undercarriage

The starboard u/c door on the example in Australia clearly shows that the blister seen on the port door is not present *(©P. Skulski)*

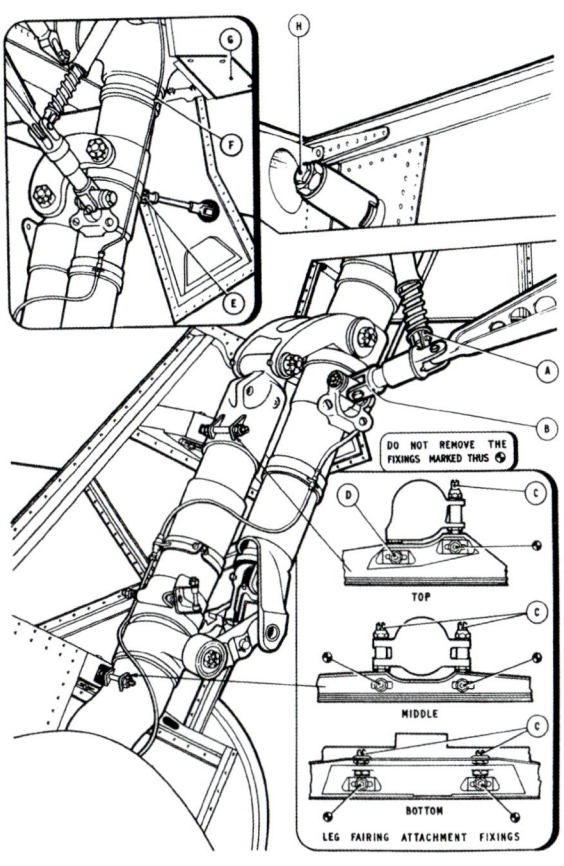

This diagram shows how the u/c doors are removed, although it also offers us a detailed look at all the linkage and attachment points for the door elements *(©Crown Copyright)*

Again the Australian example, this is fitted with a tyre that is probably more representative of what it would have had in the late 40s and early 50s, albeit we doubt it is original *(©P. Skulski)*

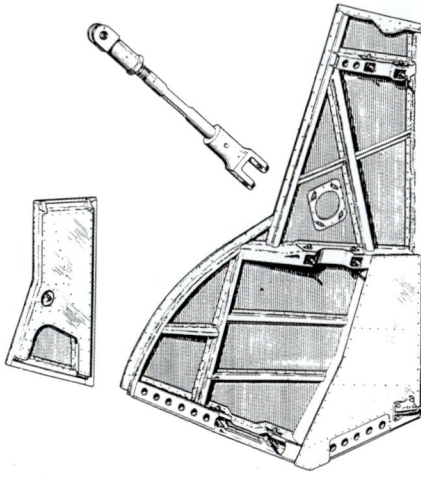

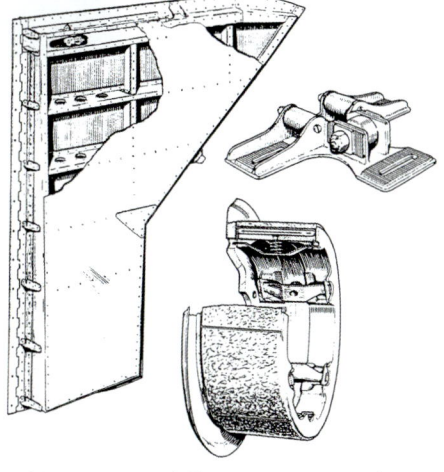

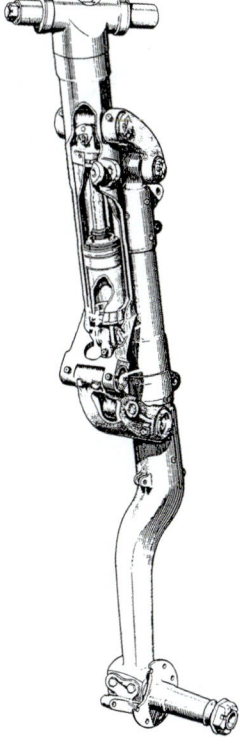

This diagram from the parts manual shows the main and small auxiliary doors along with the radius arm that links the latter to the main oleo *(©Crown Copyright)*

In this parts manual diagram you can see the inner u/c door unit, the up-lock pick-up that is attached to it and the main brake plate *(©Crown Copyright)*

This diagram from the parts manual shows the main Dowty oleo unit *(©Crown Copyright)*

Group 2 – Side 3
Undercarriage
Tailwheel & Hook

This shot of the RNHF FB.11 shows the tail hook and tailwheel assembly, the latter with a towing arm attached
(©Crown Copyright via J. Haggo)

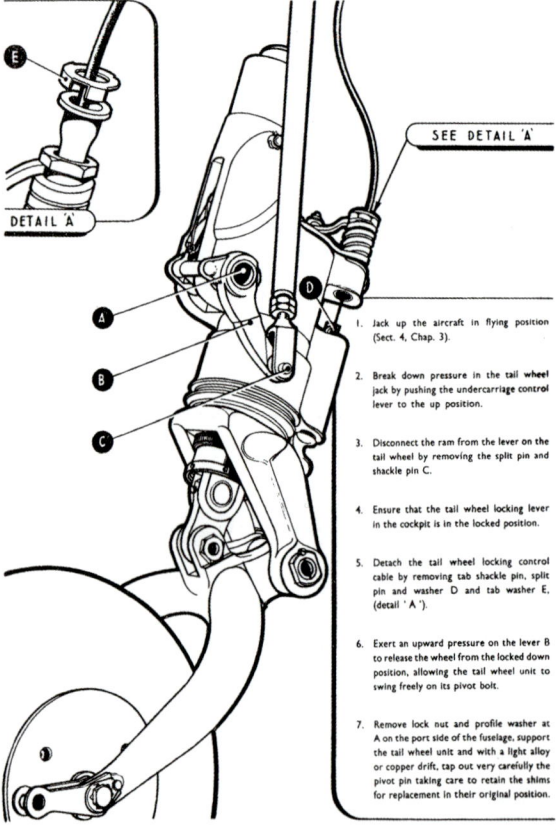

This diagram shows the construction of the tailwheel assembly
(©Crown Copyright)

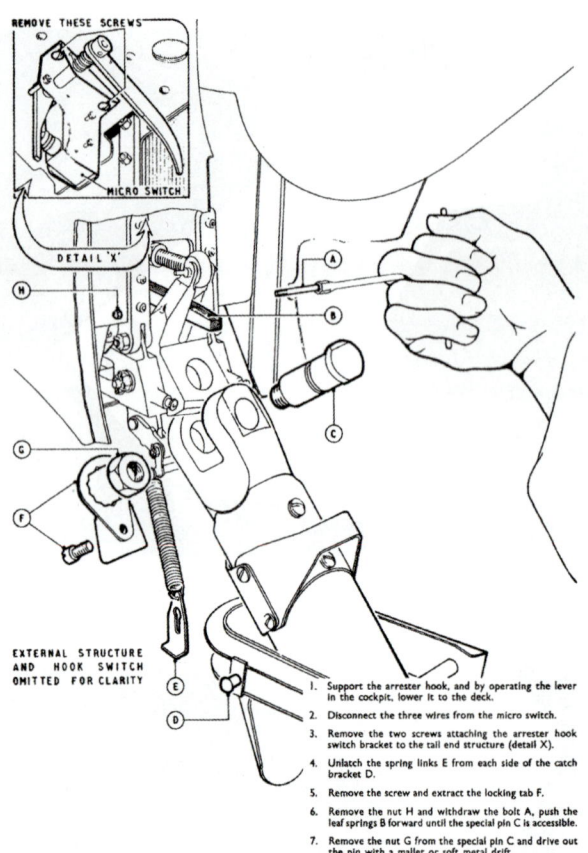

This diagram shows how the arrestor hook assembly is removed/installed (©Crown Copyright)

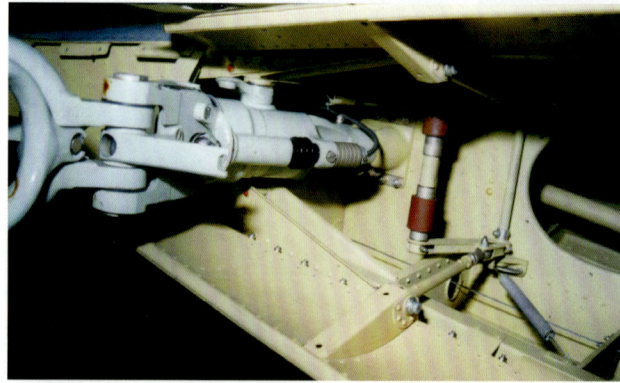

A quick look up into the tailwheel bay, here you are looking aft (left) and you can see the tailwheel unit, the door linkage and the cut-out to house the wheel

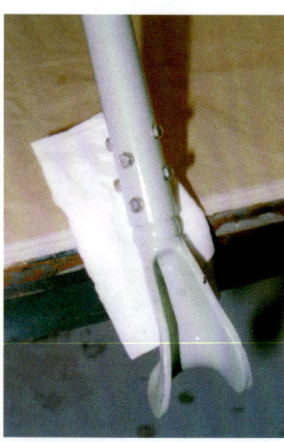

A look at the hook end of the arrestor, as you can see the cast hook is secured into the tube with numerous bolts

This is the port tailwheel door with the front of the aircraft to the right. Note the light that is only present on the port door

Group 2 – Side 4
Undercarriage
Tailwheel & Hook

27

Looking directly into the tail hook area you can see all the linkage etc

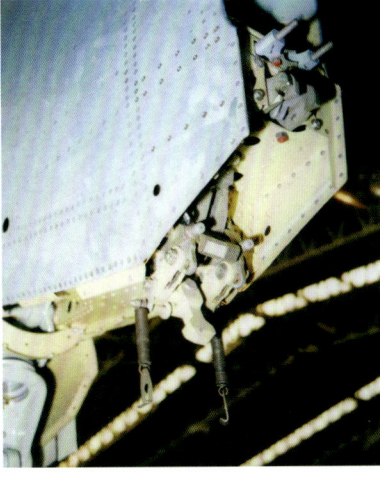

Here is the arrestor hook attachment area on the TFC FB Mk 11

The same area on the TFC example, this time with the hook installed

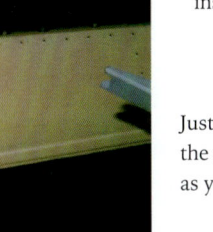

Just to prove it, this is the starboard door and as you can see, no light

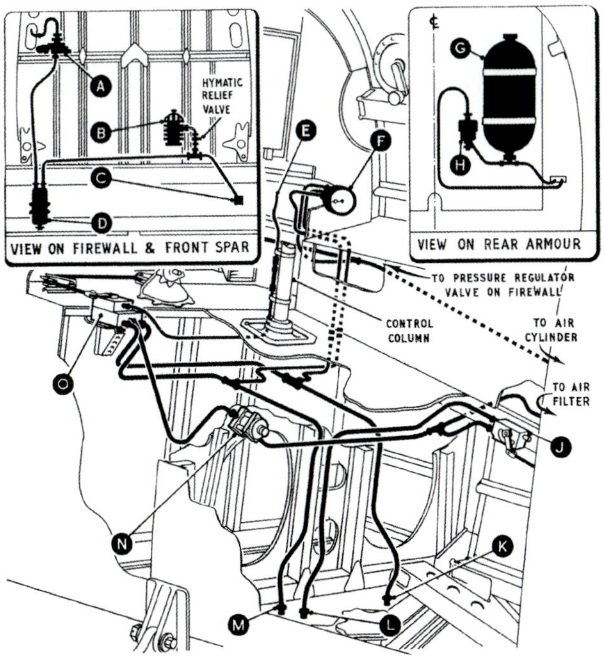

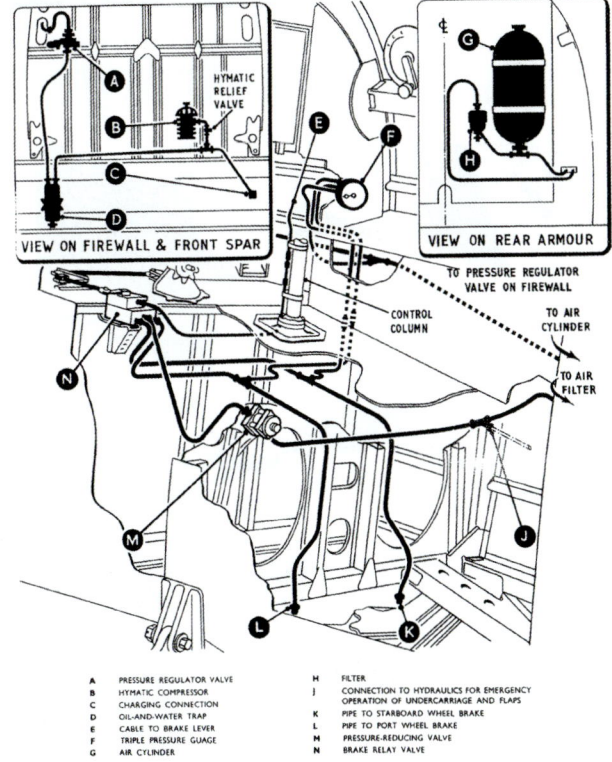

A PRESSURE REGULATOR VALVE
B HYMATIC COMPRESSOR
C CHARGING CONNECTION
D OIL-AND-WATER TRAP
E CABLE TO BRAKE LEVER
F TRIPLE PRESSURE GUAGE
G AIR CYLINDER
H FILTER
J UNDERCARRIAGE ASSISTER VALVE
K PIPE TO STARBOARD WHEEL BRAKE
L PIPE TO PORT AND STARBOARD UNDERCARRIAGE ASSISTERS
M PIPE TO PORT WHEEL BRAKE
N PRESSURE-REDUCING VALVE
O BRAKE RELAY VALVE

The pneumatic system on the Sea Fury was offered in two versions, the initial one is see here listed as Pre. Mod. N30 (#Crown Copyright)

A PRESSURE REGULATOR VALVE
B HYMATIC COMPRESSOR
C CHARGING CONNECTION
D OIL-AND-WATER TRAP
E CABLE TO BRAKE LEVER
F TRIPLE PRESSURE GUAGE
G AIR CYLINDER
H FILTER
J CONNECTION TO HYDRAULICS FOR EMERGENCY OPERATION OF UNDERCARRIAGE AND FLAPS
K PIPE TO STARBOARD WHEEL BRAKE
L PIPE TO PORT WHEEL BRAKE
M PRESSURE-REDUCING VALVE
N BRAKE RELAY VALVE

This is the Mod N.30 pneumatic system, the main change being the fitment of the undercarriage assistor unit within the fuselage instead of one in each wheel well (©Crown Copyright)

Tail

Tailplanes

Group 3 – Side 1 — 1 — 28

This shot of the starboard tailplane on the FB Mk 11 preserved at Yeovilton gives you an idea of the shape and construction. Note that the T Mk 20 series all had slightly larger tailplanes, although the leading edge remained the same *(© George Papadimitriou)*

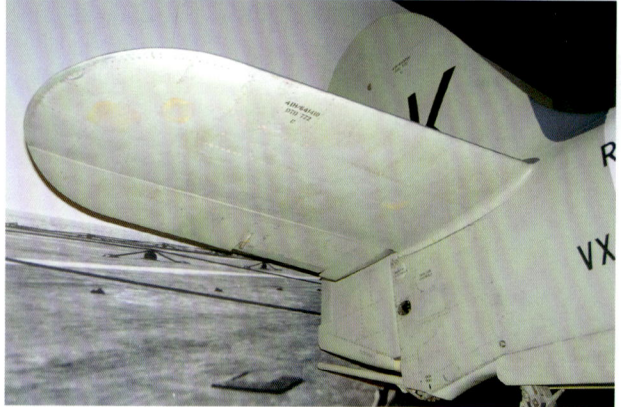

This shot of the underside of the tailplane on the Canberra example again shows construction as well as wear and the various stencils in this area *(© P. Skulski)*

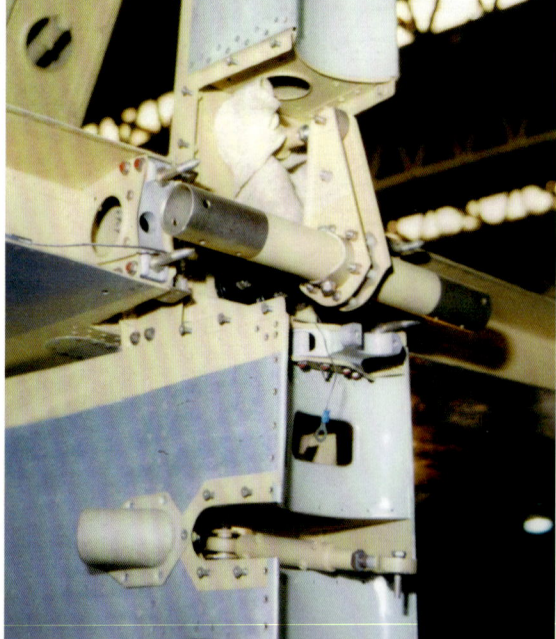

With the elevators off on the TFC example you can see the linkage and torque tube

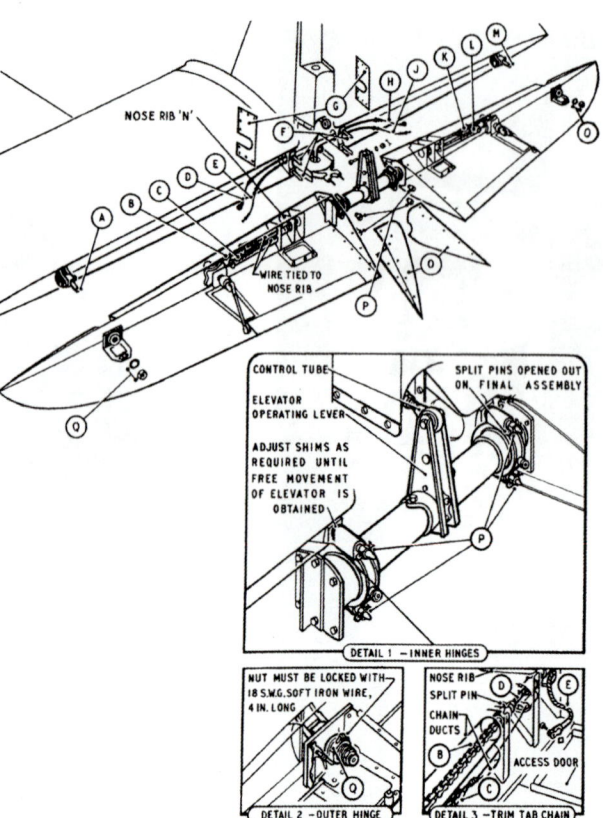

This diagram from the manual shows the elevators for all variants *(©Crown Copyright)*

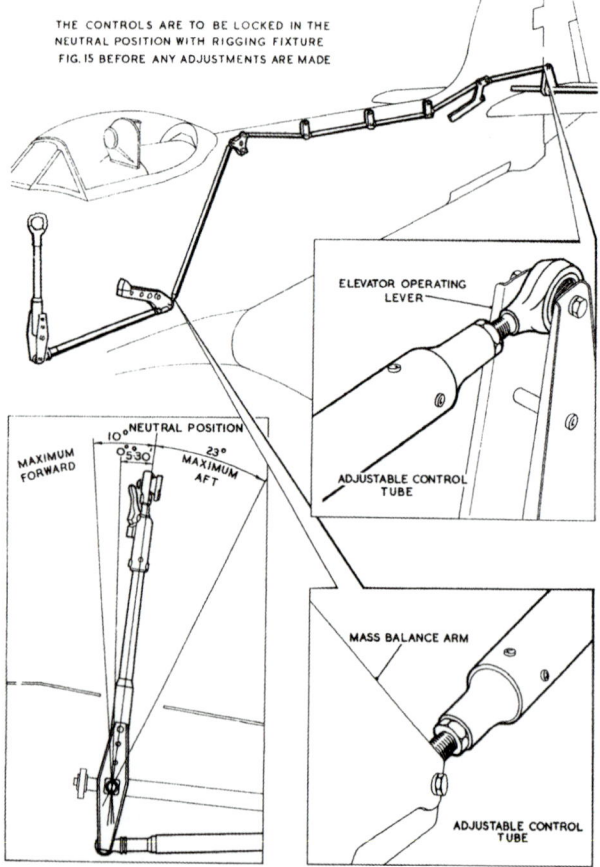

Here you can see the rather convoluted route the elevator control rods take *(©Crown Copyright)*

Group 3 – Side 2
Tail
Fin & Rudder

Compare the prototype fin and rudder with this image of the production versions on the T Mk 20 now airworthy with TFC at Duxford (©Nigel Perry)

below: In this close-up from a period image you can see the original, smaller, vertical fin and rudder fitted to the prototype NX798 (©Hawker Aircraft)

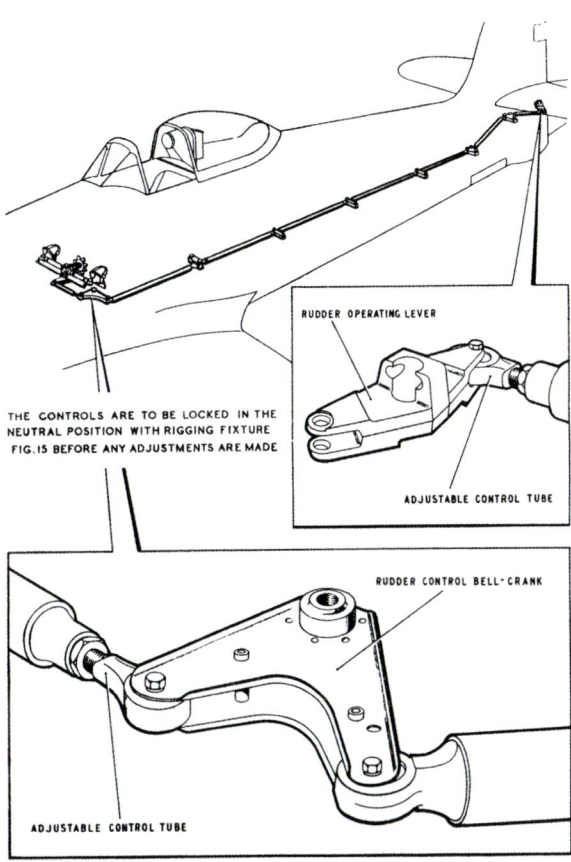
Another diagram showing the convoluted route the rudder linkage takes (©Crown Copyright)

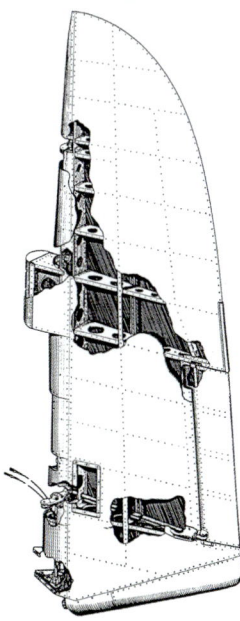
The rudder construction (©Crown Copyright)

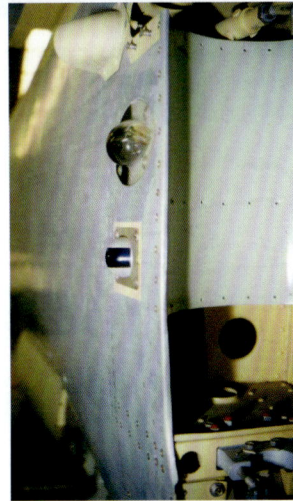
Either side of the aft fuselage, behind the rudder hinge line and under the tailplanes you will find these two lights. The upper one is clear, the lower one blue

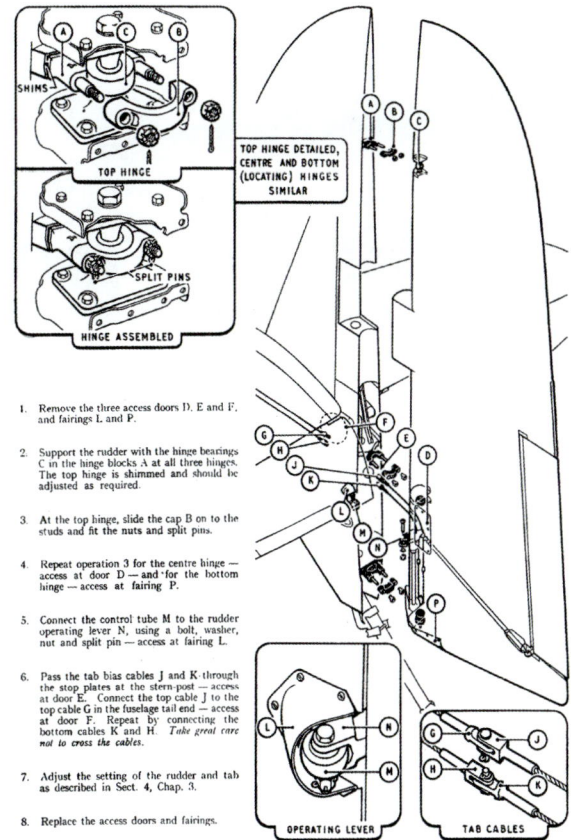
This diagram shows how the rudder is assembled (©Crown Copyright)

Wings

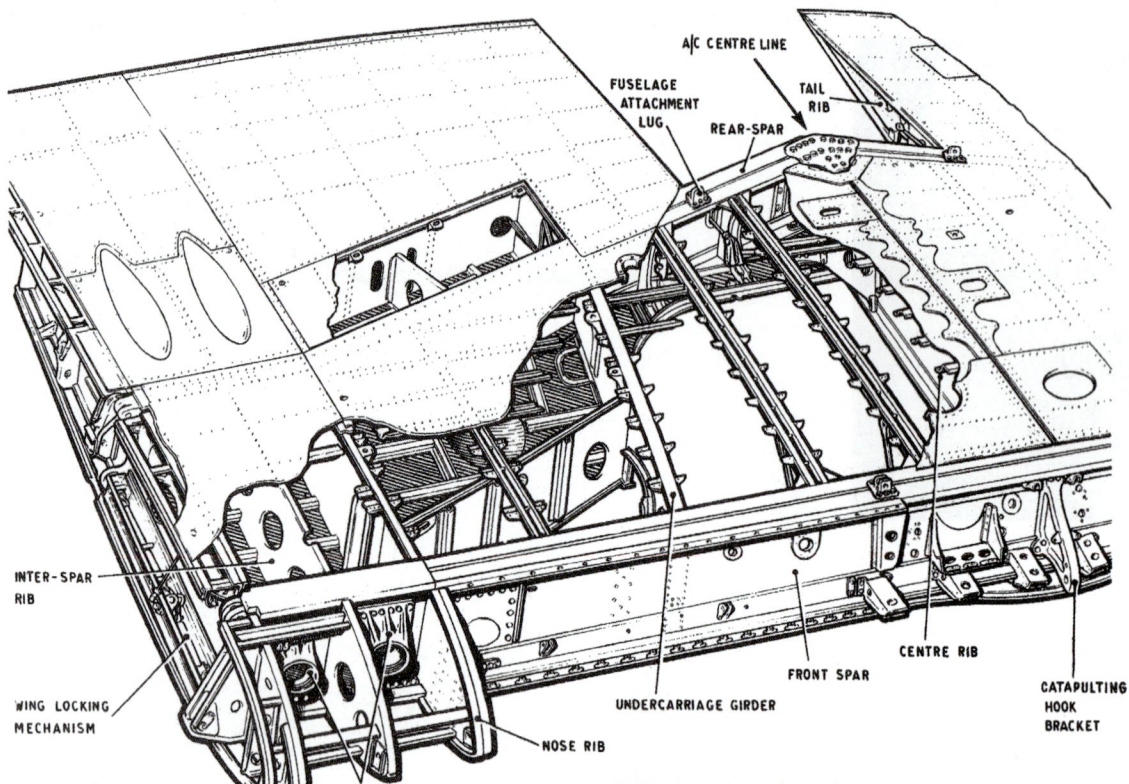

This diagram shows the construction of the centre section on the Sea Fury, as you can see both wing panels join at the centre instead of via wing attachments at the fuselage/root junction (©Crown Copyright)

This shot shows the interior of the wing fold on the port side of the T Mk 20 with TFC at Duxford. This airworthy machine lacks things like the ammo feed tracks in the rear portion, but otherwise is pretty standard. The red unit at the front is a jury strut fitted on the ground to keep the folded wing in place (©Nigel Perry)

This shot of the ex-Iraqi example now flying in the colours of the prototype SG661, does not have a lot of the details (covers, cables and pipework) you see on the two-seater shown on the left (©Nigel Perry)

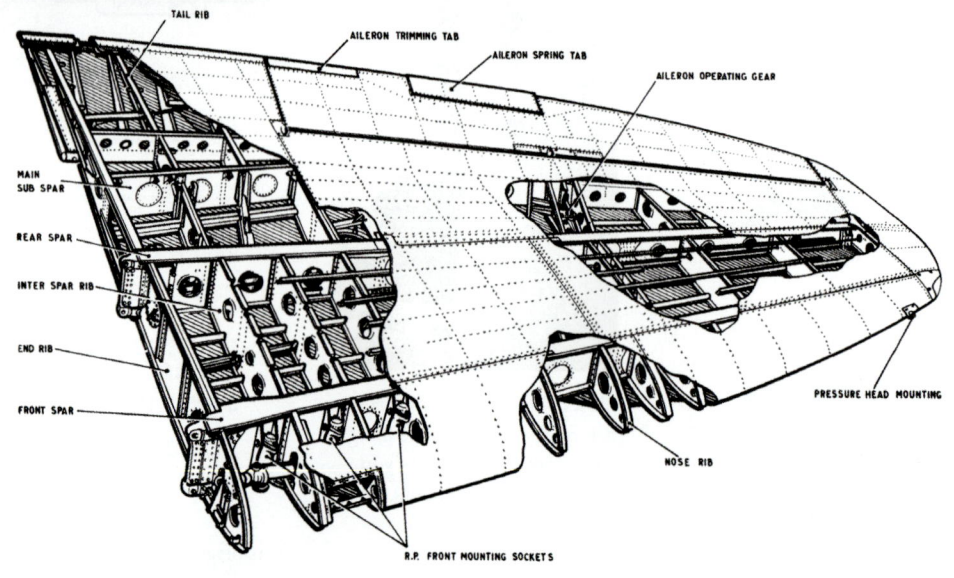

This is the outer wing panel, which is the same for all variants, the two-seater just having one gun port blanked off (©Crown Copyright)

Group 4 – Side 2
Wings

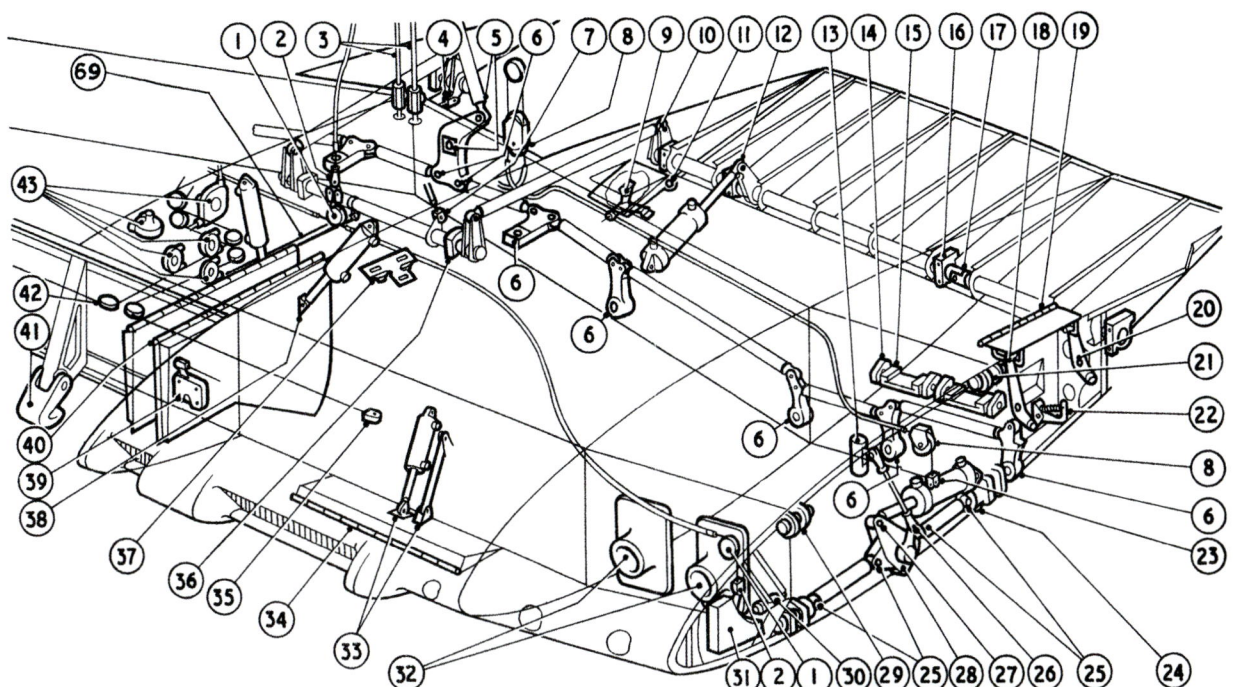

A useful diagram, taken from the manual, this shows all the various lubrication points in the wing centre section but for us it also shows all the various equipment in this area that is always hidden under the skin *(©Crown Copyright)*

Although you can still see the hinge line outboard of the cannon blisters, this ex-Iraqi example does not have the fold mechanism inside

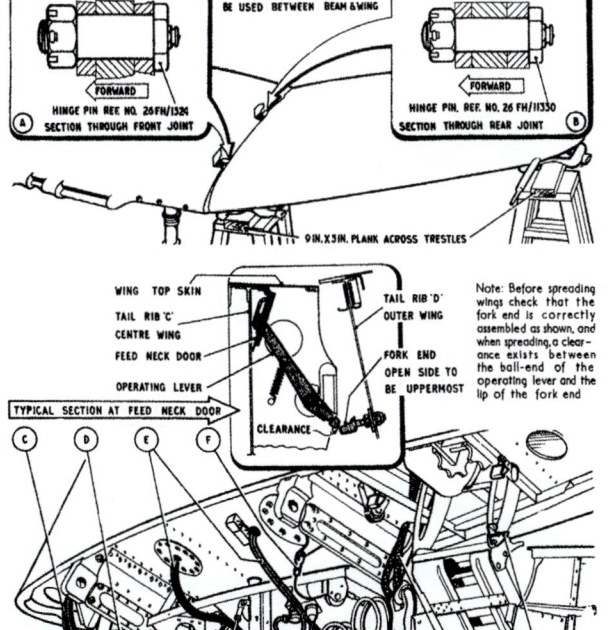

This diagram from the manual shows the wing fold in detail *(©Crown Copyright)*

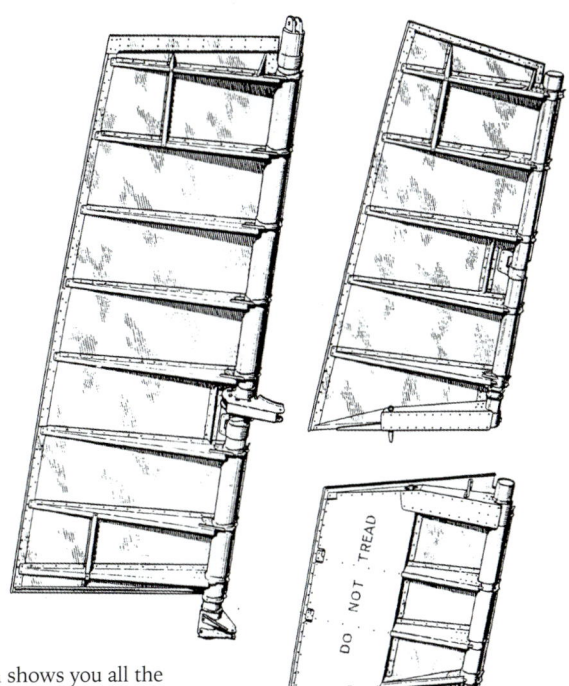

This diagram shows you all the elements of the flaps *(©Crown Copyright)*

Group 4 – Side 3
Wings

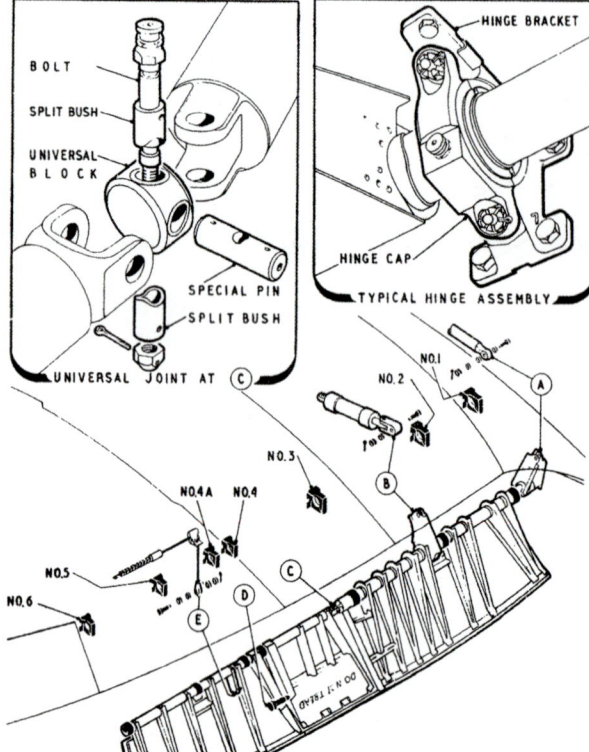

This diagram shows how the flaps are installed/removed
(©Crown Copyright)

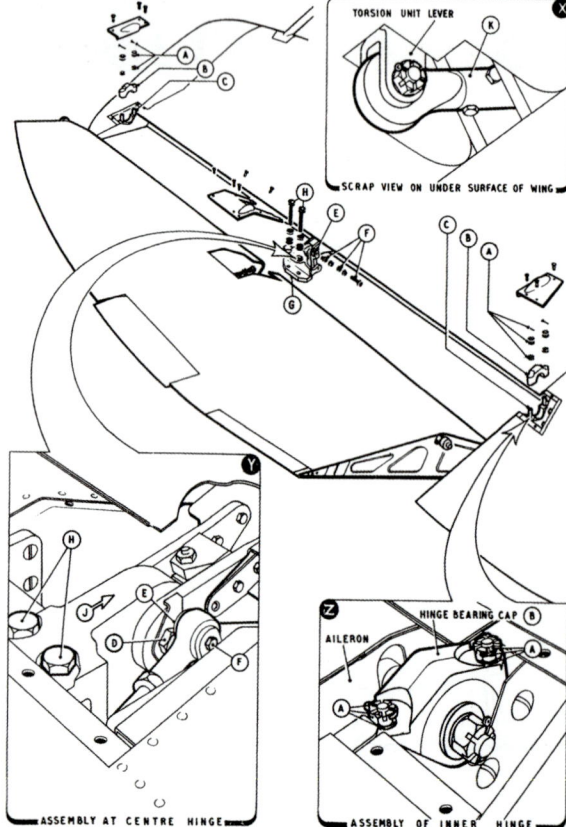

This is how the ailerons are attached/removed (©Crown Copyright)

The inboard flap assembly on the port side of the FB Mk 11

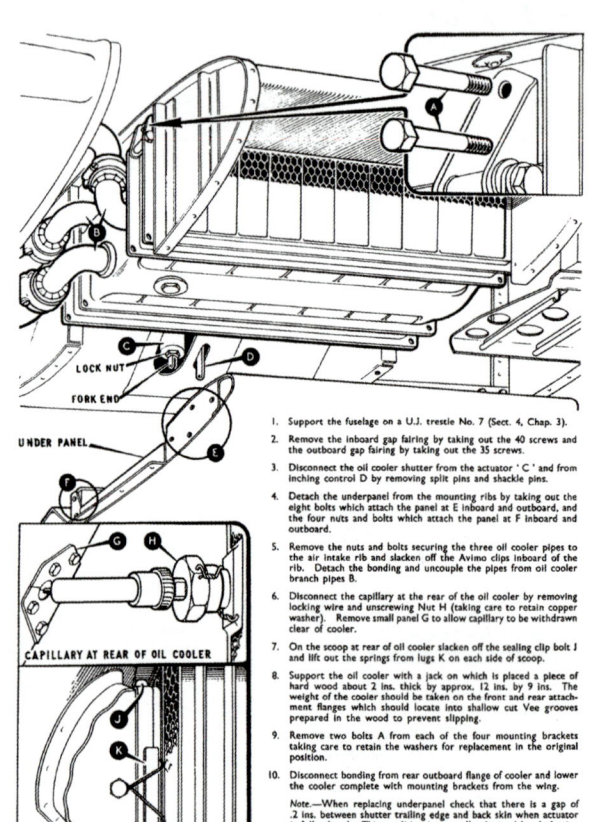

This diagrams shows how the wing leading edge radiator units are removed/installed (©Crown Copyright)

Although an odd angle, this shot looking up and forward under the port wing l/e radiator does show a lot of detail

Group 4 – Side 4
Wings

The radiator unit installed in the port wing of the TFC example

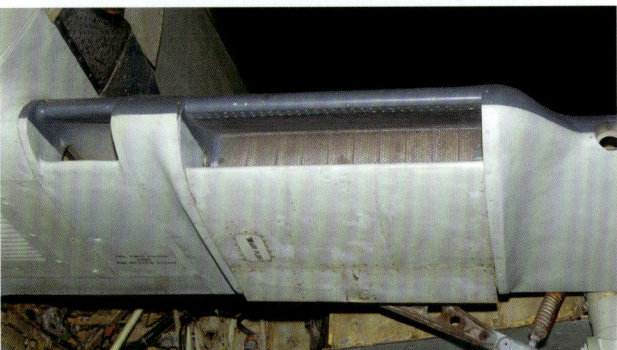

With everything in situ, this is the port wing l/e radiator as well as the carburettor intake at the root *(©P. Skulski)*

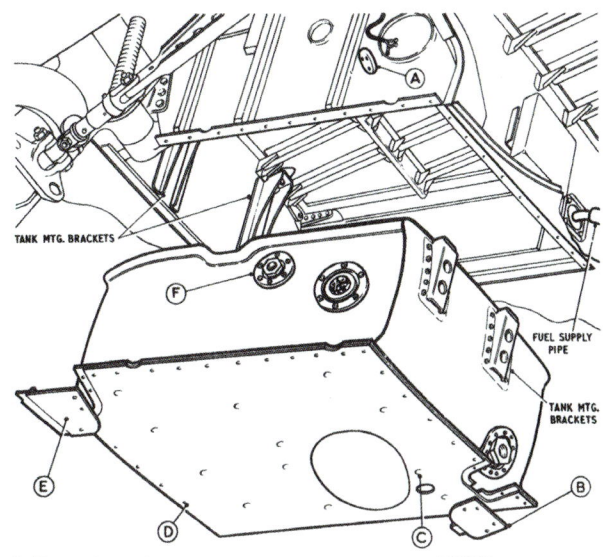

1. Disconnect the accumulator.
2. Set the fuel cocks at "OFF" and drain the tank as described in Sect. 4, Chap. 3.
3. Remove the filler cap access door (Sect. 4, Chap. 3). Disconnect the bonding wire at filler cap and unscrew the eight 2 B.A. nuts around the filler cap rubber sealing.
4. Unlock and disconnect the vent pipe (F). Disconnect the fuel gauge cable after removing terminal cover by withdrawing three screws.
5. Detach access door (B) and unlock and disconnect fuel supply pipe.
6. Remove U/C pivot access door (E) and the 23 screws (D) securing the tank fairing to the wing. When removing the tank for other than replacement purposes it is not necessary to remove the fairing, but if a new tank is being installed the fairing must be removed and retained for re-fitting.
7. Support the tank and remove the tank mounting bolts which are accessible through holes in the top surface of the wing above the tank taking care to retain the rubber washers for use in re-assembly.
To remove the fairing from the tank, gouge out the plastic filling from 12 holes (C) in the fairing and unscrew the bolts.

ASSEMBLY
The assembly is a reversal of the above operations, but the following points should be observed:
1. The tank is to be bolted to the inboard forward mounting bracket first.
2. Locking wire must be attached to the vent pipe connection on the tank before assembly to the wing.
3. To align with the wing contour it may be necessary to adjust the number of rubber washers at the mounting brackets.

The other tanks are the inter-spar ones, with one in each wing of the single-seat versions and only one in the port wing of the two-seater *(©Crown Copyright)*

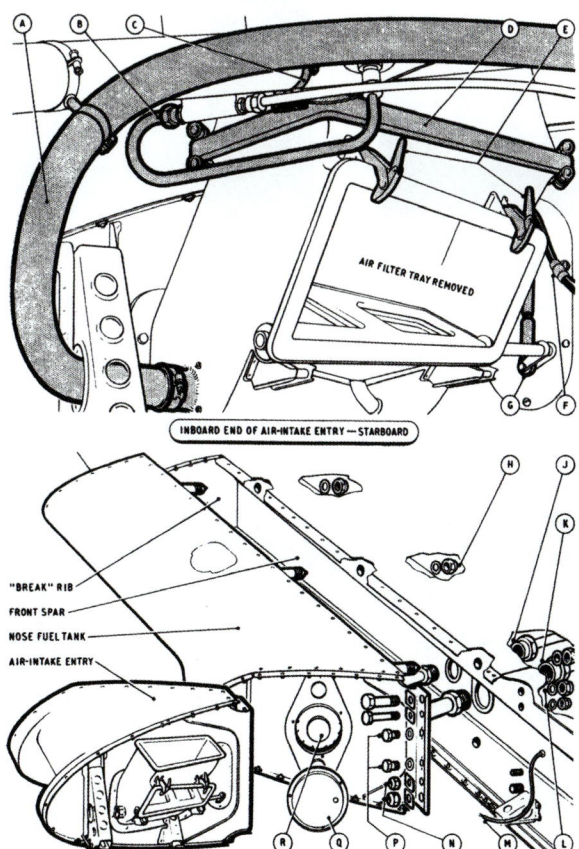

The wings contain two fuel cells and this is what are called the 'nose' tanks, although they are in the leading edge of each wing, not the fuselage *(©Crown Copyright)*

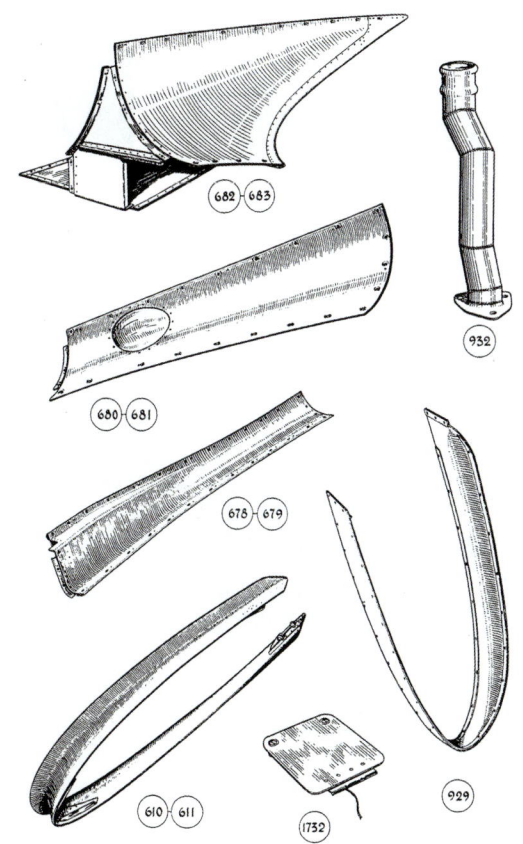

From the parts manual, this diagram shows all the various fillets and panels used at the wing root

Wings & Bays

As you can see, the inter-spar tanks are fitted aft of the wheel well, this being the port example in the TFC FB.11. The circular item in the front edge is the fuel level gauge transmitter

The wing-to-fuselage area is covered with various panels, as seen here with the mid-root one installed and the aft one missing

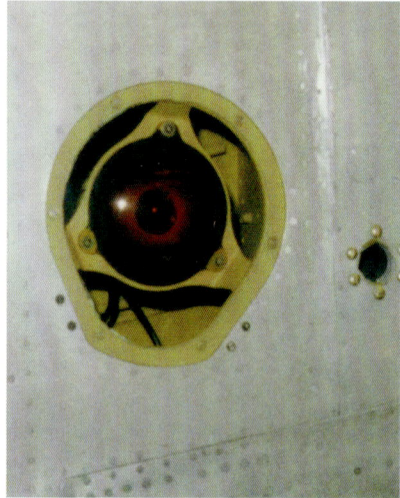

Mid-span of the outer wing panels on both sides is this downward identification lamp, seen here without the clear cover fitted

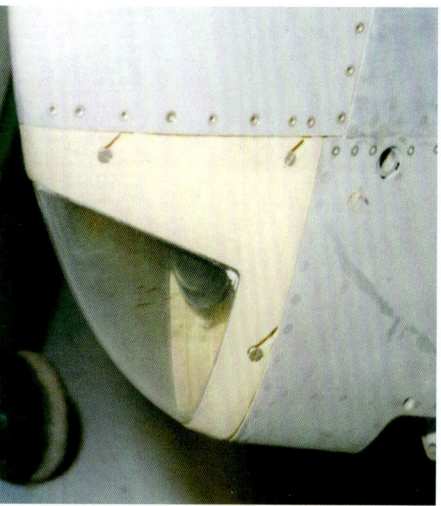

At the wingtip you get two lights, this is the one in the leading edge and the bulb is green, so this is the port one as the starboard one is red

On the trailing edge of each wingtip is this light and it is blue on both sides

An overall shot of the starboard wheel well on the RNHF airworthy FB.11. Note the access panel behind the bay open to give access under the cockpit and into the aft fuselage (©Crown Copyright via J. Haggo)

A detailed look at the inner face of the starboard wheel well (right = forward). Not all pipework etc. is installed or connected as this FB.11 was being restored when photographed

Group 4 – Side 6
Wings
Undercarriage Bays

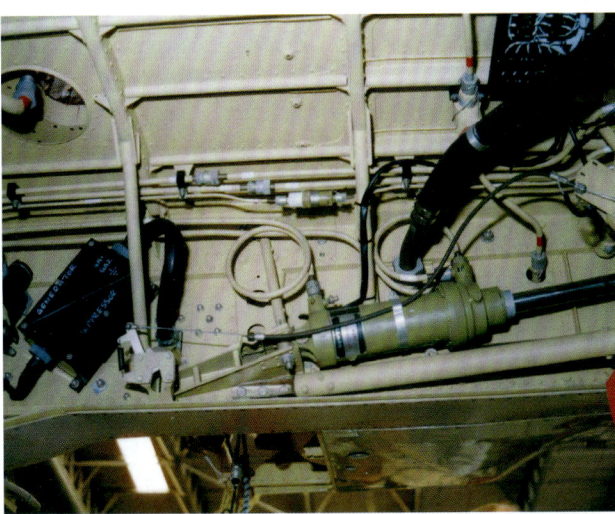

As you move round the starboard wheel well, this is the rib detail on the front (looking forward). The hydraulic ram is for the u/c retraction

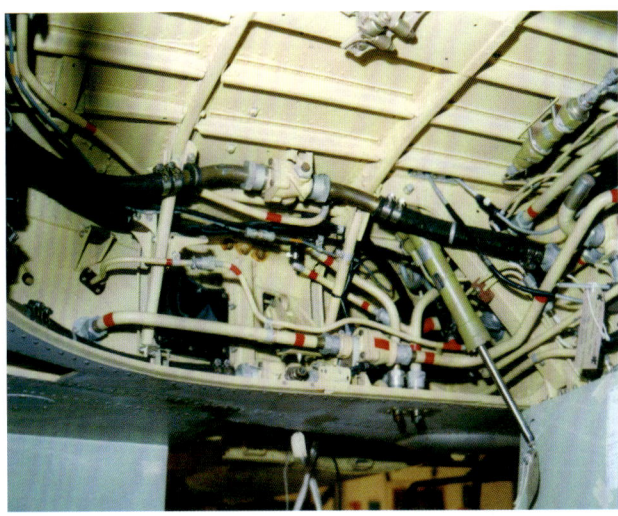

If you now turn round in the starboard wheel well, to look aft, this is the rear bulkhead area

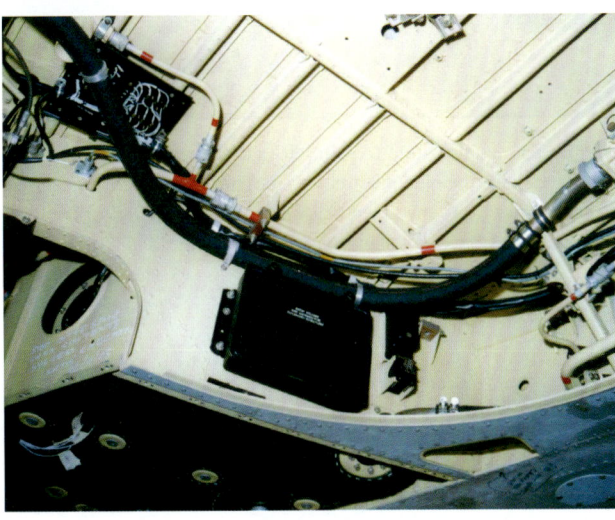

Continuing round in the starboard bay, this is the area forward of the inter-spar tank, which you can see in the background, it contains various electrical distribution boxes

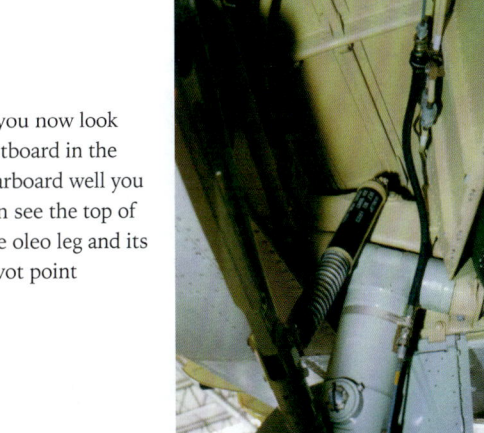

If you now look outboard in the starboard well you can see the top of the oleo leg and its pivot point

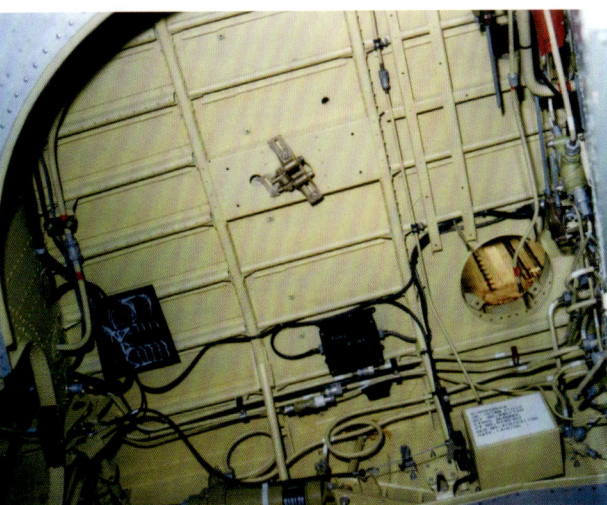

Looking directly up into the roof of the wheel well here you can see things like the wheel up-lock catch in the centre

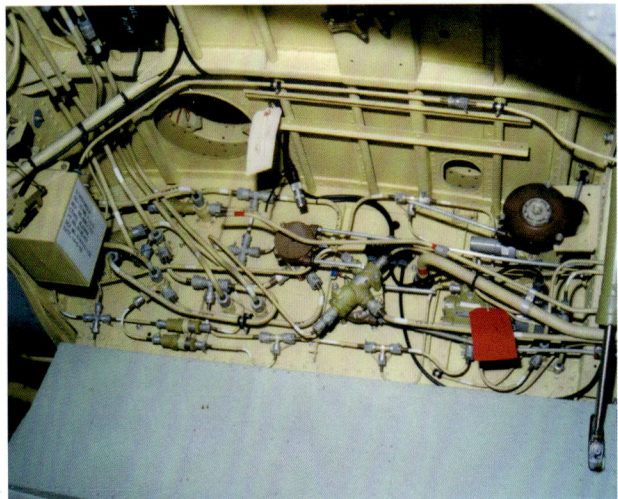

Moving over to the port side, this is the inboard face with the front of the aircraft to the left

Wings
Undercarriage Bays

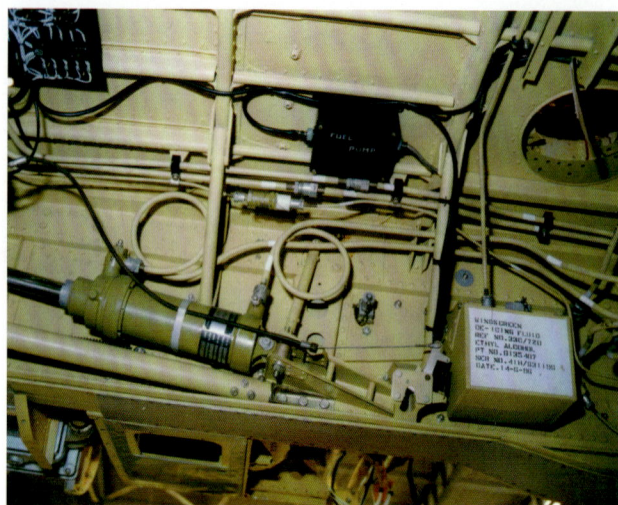

Swinging round in the port bay, this is the front rib area, looking forward. Again the u/c retraction jack dominates the area, but you can also see the windscreen de-icer tank

Continuing on round to the left in the port bay, this is the bulkhead inboard of the inter-spar tank you can see in the background and it contains this electrical distribution box

If you move round to the left once more in the port bay this is the rear bulkhead area, looking aft

If you keep moving round to your left in the port bay, this is the outer area with the oleo pivot point etc. The dark object you can see on the central rib is a wooden block that acts as a buffer for the oleo as it retracts, stopping it slamming into the wing rib in that area

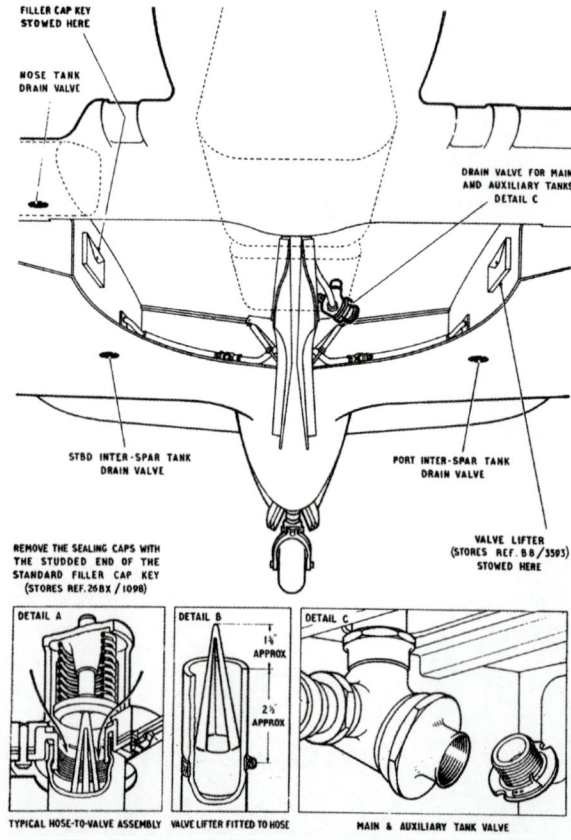

Not installed in the previous photos, this diagram shows the fuel tank sump in the port wheel well used to drain the main and auxiliary tanks in the fuselage (©Crown Copyright)

Group 5 – Side 1
Engine

A nice shot of the Centaurus from the TFC FB Mk 11
(© George Papadimitriou)

Another shot of the TFC engine, showing all the various colours seen on such an engine *(© George Papadimitriou)*

A closer look at the unit on display at Yeovilton – note the 'front' and 'back' cast into the baffle plates on the cylinder heads
(© George Papadimitriou)

A nice view of seven of the exhaust outlets, which go out of the starboard side; there are two banks of eight, but one exhaust from each bank goes out through the underside of the airframe *(© George Papadimitriou)*

This is the back of the Centaurus, showing the anciliary equipment in this area
(© George Papadimitriou)

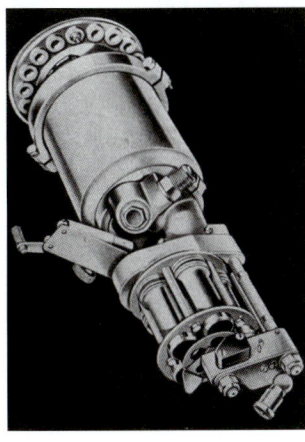

This period photo shows a Coffman starter unit

Under the nose of the Sea Fury you will find these louvre vents to allow hot air to come out of the engine bay *(© P. Skulski)*

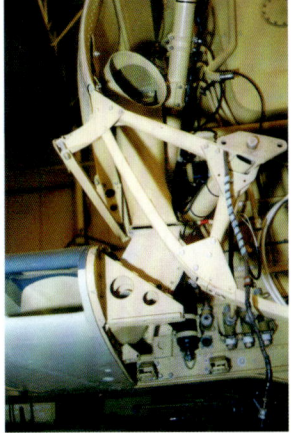

This photo shows how the carburettor intake in the wing root is ducted into the engine compartment area

Group 5 – Side 2
Engine
Engine & Cowling

This is what is termed as the 'break point', namely where the engine meets the mounts/bulkhead (© George Papadimitriou)

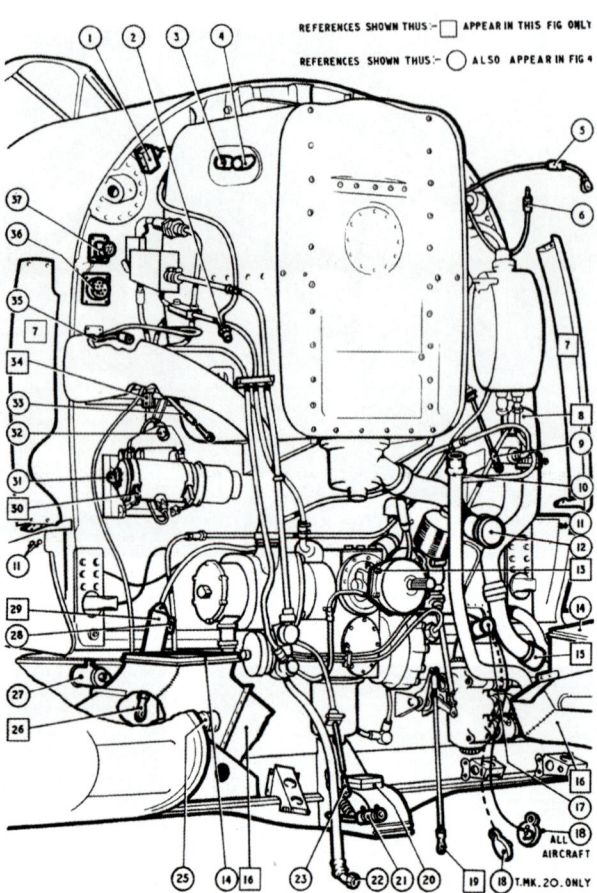

This diagram from the manual shows the fuselage bulkhead area of the 'break point' (©Crown Copyright)

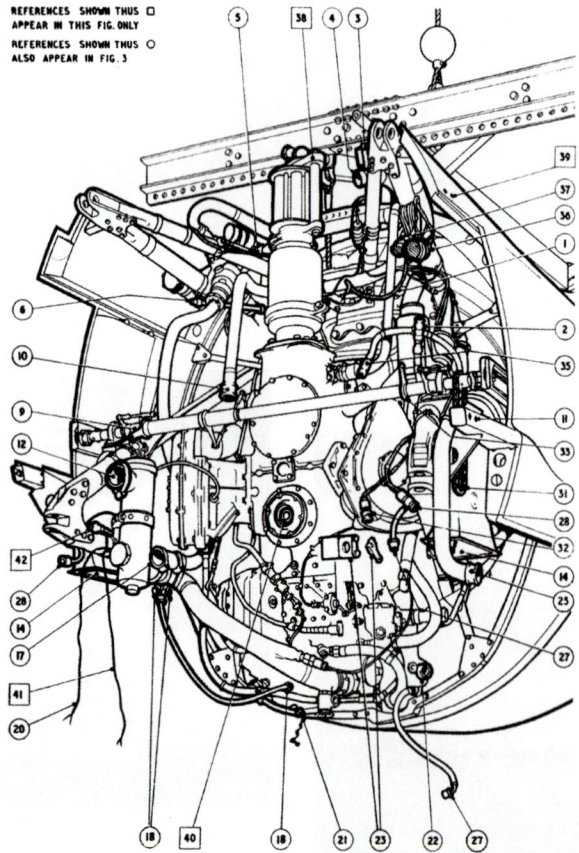

This diagram shows the engine power egg and the 'break point'. The item marked as '38' is the Coffman starter unit – see photo on previous page (©Crown Copyright)

A quick look from the front into the 'break point', the cast aluminium unit is the gearbox for the propeller pitch mechanism

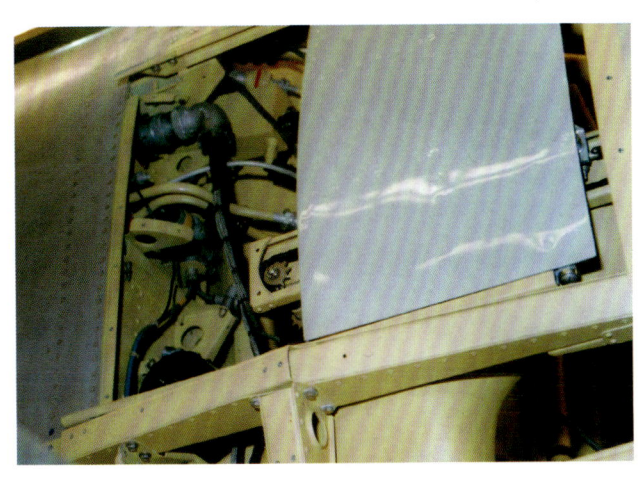

Group 5 – Side 3
Engine
Cowling & Propeller

Now people have told me there is no such things as 'cowl gills' on aircraft, they are 'cowl flaps', well they're not on the Sea Fury. According to the manual the chain driven unit seen here is for the 'gills' and it's aft of the exhaust outlets on both side of the nose

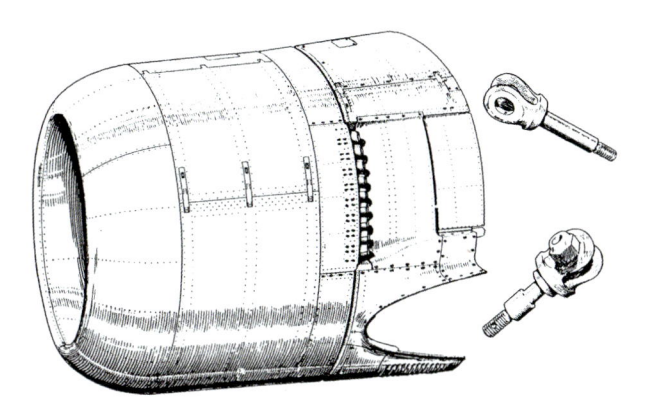

This diagram shows the cowlings fitted to all Sea fury variants, and their fixtures *(©Crown Copyright)*

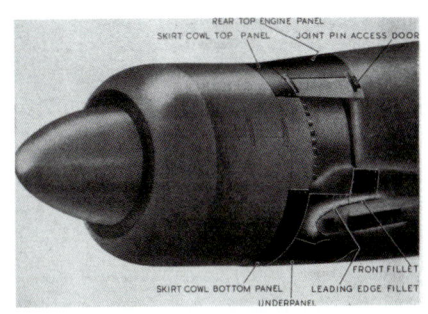

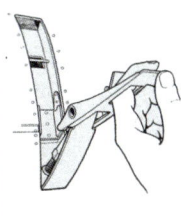

This photograph from the manual shows all the various other panels fitted around the cowl area, along with how the cowl panels are latched *(©Crown Copyright)*

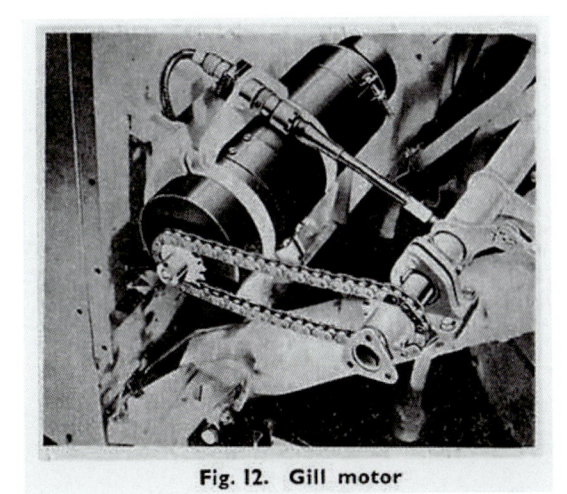

Just to prove the point, here is the photo from the manual with its title, definitely the 'gill motor'! *(©Crown Copyright)*

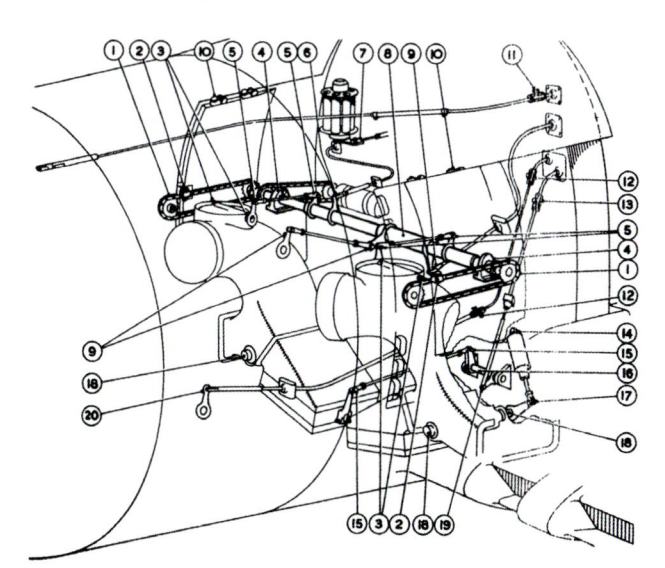

This lubrication diagram shows the chain-driven linkage for the cowl gills much better, as well as the Coffman starter (7) and both air intakes *(©Crown Copright)*

The Sea Fury had a whopping great big five-blade Rotol propeller, as illustrated nicely here with this shot of the RNHF airworthy example during a visit to Duxford

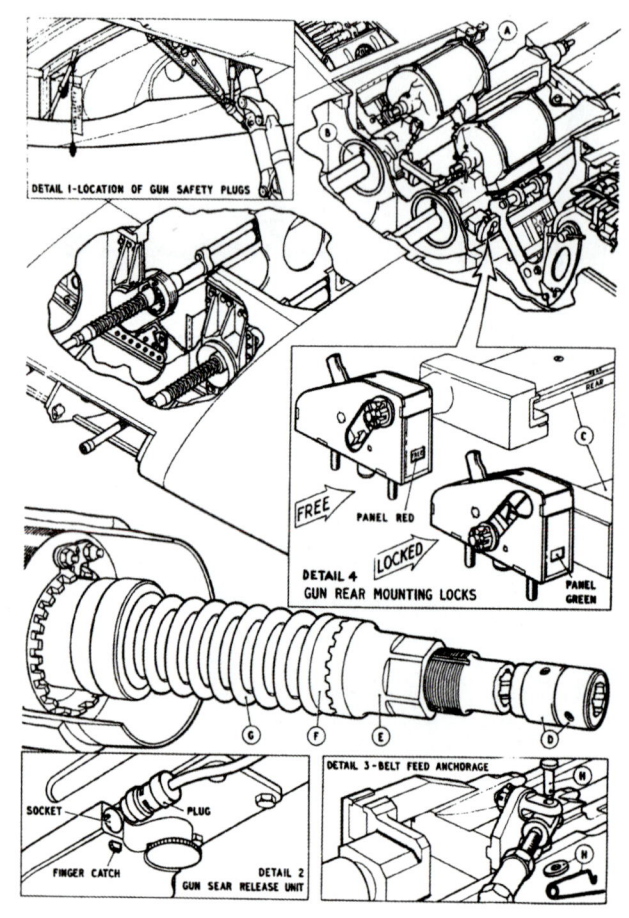

Group 6 – Side 1
Weaponry
Armament

All Sea Furies had Hispano 20mm cannon, four in the fighter/fighter-bomber versions and two in the trainer. This diagram shows the basic four-gun installation *(©Crown Copyright)*

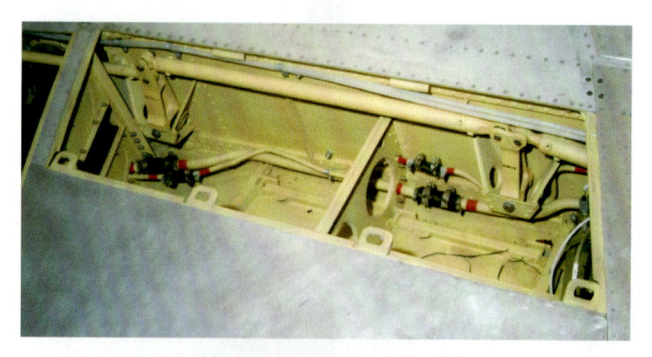

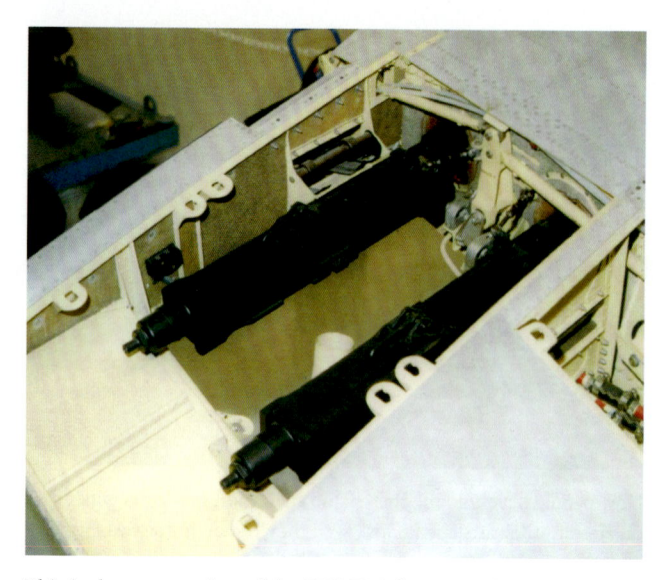

This is the port gun bay of the TFC FB Mk 11, just the bare elements are fitted at present

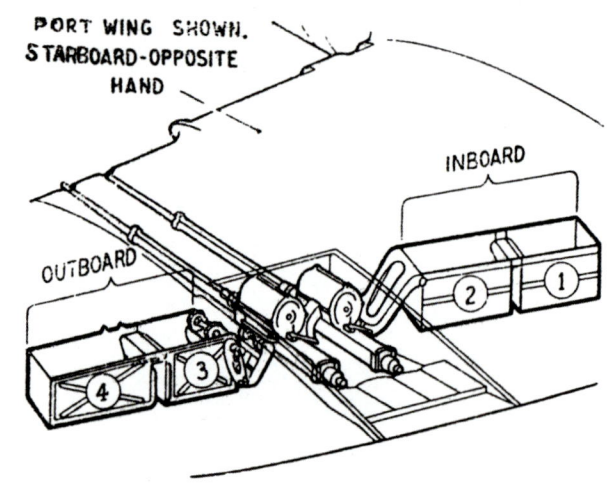

This diagram shows the ammo tracks for the cannon *(©Crown Copyright)*

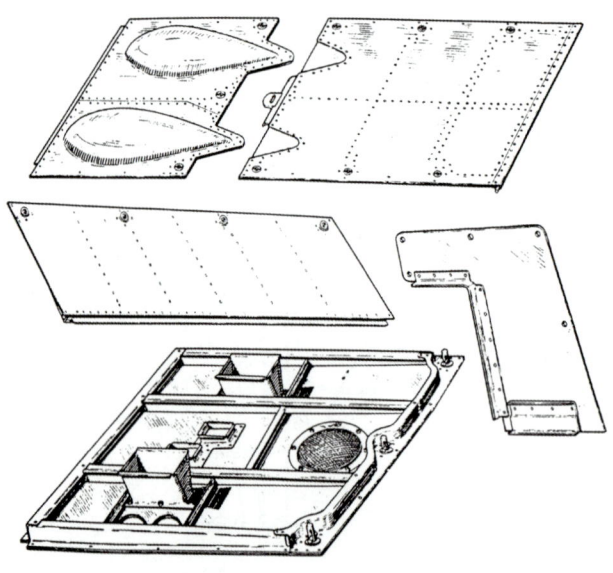

This is the inboard ammunition bay in the port wing

If you look into the gun bay from the trailing edge this is the view of the front spar, with the ports for each cannon going through it

A nice set of diagrams from the parts manual showing the gun access panels in more detail *(©Crown Copyright)*

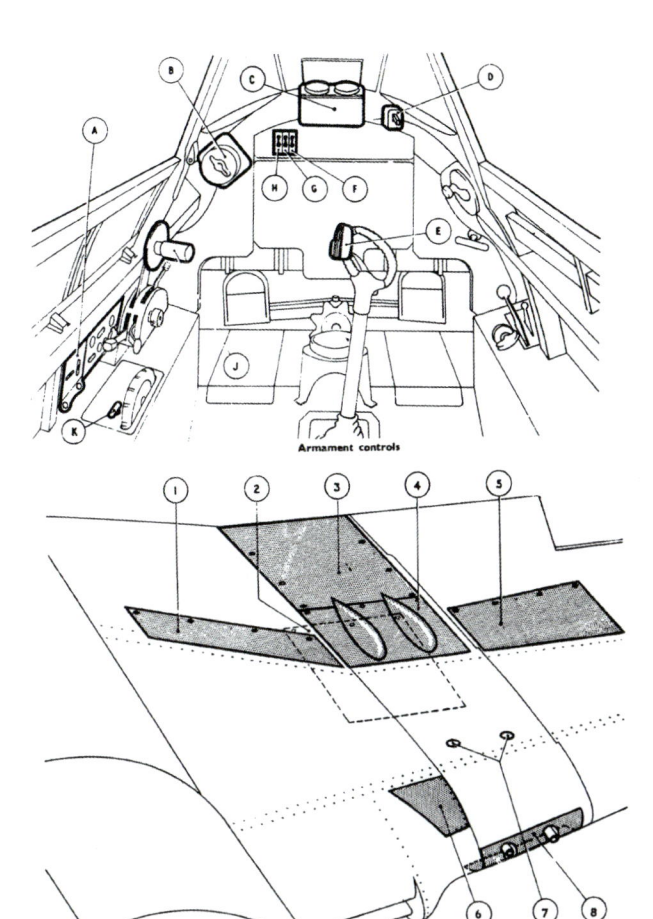

Group 6 – Side 2
Weaponry
Armament

With the front access panel in place you can see how the guns line up with the leading edge – this is the starboard side, hence the outer one this time projects further forward (©P. Skulski)

These two diagrams show the armament related controls in the cockpit (top) and access doors in the wing (bottom)
(©Crown Copyright)

What you cannot see in the below photo is the fixed element in the inner wing, this is it and the track seen in the below photo 'runs' round it when the wing is folded

Key
- A. External stores control switch
- B. Gyro Gunsight dimmer/selector control
- C. Gyro Gunsight (GGS)
- D. GGS – guns/R.P. switch
- E. Gun firing, bombs, R.P. and ciné camera control
- F. Ciné camera – sunny/cloudy switch
- G. Ciné camera master switch
- H. GGS master switch
- J. GGS – range control
- K. Universal camera release toggle
- 1. Inboard ammunition tanks
- 2. Guns – under wings
- 3. Guns – upper rear
- 4. Guns – upper front
- 5. Outboard ammunition tanks
- 6. Ciné camera – port only
- 7. Gun gas plugs
- 8. Gun front mountings

Here you can see the cannon in the port wing, note that the outboard cannon is further forward

Now, with the gun bays so near the wing fold the ammo tracks have to fold. Here you can see how this is achieved with the starboard wing folded (©P. Skulski)

Group 6 – Side 3
Weaponry
Ordnance

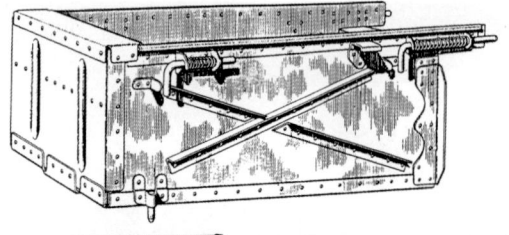

This is a more detailed diagram of the ammo bins seen on page 40 (mid-right) in the diagram about ammunition tracks, the top one is (1) & (4) in the previous diagram, the bottom-left is (2) and the bottom-right (3) *(©Crown Copyright)*

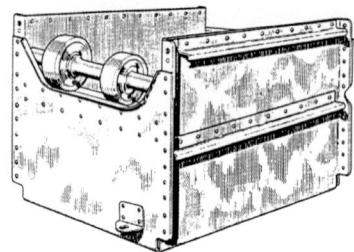

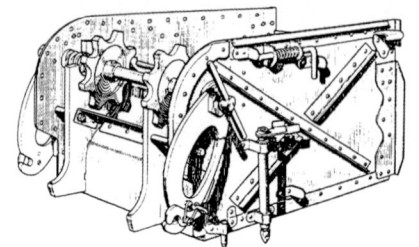

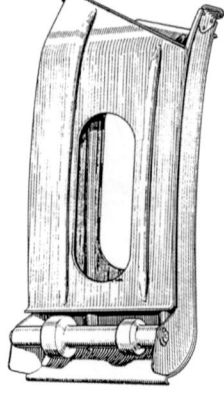

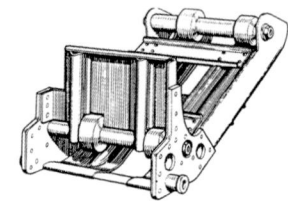

Here is a diagram from the parts manual showing the track (top) and fixed element (below) seen in the photos on previous page *(©Crown Copyright)*

In this period photo, RCN WG573 is being loaded with a 1,000lb GP bomb on the starboard wing rack
(©Public Archives of Canada)

Armourers attach dummy rockets with concrete heads for practice firing. This was a common scene at HMS Falcon (Hal Far, Malta). Such live firing practice usually had the uninhabited islet of Filfla, to the south of Malta, as target – photo dated 13th June 1952. Note the bar still in place between the posts in this single rocket installation, and the fact that only two rockets per wing are being carried
(©R.J. Caruana Archives)

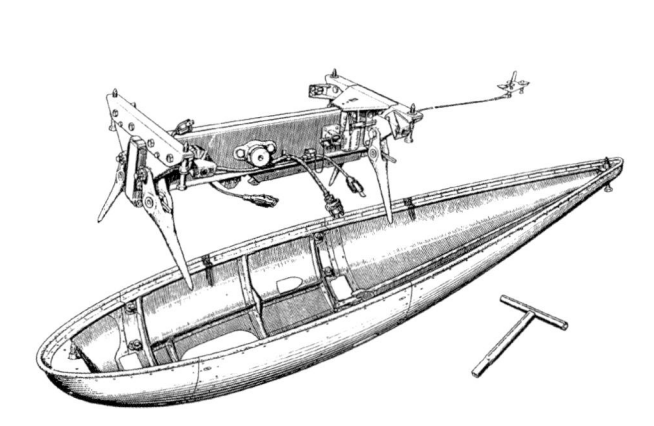

Group 6 – Side 4	**1**
Weaponry	
Ordnance	43

Although not a great image, this does show the fitment of practice bomb racks on the Sea Fury. This was often seen when the RNVR squadrons operated the type

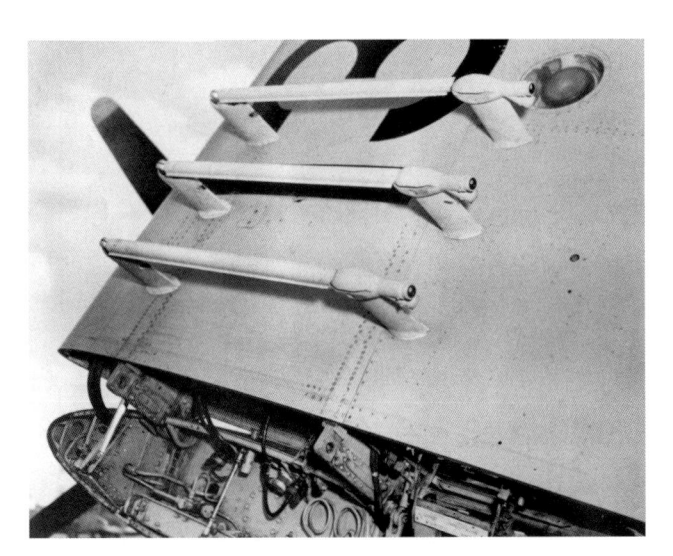

The FB Mk 11 had the capacity to carry up to 2,000lb of bombs on the two underwing racks seen here *(©Crown Copyright)*

A nice period photo showing the rocket rails fitted under the outer wing panel. Only three are visible here, although two or three could be installed. As seen here these are for single-rocket carriage, when the two-tier system was used the connecting bar between the two posts was removed *(©RCN)*

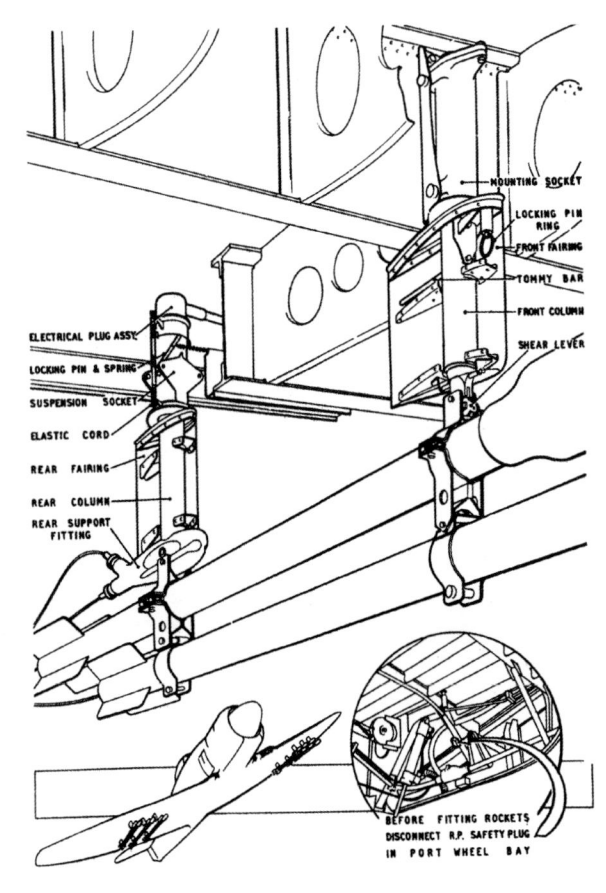

In this diagram from the manual you can see the top stubs of the zero-length rails used on the Sea Fury, as well as the two-tier rocket set-up *(©Crown Copyright)*

This nice period image of VX642 shows the huge wealth of ordnance the type could carry *(©Hawker Aircraft)*

Group 6 – Side 5
Weaponry
Sighting / Drop Tanks

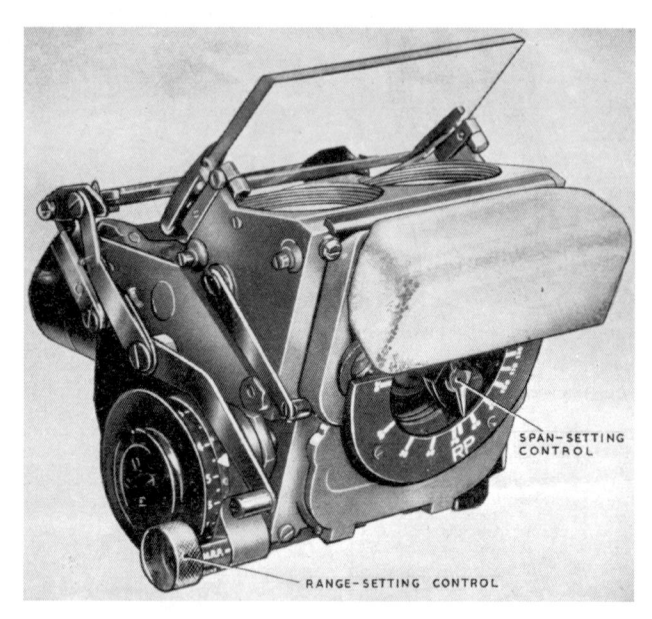

The Sea Fury used a Gyroscopic Gun Sight (GGS) like this Mk 7 version seen here *(©Crown Copyright)*

This close-up of an RCN machine shows it fitted with the 90Imp. Gal. tanks *(©RCN)*

The Sea Fury could carry two sizes of drop tank (45 & 90Imp. Gal.), both designed by Hawker and seen here in this close-up of the photo of VX642 *(©Hawker Aircraft)*

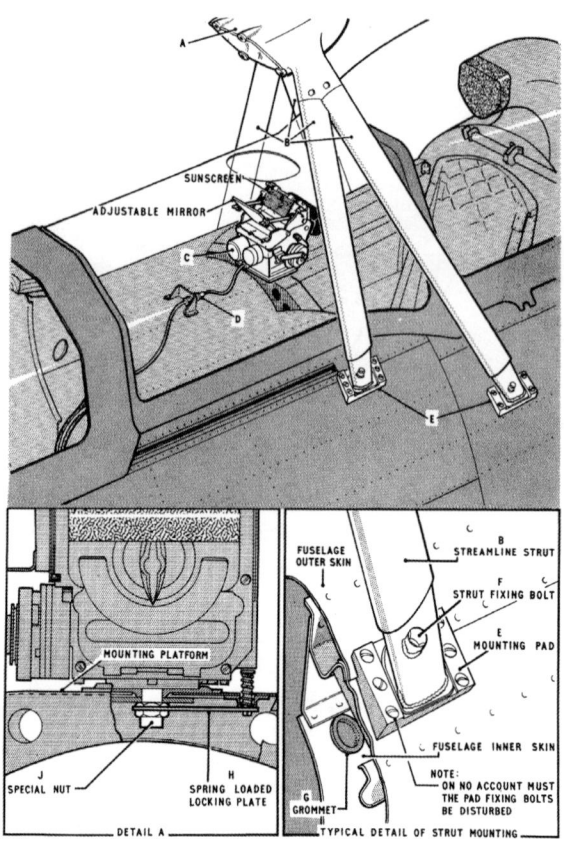

The trainer versions were fitted with this simple mirror periscope to allow the instructor in the back seat to keep an eye on the front seat's (the pupil's) instrument panel and GGS *(©Crown Copyright)*

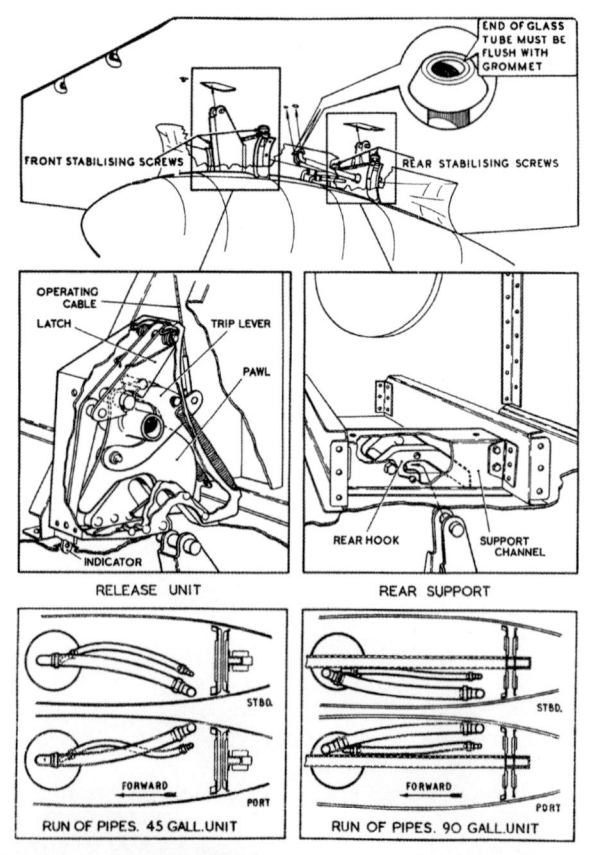

This diagram from the manual shows how the drop tanks were installed/removed *(©Crown Copyright)*

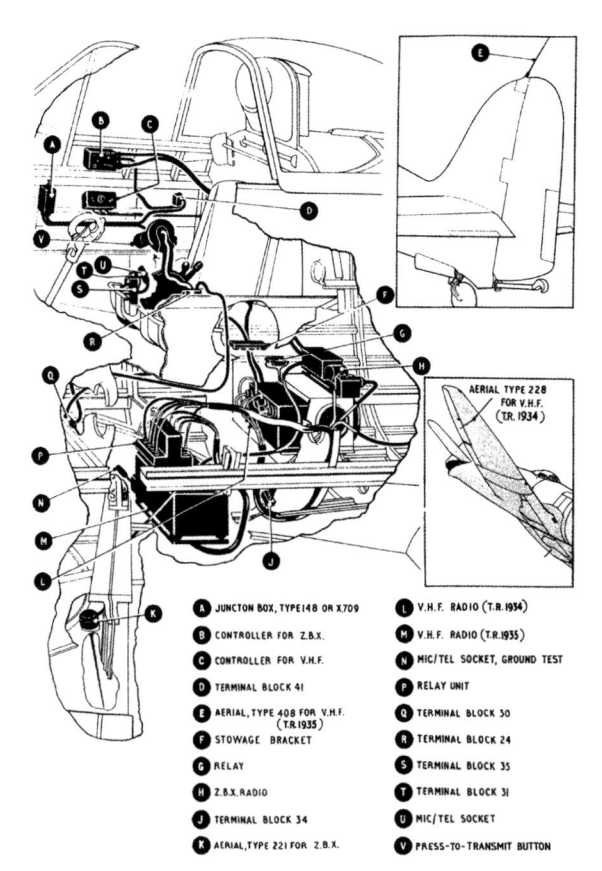

Group 7 – Side 1
Electrical
Radio

- A JUNCTION BOX, TYPE 148 OR X709
- B CONTROLLER FOR Z.B.X.
- C CONTROLLER FOR V.H.F.
- D TERMINAL BLOCK 41
- E AERIAL, TYPE 408 FOR V.H.F. (T.R.1935)
- F STOWAGE BRACKET
- G RELAY
- H Z.B.X. RADIO
- J TERMINAL BLOCK 34
- K AERIAL, TYPE 221 FOR Z.B.X.
- L V.H.F. RADIO (T.R.1934)
- M V.H.F. RADIO (T.R.1935)
- N MIC/TEL SOCKET, GROUND TEST
- P RELAY UNIT
- Q TERMINAL BLOCK 30
- R TERMINAL BLOCK 24
- S TERMINAL BLOCK 35
- T TERMINAL BLOCK 31
- U MIC/TEL SOCKET
- V PRESS-TO-TRANSMIT BUTTON

This diagram shows the later radio equipment installation, with the whip antenna on the top of the fin. The earlier installation had the SCR.522 unit and the whip antenna on the dorsal spine
(©Crown Copyright)

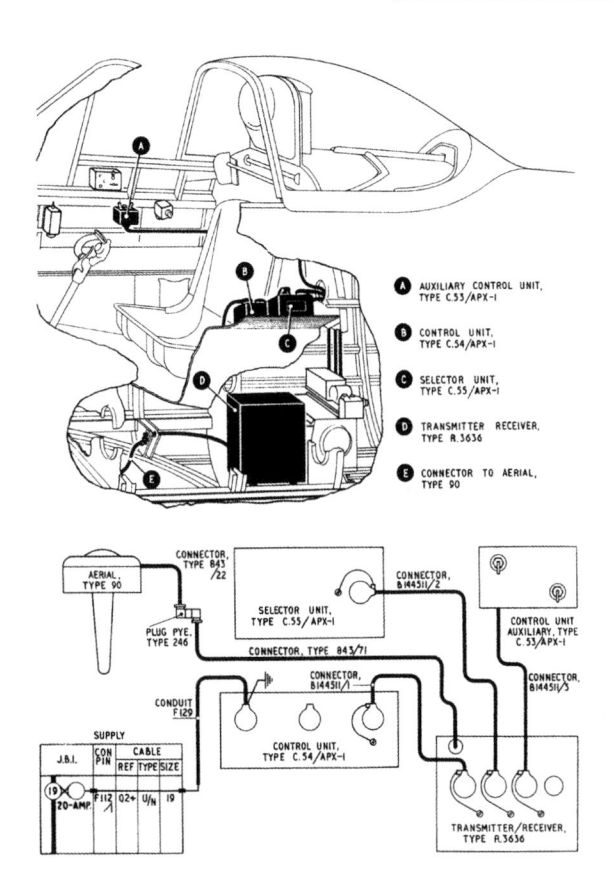

- A AUXILIARY CONTROL UNIT, TYPE C.53/APX-1
- B CONTROL UNIT, TYPE C.54/APX-1
- C SELECTOR UNIT, TYPE C.55/APX-1
- D TRANSMITTER RECEIVER, TYPE R.3636
- E CONNECTOR TO AERIAL, TYPE 90

This diagram shows the location of the ARI.5679 intercommunication system *(©Crown Copyright)*

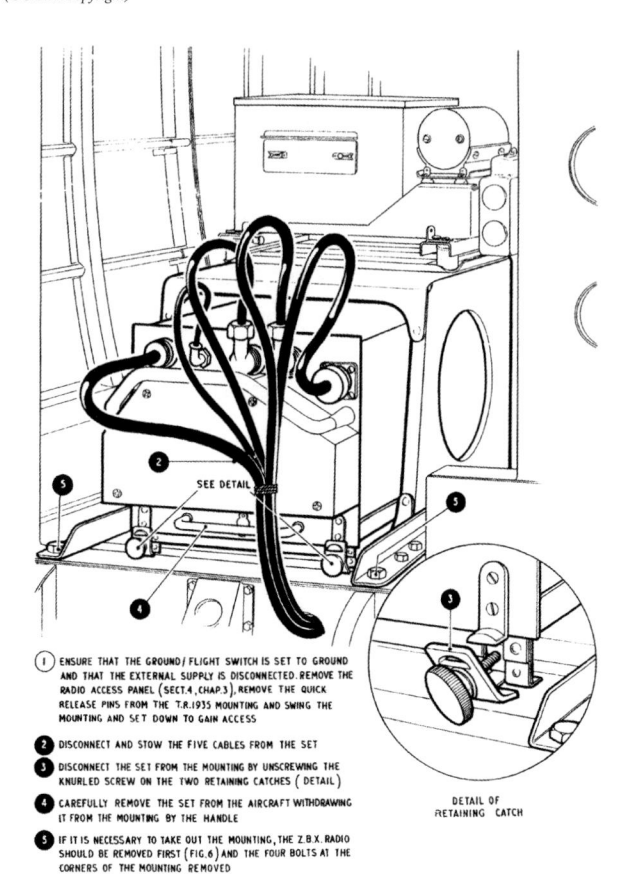

1. ENSURE THAT THE GROUND/FLIGHT SWITCH IS SET TO GROUND AND THAT THE EXTERNAL SUPPLY IS DISCONNECTED. REMOVE THE RADIO ACCESS PANEL (SECT.4, CHAP.3), REMOVE THE QUICK RELEASE PINS FROM THE T.R.1935 MOUNTING AND SWING THE MOUNTING AND SET DOWN TO GAIN ACCESS
2. DISCONNECT AND STOW THE FIVE CABLES FROM THE SET
3. DISCONNECT THE SET FROM THE MOUNTING BY UNSCREWING THE KNURLED SCREW ON THE TWO RETAINING CATCHES (DETAIL)
4. CAREFULLY REMOVE THE SET FROM THE AIRCRAFT WITHDRAWING IT FROM THE MOUNTING BY THE HANDLE
5. IF IT IS NECESSARY TO TAKE OUT THE MOUNTING, THE Z.B.X. RADIO SHOULD BE REMOVED FIRST (FIG.6) AND THE FOUR BOLTS AT THE CORNERS OF THE MOUNTING REMOVED

The TR.1934 VHF receiver/transmitter *(©Crown Copyright)*

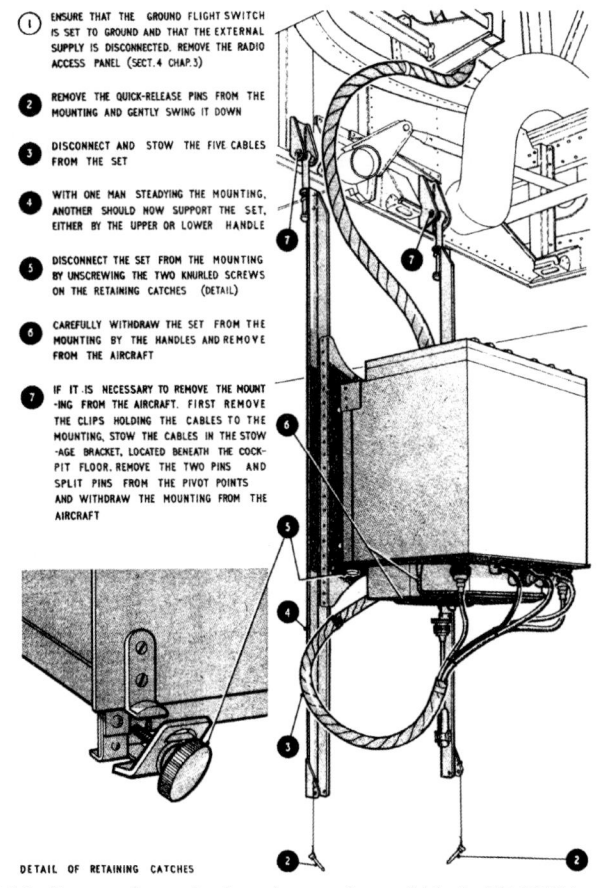

1. ENSURE THAT THE GROUND FLIGHT SWITCH IS SET TO GROUND AND THAT THE EXTERNAL SUPPLY IS DISCONNECTED. REMOVE THE RADIO ACCESS PANEL (SECT.4 CHAP.3)
2. REMOVE THE QUICK-RELEASE PINS FROM THE MOUNTING AND GENTLY SWING IT DOWN
3. DISCONNECT AND STOW THE FIVE CABLES FROM THE SET
4. WITH ONE MAN STEADYING THE MOUNTING, ANOTHER SHOULD NOW SUPPORT THE SET, EITHER BY THE UPPER OR LOWER HANDLE
5. DISCONNECT THE SET FROM THE MOUNTING BY UNSCREWING THE TWO KNURLED SCREWS ON THE RETAINING CATCHES (DETAIL)
6. CAREFULLY WITHDRAW THE SET FROM THE MOUNTING BY THE HANDLES AND REMOVE FROM THE AIRCRAFT
7. IF IT IS NECESSARY TO REMOVE THE MOUNTING FROM THE AIRCRAFT, FIRST REMOVE THE CLIPS HOLDING THE CABLES TO THE MOUNTING, STOW THE CABLES IN THE STOWAGE BRACKET, LOCATED BENEATH THE COCKPIT FLOOR. REMOVE THE TWO PINS AND SPLIT PINS FROM THE PIVOT POINTS AND WITHDRAW THE MOUNTING FROM THE AIRCRAFT

This diagram shows the drop-down rack on which the TR.1935 is removed *(©Crown Copyright)*

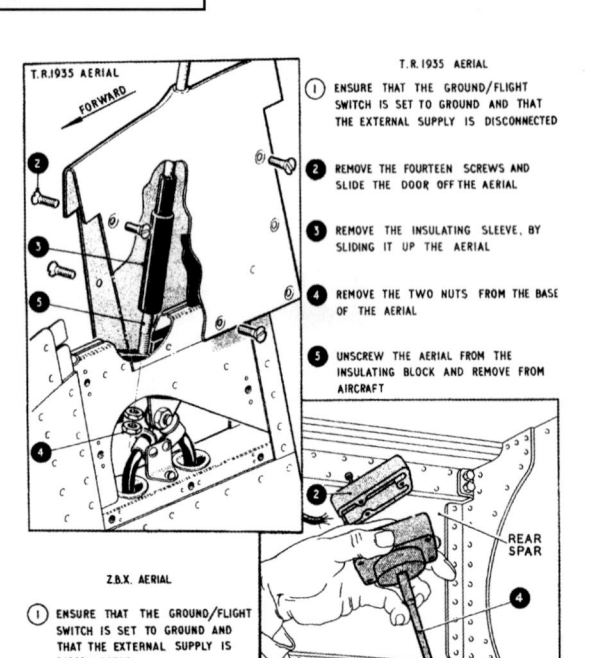

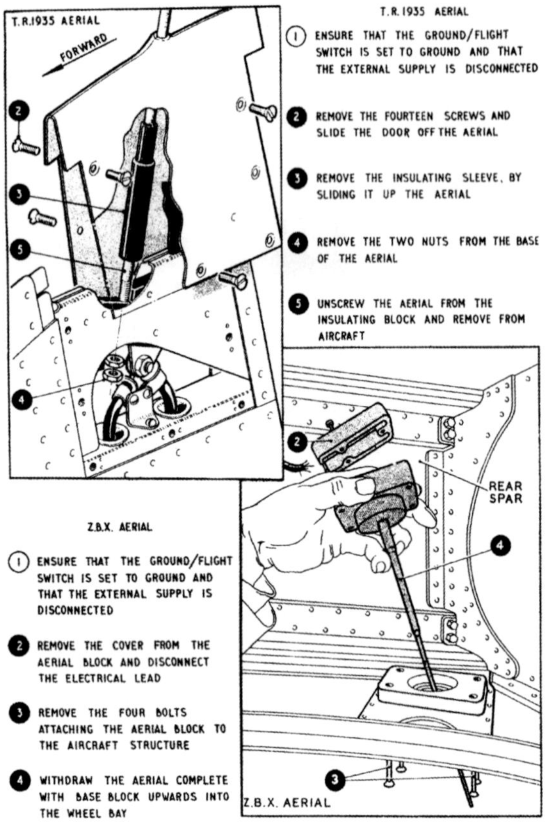

Group 7 – Side 2
Electrical
Radio

The TR.1935 aerial is in the tip of the vertical fin, whilst the ARI.5307 is in the wheel well, this diagram shows the removal of both (#Crown Copyright)

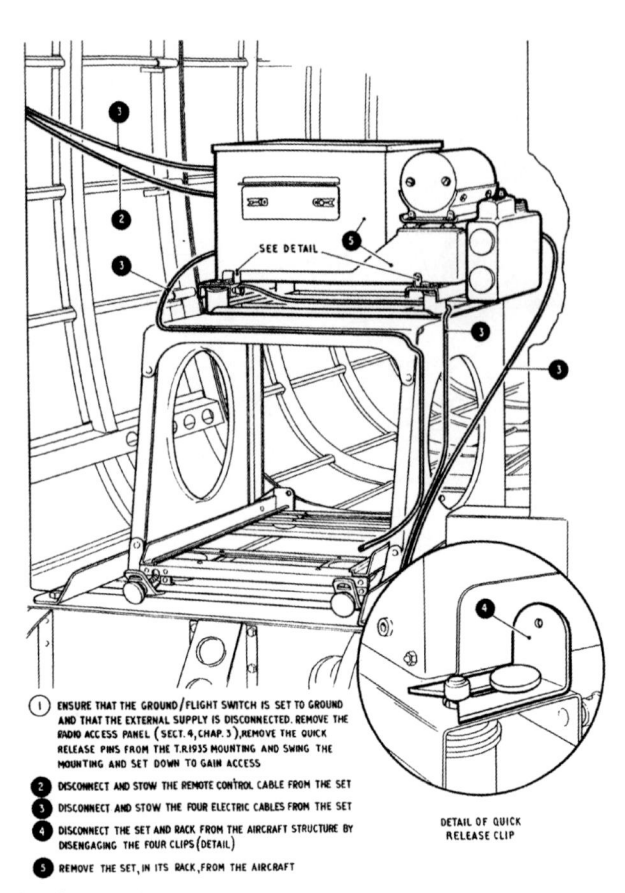

This diagram shows the installation of the ARI.5307 (Z.B.X) system

(©Crown Copyright)

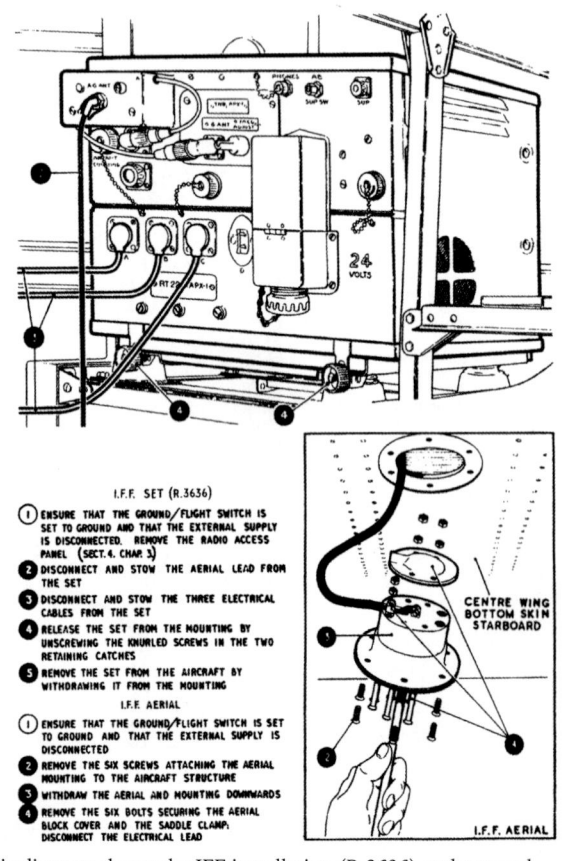

This diagram shows the IFF installation (R.3636) and removal

(©Crown Copyright)

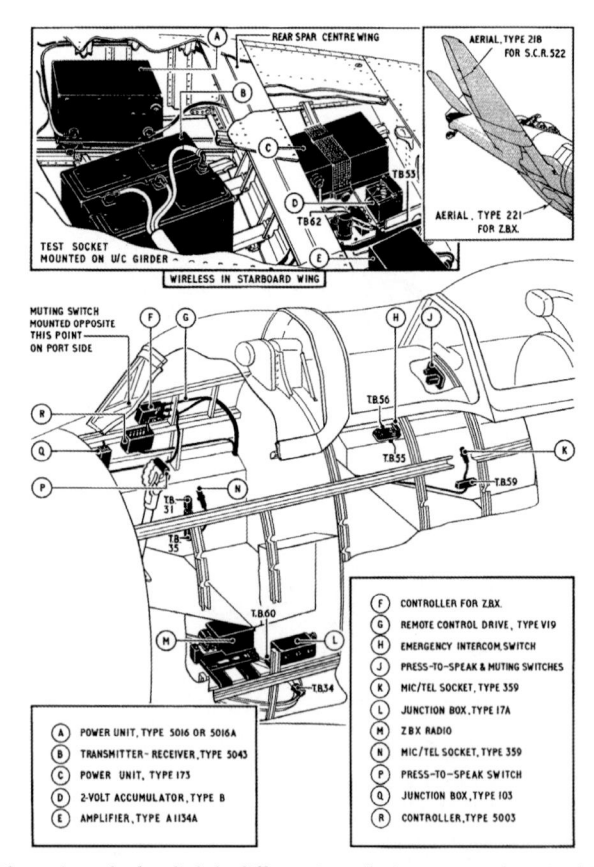

The trainers had a slightly different installation, as seen here in this diagram. Note that this shows the early SCR.522 system

(©Crown Copyright)

Group 7 – Side 3
Electrical
Radio / Miscellaneous

TR.5043 installation — labels and instructions:

- UNDERCARRIAGE GIRDER
- MEMBER FORWARD OF TANK
- ACCESS DOOR FASTENER MOUNTING
- RADIO MOUNTING
- DETAIL

1. ENSURE THAT THE GROUND/FLIGHT SWITCH IS SET TO GROUND AND THAT THE EXTERNAL SUPPLY IS DISCONNECTED
2. REMOVE THE RADIO ACCESS PANEL FROM BENEATH THE STARBOARD CENTRE WING BY DISENGAGING THE FOUR FASTENERS
3. REMOVE THE TWO FORWARD QUICK RELEASE PINS (B), THEN, SUPPORTING RADIO MOUNTING, REMOVE THE TWO REAR QUICK RELEASE PINS (C) AND SLIDE THE MOUNTING FORWARD UNTIL IT CAN BE SWUNG DOWN
4. DISCONNECT AND STOW THE THREE CABLES (E) FROM THE SET
5. WITH ONE MAN SUPPORTING THE SET, DISCONNECT FROM THE MOUNTING BY REMOVING THE FOUR BOLTS, SPRING WASHERS AND CHECK-WASHERS (D) ON THE UNDERSIDE CORNERS OF THE SET (DETAIL). REMOVE THE SET
6. IF IT IS NECESSARY TO TAKE OUT THE MOUNTING, THE TWO BOLTS, SPLIT PINS AND NUTS (A) SHOULD BE REMOVED

This is the TR.5043 installation in the T Mk 20 (*©Crown Copyright*)

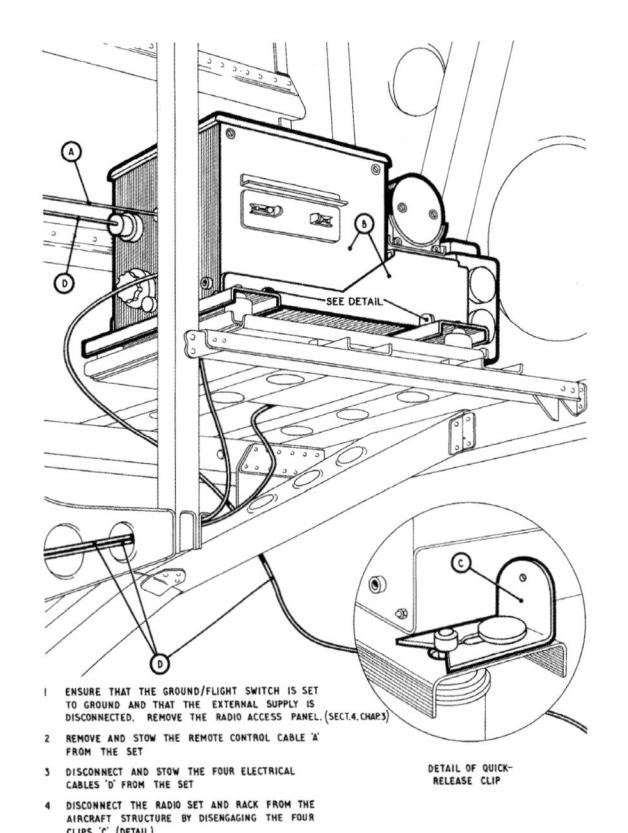

ARI.5307 (Z.B.X.) installation — instructions:

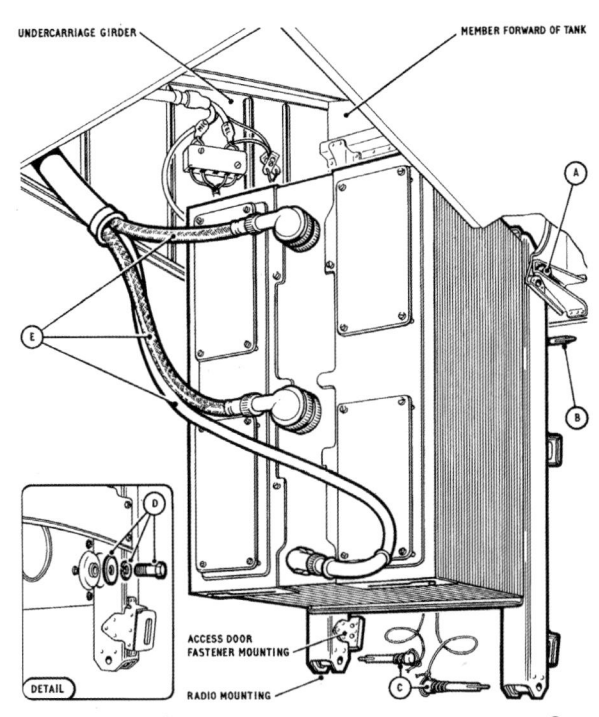

- DETAIL OF QUICK-RELEASE CLIP

1. ENSURE THAT THE GROUND/FLIGHT SWITCH IS SET TO GROUND AND THAT THE EXTERNAL SUPPLY IS DISCONNECTED. REMOVE THE RADIO ACCESS PANEL. (SECT.4, CHAP.3)
2. REMOVE AND STOW THE REMOTE CONTROL CABLE 'A' FROM THE SET
3. DISCONNECT AND STOW THE FOUR ELECTRICAL CABLES 'D' FROM THE SET
4. DISCONNECT THE RADIO SET AND RACK FROM THE AIRCRAFT STRUCTURE BY DISENGAGING THE FOUR CLIPS 'C' (DETAIL)
5. REMOVE THE RADIO SET IN ITS RACK FROM THE AIRCRAFT

And this diagram shows the ARI.5307 (Z.B.X.) installation in the T Mk 20 (*©Crown Copyright*)

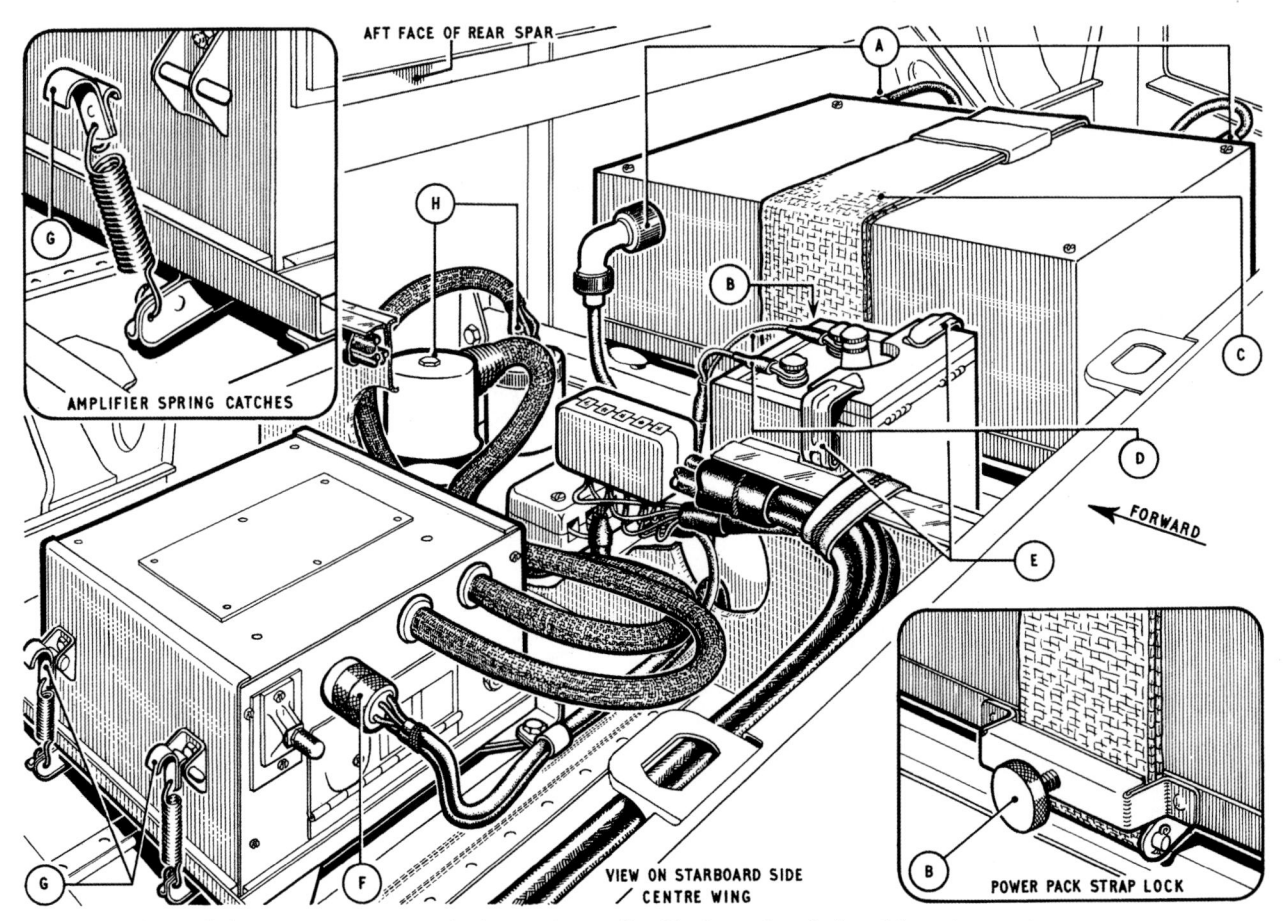

Intercommunication equipment labels:

- AFT FACE OF REAR SPAR
- AMPLIFIER SPRING CATCHES
- FORWARD
- VIEW ON STARBOARD SIDE / CENTRE WING
- POWER PACK STRAP LOCK

This diagram shows all the various intercommunication equipment fitted in the starboard wing of the trainer versions (*©Crown Copyright*)

Group 7 – Side 4
Electrical
Miscellaneous

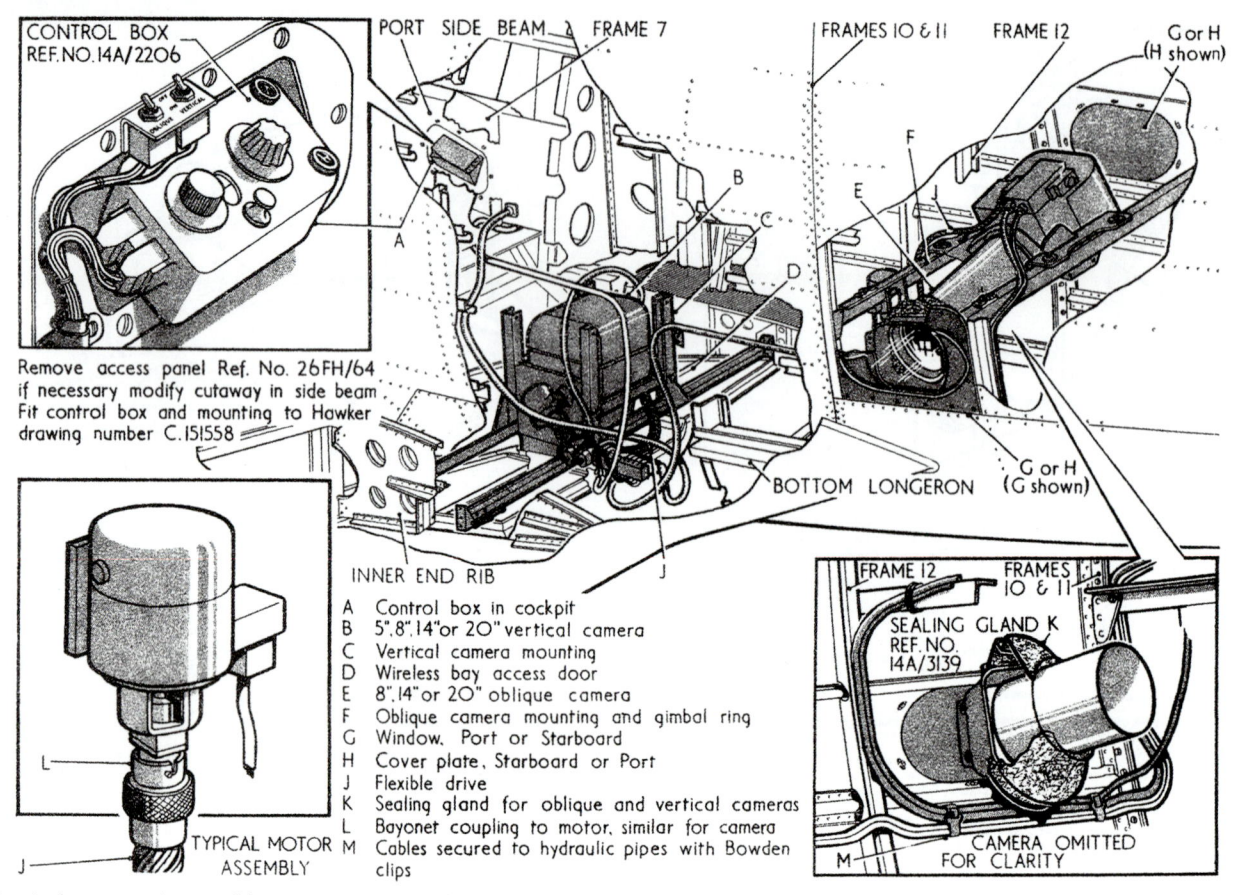

CONTROL BOX REF. NO. 14A/2206

Remove access panel Ref. No. 26FH/64 if necessary modify cutaway in side beam. Fit control box and mounting to Hawker drawing number C.151558

PORT SIDE BEAM — FRAME 7 — FRAMES 10 & 11 — FRAME 12 — G or H (H shown)

BOTTOM LONGERON — G or H (G shown)

INNER END RIB

TYPICAL MOTOR ASSEMBLY

A — Control box in cockpit
B — 5", 8", 14" or 20" vertical camera
C — Vertical camera mounting
D — Wireless bay access door
E — 8", 14" or 20" oblique camera
F — Oblique camera mounting and gimbal ring
G — Window, Port or Starboard
H — Cover plate, Starboard or Port
J — Flexible drive
K — Sealing gland for oblique and vertical cameras
L — Bayonet coupling to motor, similar for camera
M — Cables secured to hydraulic pipes with Bowden clips

FRAME 12 — FRAMES 10 & 11 — SEALING GLAND K REF. NO. 14A/3139 — CAMERA OMITTED FOR CLARITY

The single-seat versions could carry two camera in three locations, this diagram shows both vertical and oblique installations (©*Crown Copyright*)

This is the port for the oblique camera in the starboard side (©*P. Skulski*)

While this photo shows the hole for the camera in the port side. These would be covered with plates when a camera was not installed (©*P. Skulski*)

DUMMY T.B. MOUNTED UNDER COCKPIT FLOOR ABOVE BATTERIES

BATTERY SUPPORT BRACKET — BATTERY PLATFORM — VOLTAGE REGULATOR AND CUT-OUT UNIT

1. ENSURE THAT THE GROUND/FLIGHT SWITCH IS SET TO GROUND & THAT THE EXTERNAL SUPPLY IS DISCONNECTED. REMOVE THE RADIO ACCESS PANEL (SECT. 4, CHAP. 3)
2. DISCONNECT THE ELECTRICAL CABLES FROM THE FOUR TERMINALS AND STOW ON DUMMY T.B.
3. SLACKEN OFF THE FOUR WING NUTS
4. DISENGAGE THE MOUNTING CLAMPS FROM THE ANCHOR BOLTS
5. LIFT THE BATTERIES OUT BY THE STRAPS

This period photo shows the vertical camera installation under the fuselage of a RCN FB Mk 11 (©*Public Archive of Canada/RCN*)

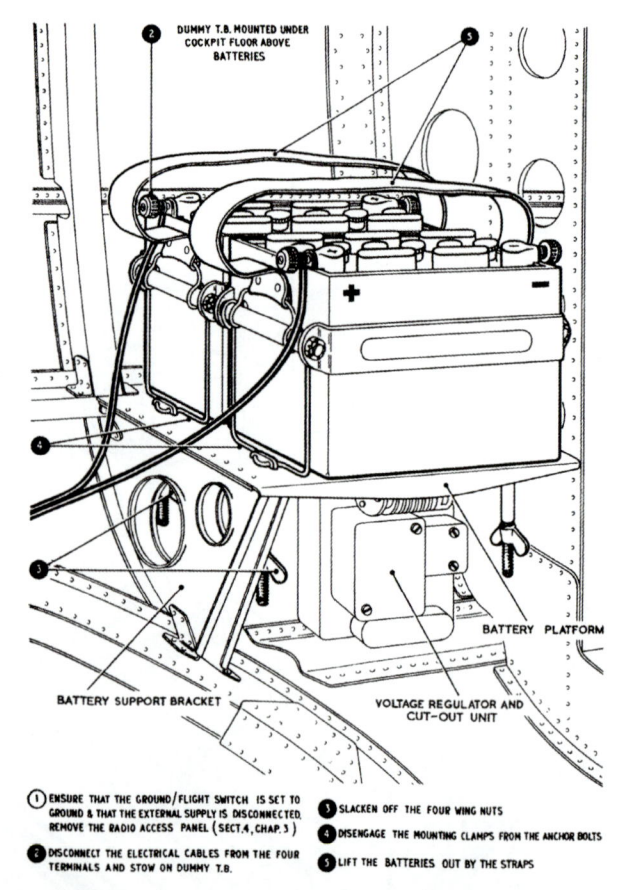

This diagram shows the removal of the batteries under the floor in the fuselage of the fighter variants (©*Crown Copyright*)

Group 8 – Side 1	**1**
Miscellaneous	
Access Panels	49

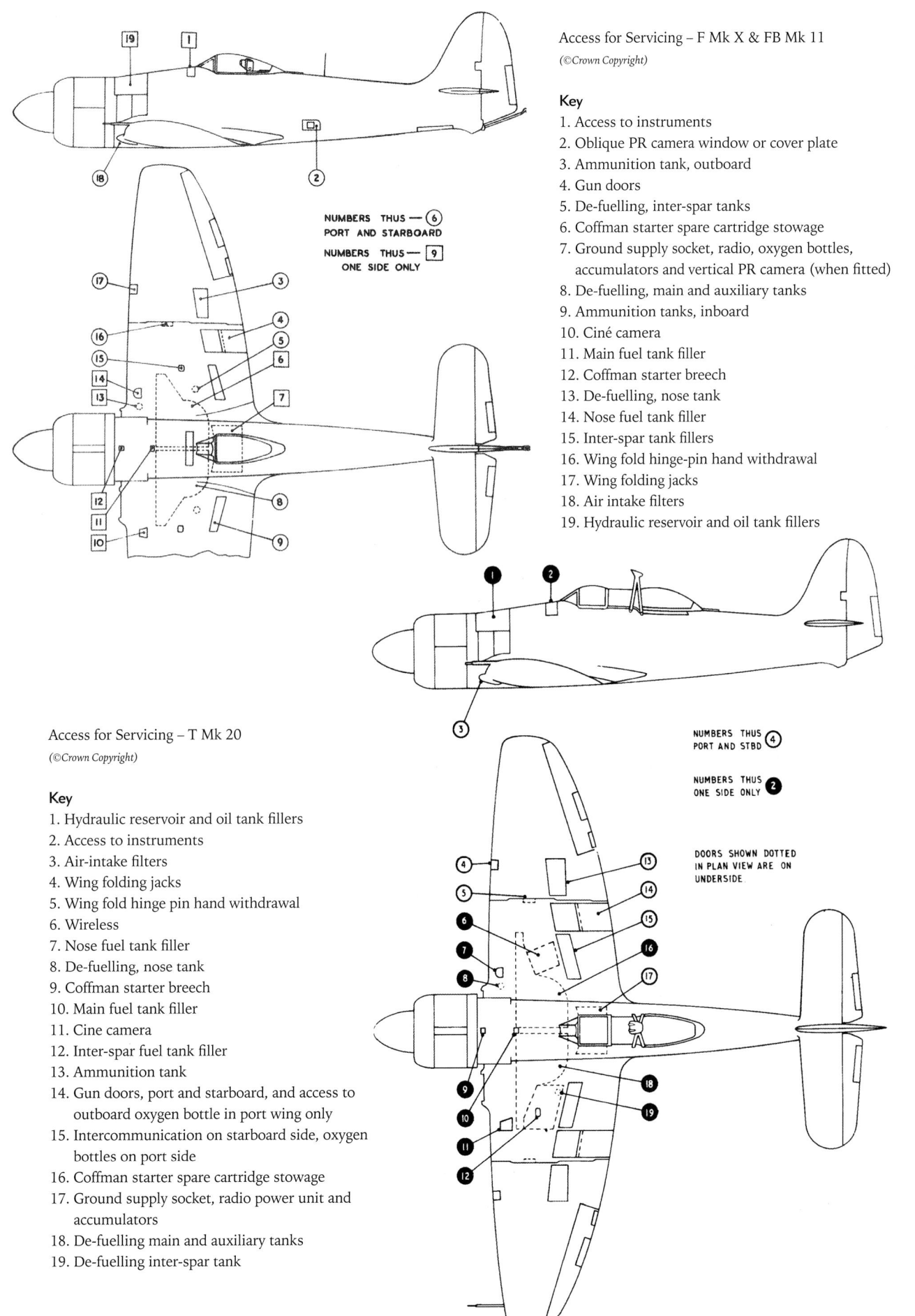

Access for Servicing – F Mk X & FB Mk 11
(©Crown Copyright)

Key
1. Access to instruments
2. Oblique PR camera window or cover plate
3. Ammunition tank, outboard
4. Gun doors
5. De-fuelling, inter-spar tanks
6. Coffman starter spare cartridge stowage
7. Ground supply socket, radio, oxygen bottles, accumulators and vertical PR camera (when fitted)
8. De-fuelling, main and auxiliary tanks
9. Ammunition tanks, inboard
10. Ciné camera
11. Main fuel tank filler
12. Coffman starter breech
13. De-fuelling, nose tank
14. Nose fuel tank filler
15. Inter-spar tank fillers
16. Wing fold hinge-pin hand withdrawal
17. Wing folding jacks
18. Air intake filters
19. Hydraulic reservoir and oil tank fillers

Access for Servicing – T Mk 20
(©Crown Copyright)

Key
1. Hydraulic reservoir and oil tank fillers
2. Access to instruments
3. Air-intake filters
4. Wing folding jacks
5. Wing fold hinge pin hand withdrawal
6. Wireless
7. Nose fuel tank filler
8. De-fuelling, nose tank
9. Coffman starter breech
10. Main fuel tank filler
11. Cine camera
12. Inter-spar fuel tank filler
13. Ammunition tank
14. Gun doors, port and starboard, and access to outboard oxygen bottle in port wing only
15. Intercommunication on starboard side, oxygen bottles on port side
16. Coffman starter spare cartridge stowage
17. Ground supply socket, radio power unit and accumulators
18. De-fuelling main and auxiliary tanks
19. De-fuelling inter-spar tank

AA02/18/49 — Valiant Wings Publishing — Issued: March 2018

Group 8 – Side 2
Miscellaneous
50 Access Panels

Doors & Removable Panels
– F Mk X & FB Mk 11

(©Crown Copyright)

Key
1. Navigation lamps (wings)
2. Aileron outer hinges
3. Aileron operating gear
4. Aileron spring tab gear
5. Aileron inner hinges
6. Door for withdrawing hinge pin by hand
7. Wing rear hinge
8. Guns
9. Inboard ammunition tank
10. Radio access panel
11. Elevator outer hinge
12. Elevator trim tab control gear
13. Elevator trim tab control cables
14. Flap jacks
15. Fuel tank fillers
16. Guns
17. Guns
18. Outboard ammunition tank
19. Downward identification lamps
20. Aileron operating gear
21. Doors in cockpit walls
22. Pitot tube
23. Emergency exit panel
24. Emergency hood release
25. Door for tailplane assembly
26. Elevator trimming tab control pulleys
27. Rudder tab lever fairing
28. Rudder spring tab operating gear
29. Rudder bottom fairing
30. Rudder lever fairing
31. Navigation lamps (tail)
32. Rudder control rods and tail trim cables
33. Access door for rudder control gear
34. Dished diaphragm over tailwheel
35. Access to instruments
36. Tank panel
37. Rear top engine panel
38. Rear top detachable panel
39. Engine cooling shutter and fairings
40. Undercarriage shock-absorber pin
41. Undercarriage fairing attachments
42. Front fillet
43. Underpanel
44. Leading edge fillet
45. Top and bottom skirt panels
46. Bottom fixed hinge panel
47. Lower cowl panel
48. Upper cowl panel
49. Top fixed hinge panel
50. Nose cowl
51. Pitot tube
52. Gun gas plug
53. Wing folding jack
54. Front wing hinge
55. Ciné camera
56. Inching control and actuator, and oil cooler drain plug
57. Oil pipe connections
58. Top and bottom sparking plugs
59. Signal discharger
60. Fuel pipe connections
61. Fuel tank fairings
62. Gun front mounts
63. Undercarriage pivot bracket
64. Fuel tank bolts
65. Aircraft front alignment sight
66. Oblique PR camera window or cover plate
67. Undercarriage emergency lowering (Mod. N.30)
68. Access to RATOG fixed parts

DOORS SHOWN DOTTED IN TOP FIG ARE ON UNDERSIDE WHILE THOSE DOTTED IN LOWER FIG. ARE EITHER INSIDE OR ON STBD. SIDE

NUMBERS THUS ① PORT AND STBD.

NUMBERS THUS ❿ ONE SIDE ONLY

PORT SIDE OF COCKPIT LOOKING FORWARD

SEE SCRAP VIEW

Group 8 – Side 3
Miscellaneous
Access Panels

Doors & Removable Panels – T Mk 20

(©Crown Copyright)

Key

1. Navigation lamps (wings)
2. Aileron outer hinges
3. Aileron operating gear
4. Aileron spring tab gear
5. Downward identification lamps
6. Aileron inner hinges
7. Door for withdrawing hinge pin by hand
8. Gun gas plug
9. Guns
10. Intercommunication on starboard side, oxygen bottles on port side
11. Access panels in cockpit side beams
12. Elevator outer hinge
13. Elevator trim tab control
14. Elevator trim tab control cables
15. Ground supply socket, radio power unit and accumulators
16. Flap jacks
17. Fuel pipe connections
18. Fuel tank bolts
20. Rear wing hinge
21. Access door for bomb gear
22. Pitot tube
23. Access panel in rear cockpit port side beam
24. Acces panel in rear cockpit starboard side beam
25. Nose cowl
26. Tank panel
27. Access to instruments
28. Emergency exit panel
29. Emergency hood release
31. Elevator trimming tab control pulleys
32. Rudder tab lever fairing
33. Rudder spring tab operating gear
34. Rudder bottom fairing
35. Navigation lamps (tail)
36. Rudder lever fairing
37. Rudder control rods and tail trim cables
38. Access door for rudder control gear
39. Dished diaphragm over tailwheel
40. Rear top engine panel
41. Rear top detachable panel
42. Engine cooling shutter and fairings
43. Undercarriage shock-absorber pin
44. Undercarriage fairing attachments
45. Front fillet
46. Underpanel
47. Leading edge fillet
48. Top and bottom skirt panels
49. Lower fixed hinge panel
50. Lower cowl panel
51. Upper cowl panel
52. Top fixed hinge panel
53. Pitot tube
54. Bomb release cover
55. Undercarriage pivot bracket
56. Inter-spar fuel tank filler
57. Ciné camera
58. Fuel tank fairing
59. Oil pipe connections
60. Main fuel tank filler (top surface), aircraft front alignment sight (bottom surface)
61. Coffman starter breech
62. Top and bottom sparking plugs
63. Emptying nose tank
64. Nose tank filler
65. Wireless
66. Front gun mounting
67. Front wing hinge
68. Wing folding jack
69. Aileron operating gear
70. Ammunition tanks
71. Undercarriage emergency lowering
72. Access to RATOG fixed parts

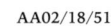

NUMBERS THUS PORT AND STBD
NUMBERS THUS ONE SIDE ONLY

DOORS SHOWN DOTTED IN TOP FIG. ARE ON UNDER SIDE WHILE THOSE DOTTED IN LOWER FIG. ARE EITHER INSIDE OR ON STBD. SIDE.

PORT SIDE OF FRONT COCKPIT LOOKING FORWARD

REAR COCKPIT

SEE SCRAP VIEWS

Group 8 – Side 4
Miscellaneous Equipment

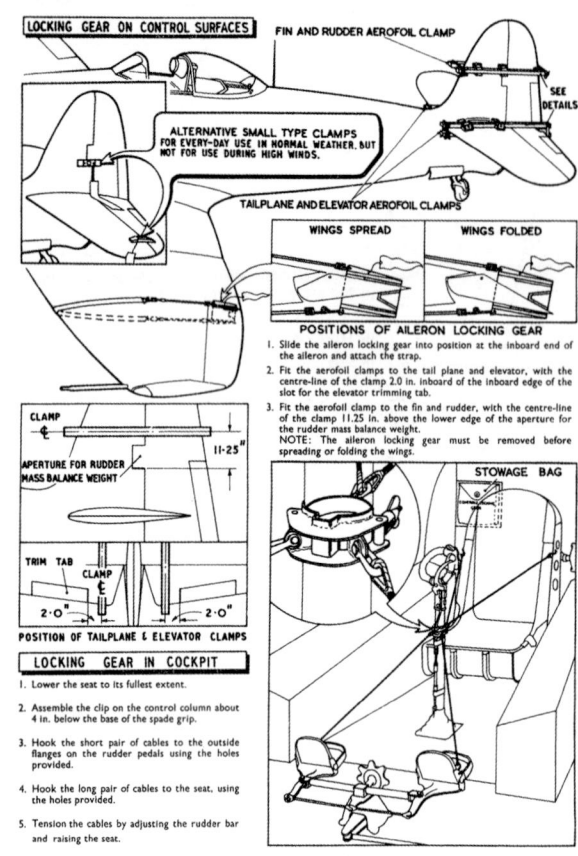

This diagram shows the control surface locking gear used on the Sea Fury (©Crown Copyright)

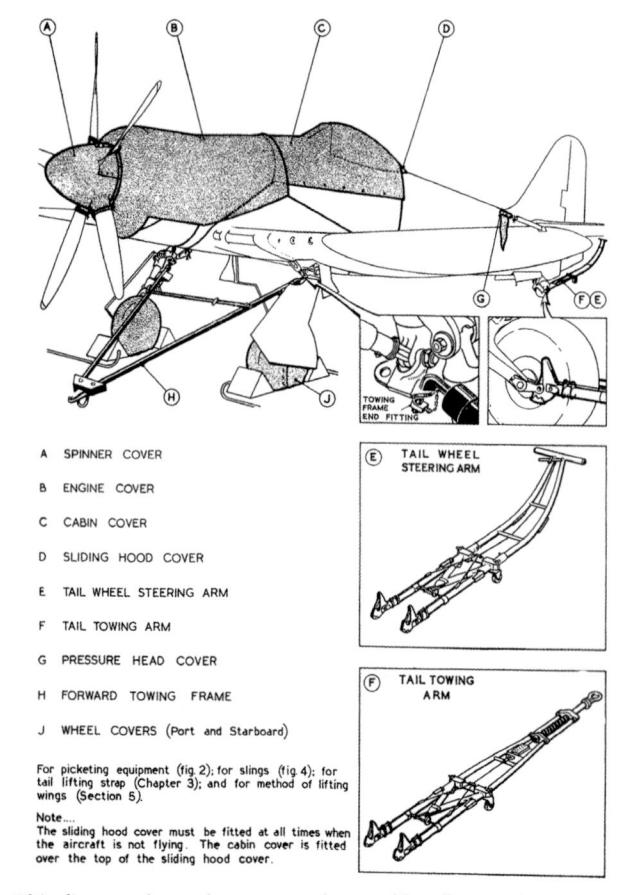

This diagram shows the covers and ground handling equipment used for the single-seat versions (©Crown Copyright)

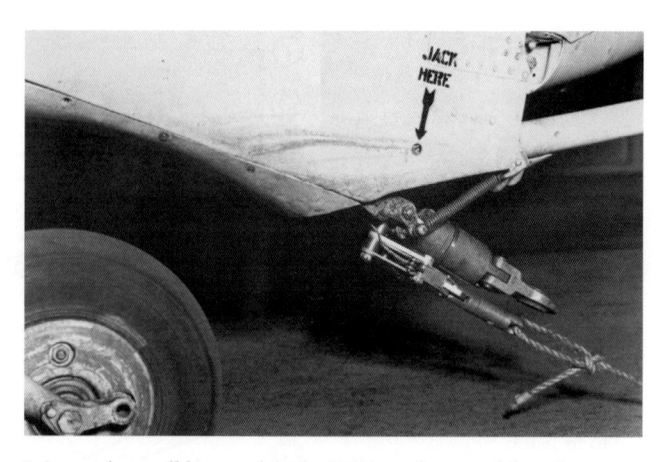

It is not that well known, but the RCN used some of their Sea Furies for target towing, and this is how the banner/cable was connected (©Public Archive of Canada/RCN)

This close-up of a period photo shows the RATOG installed under a Sea Fury

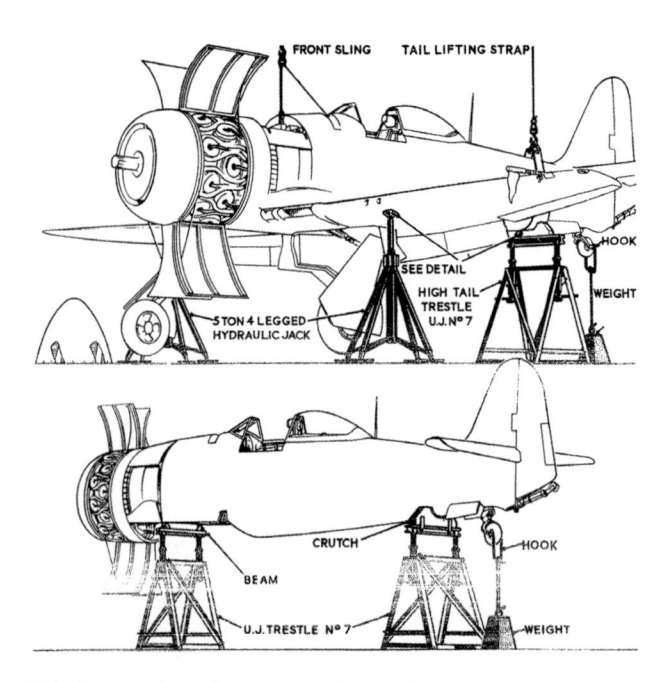

This diagram shows how you trestle or jack up a single-seat Sea Fury (©Crown Copyright)

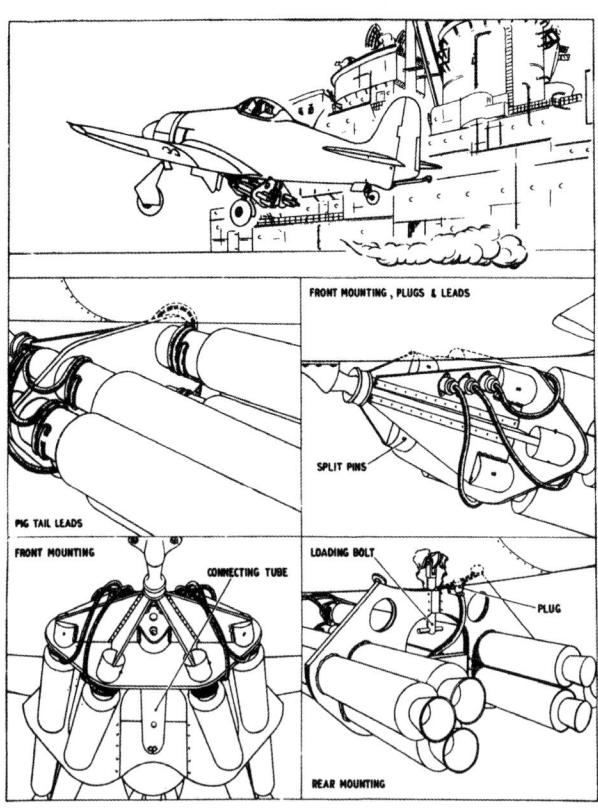

Group 8 – Side 5
Miscellaneous
Equipment

Here is the Rocket-assisted Take-Off Gear (RATOG) used on the Sea Fury *(©Crown Copyright)*

The German TT Mk 20s were fitted with this winch unit that was made in Switzerland, it was fitted with a six-blade propeller that is not shown here *(©Hawker Aircraft)*

Here you can see a Sea Fury leaving the deck with the RATOG firing *(via K. Darling)*

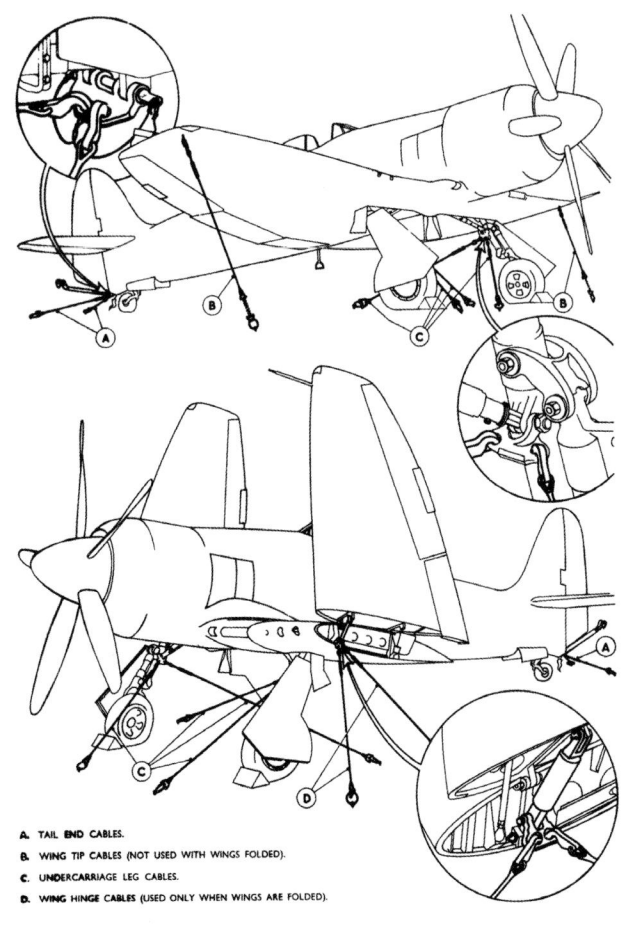

A. TAIL END CABLES.
B. WING TIP CABLES (NOT USED WITH WINGS FOLDED).
C. UNDERCARRIAGE LEG CABLES.
D. WING HINGE CABLES (USED ONLY WHEN WINGS ARE FOLDED).

This diagram shows all the picketing points for the single-seat versions *(©Crown Copyright)*

Sea Fury Evolution 2
Prototypes

Evolution
Prototype, Production and Projected Variants

The evolution of the Fury and Sea Fury series involved a series of prototype machines as well as production and projected designs. What follows therefore is a list of all the former airframes which were actually built, along with details of any the later projects that never got further than the design stage.

As you would expect with a subject now 70 years old, there is much contradiction in both period and subsequent documentation, so we have based all our drawings, where possible, on existing photos and when not, on the most likely layout based on other developments from other British aircraft manufacturers during the period.

Fury NX798

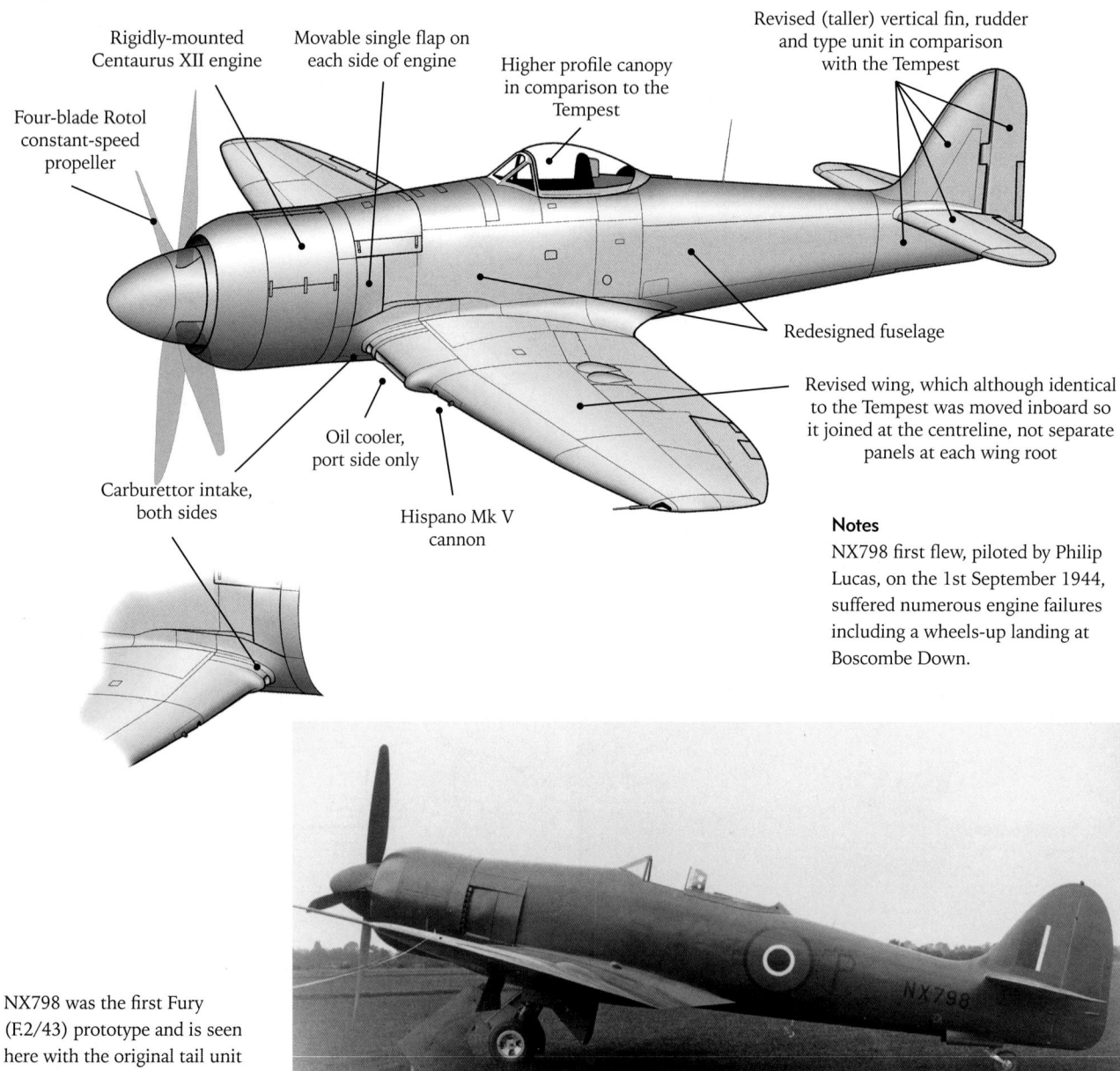

- Rigidly-mounted Centaurus XII engine
- Movable single flap on each side of engine
- Higher profile canopy in comparison to the Tempest
- Revised (taller) vertical fin, rudder and type unit in comparison with the Tempest
- Four-blade Rotol constant-speed propeller
- Redesigned fuselage
- Revised wing, which although identical to the Tempest was moved inboard so it joined at the centreline, not separate panels at each wing root
- Oil cooler, port side only
- Carburettor intake, both sides
- Hispano Mk V cannon

Notes
NX798 first flew, piloted by Philip Lucas, on the 1st September 1944, suffered numerous engine failures including a wheels-up landing at Boscombe Down.

NX798 was the first Fury (F.2/43) prototype and is seen here with the original tail unit and no arrestor hook. This aircraft was later refurbished and sold to Egypt (©MoS)

Sea Fury
Evolution
Prototypes

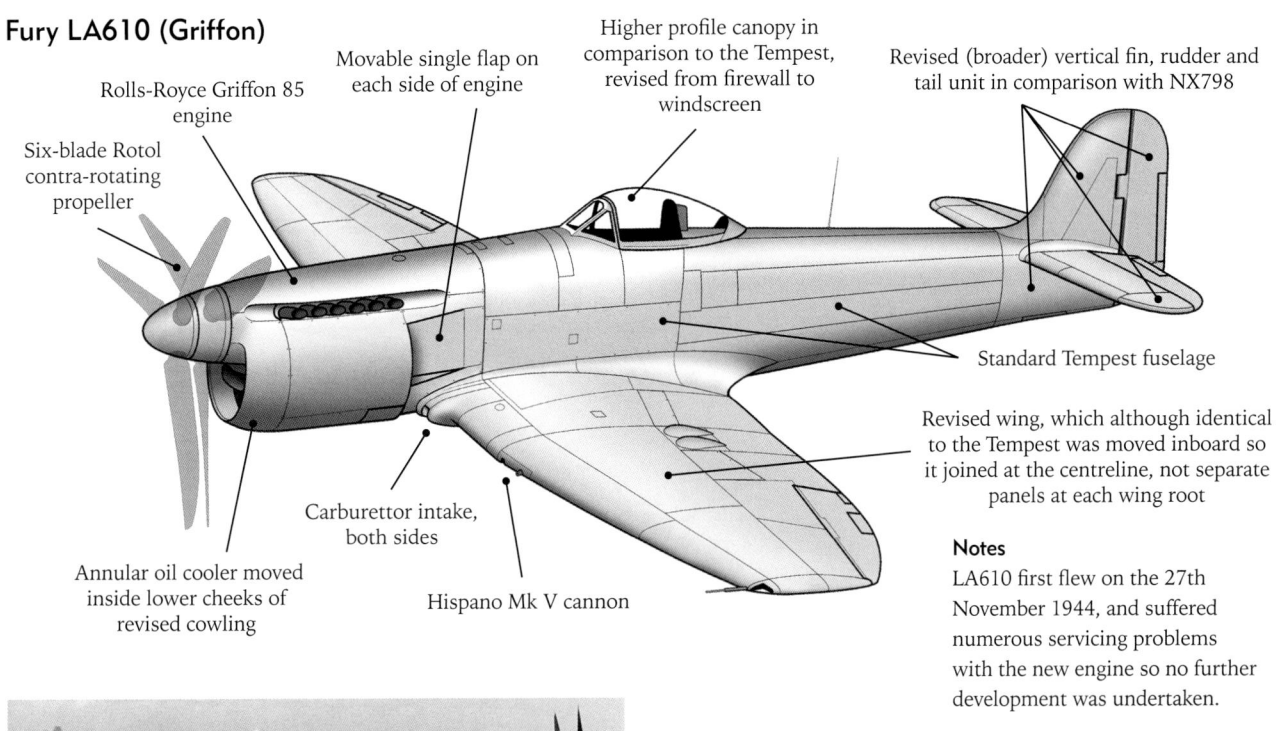

Fury LA610 (Griffon)

- Rolls-Royce Griffon 85 engine
- Six-blade Rotol contra-rotating propeller
- Movable single flap on each side of engine
- Higher profile canopy in comparison to the Tempest, revised from firewall to windscreen
- Revised (broader) vertical fin, rudder and tail unit in comparison with NX798
- Standard Tempest fuselage
- Revised wing, which although identical to the Tempest was moved inboard so it joined at the centreline, not separate panels at each wing root
- Annular oil cooler moved inside lower cheeks of revised cowling
- Carburettor intake, both sides
- Hispano Mk V cannon

Notes
LA610 first flew on the 27th November 1944, and suffered numerous servicing problems with the new engine so no further development was undertaken.

The initial form for LA610, fitted with a Griffon 85 and contra-rotating propellers (©R.J. Caruana Archive)

Fury I prototype LA610 with Sabre VII seen in June 1946 (©MoS/British Official)

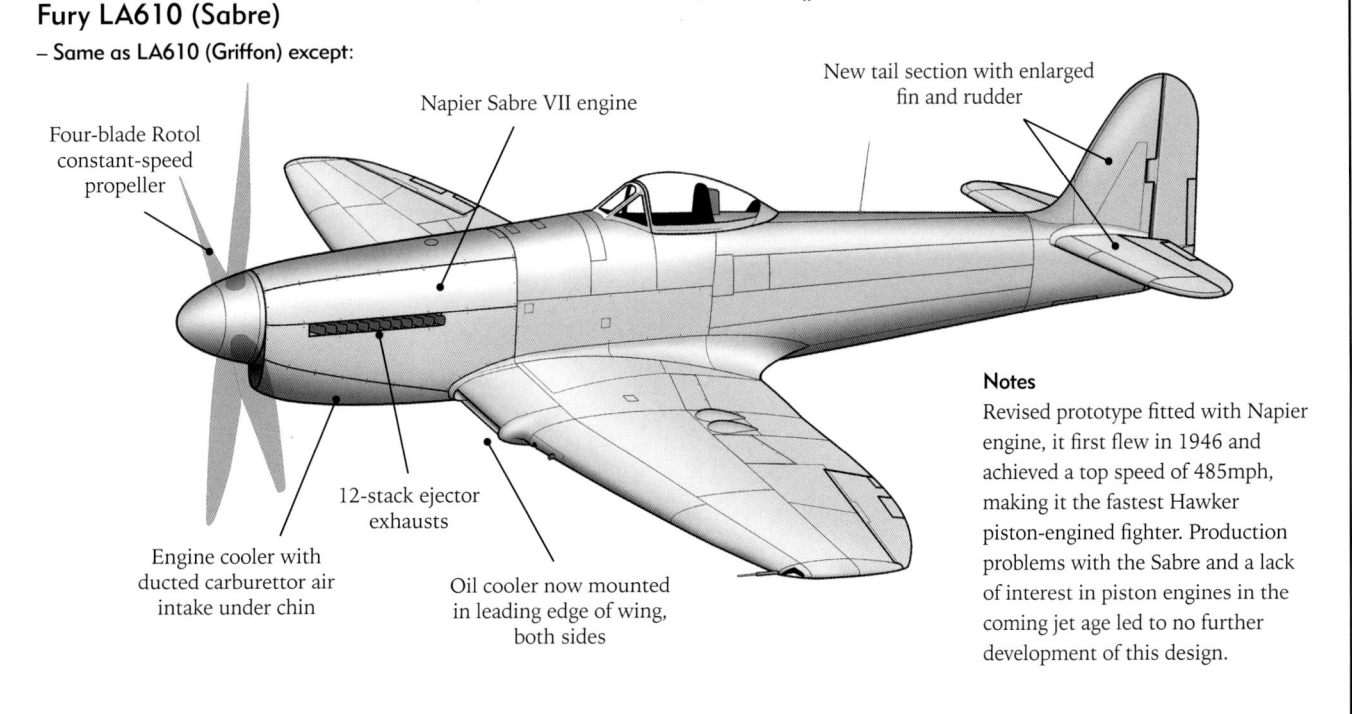

Fury LA610 (Sabre)
– Same as LA610 (Griffon) except:

- Four-blade Rotol constant-speed propeller
- Napier Sabre VII engine
- New tail section with enlarged fin and rudder
- 12-stack ejector exhausts
- Engine cooler with ducted carburettor air intake under chin
- Oil cooler now mounted in leading edge of wing, both sides

Notes
Revised prototype fitted with Napier engine, it first flew in 1946 and achieved a top speed of 485mph, making it the fastest Hawker piston-engined fighter. Production problems with the Sabre and a lack of interest in piston engines in the coming jet age led to no further development of this design.

Sea Fury Evolution 2
Prototypes

Fury SR661
– Same as NX798 except:

Rigidly-mounted Centaurus XVII engine

Modified rear lower fuselage with bulge and arrestor hook assembly

Notes
SR661 first flew from Langley on the 21st February 1945, was only 'semi-navalised' as it had non-folding wings and an arrestor hook.

Fury SR661 was semi-navalised, as it had an arrestor hook but non-folding wings (©Hawker Aircraft)

Fury NX802
– Same as NX798 except:

Production standard Centaurus XVII engine

Five-blade Rotol propeller

Notes
NX802 first flew 25th July 1945 fitted with the first production Centaurus XVII, cancelled soon after but purchased back by Hawkers and entered into various air races before being given military equipment and Centaurus XVIII and sold to Pakistan as K875.

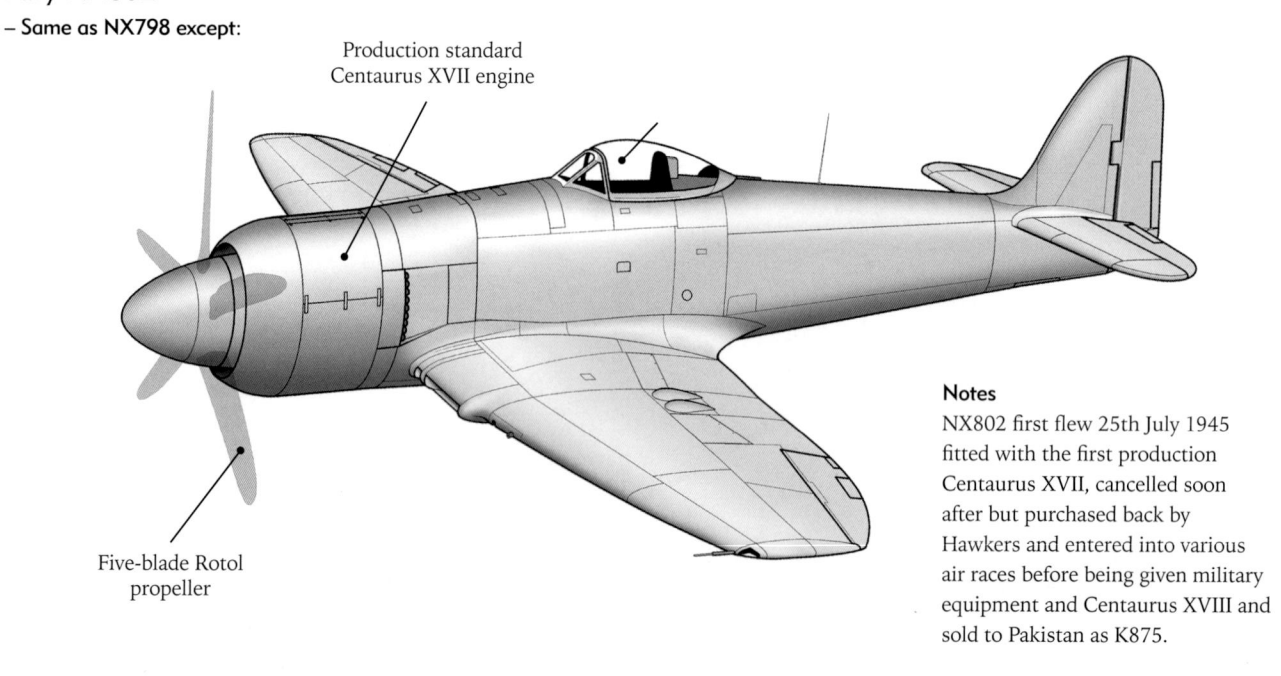

Sea Fury SR666 & VB857
– Same as NX798 except:

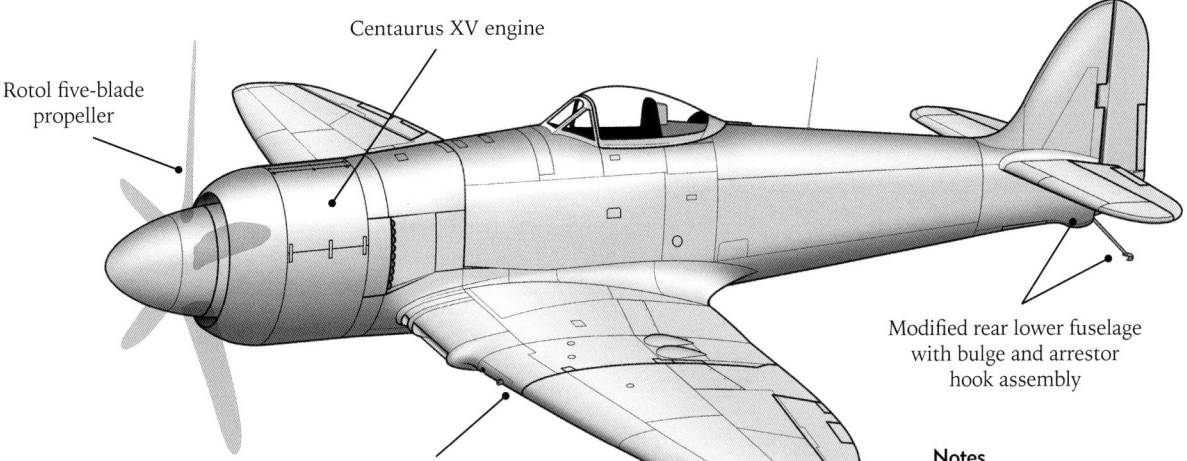

- Rotol five-blade propeller
- Centaurus XV engine
- Folding wings
- Modified rear lower fuselage with bulge and arrestor hook assembly

This image shows SR666 in its original form complete with pitot on the port wing and the short arrestor hook (*©MoS/British Official*)

Notes
SR666 first flew on the 12th October 1945, was fully navalised with folding wings, armament, naval radio equipment and arrestor hook. Undertook service trials at A&AEE Boscombe Down in 1946, and performed deck landing trials on HMS Victorious. Suffered tail hook failure during one landing, only instant response from the engine allowed the pilot to climb over parked aircraft on the deck and land safely back ashore! VB857 first flew on the 31st January 1946, was the first airframe to not feature rigid engine mounts, instead having the new dynafocal mounting. First aircraft to also fly safely without engine problems thanks to revised crankcase lubrication.

Fury VP207
– Same as NX798 except:

- Five-blade propeller
- Sabre VII engine
- 12-stack ejector exhausts
- Cooler and carburettor intake under nose

Notes
Constructed from spare components by Hawkers who felt that post-war jet aircraft would be too expensive for emergent nations, however this proved not to be the case and this aircraft was probably broken up (*first flight date not known*).

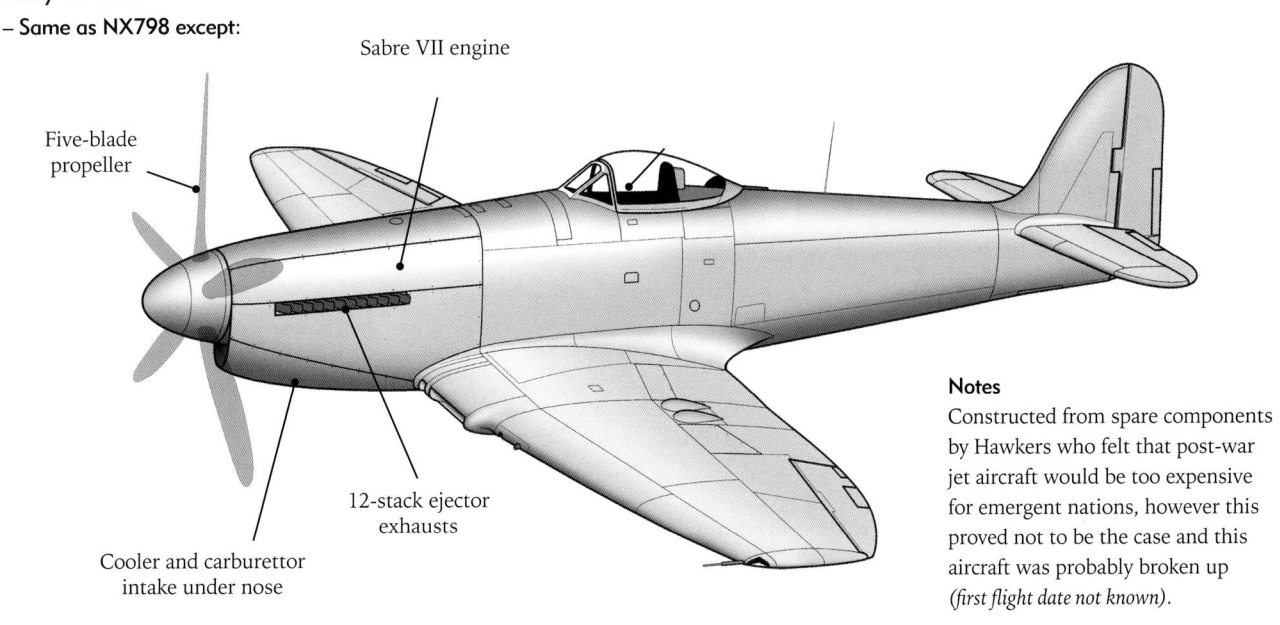

Sea Fury Evolution 2

Production Versions

Sea Fury F Mk X
– Same as SR666 & VB857 except:

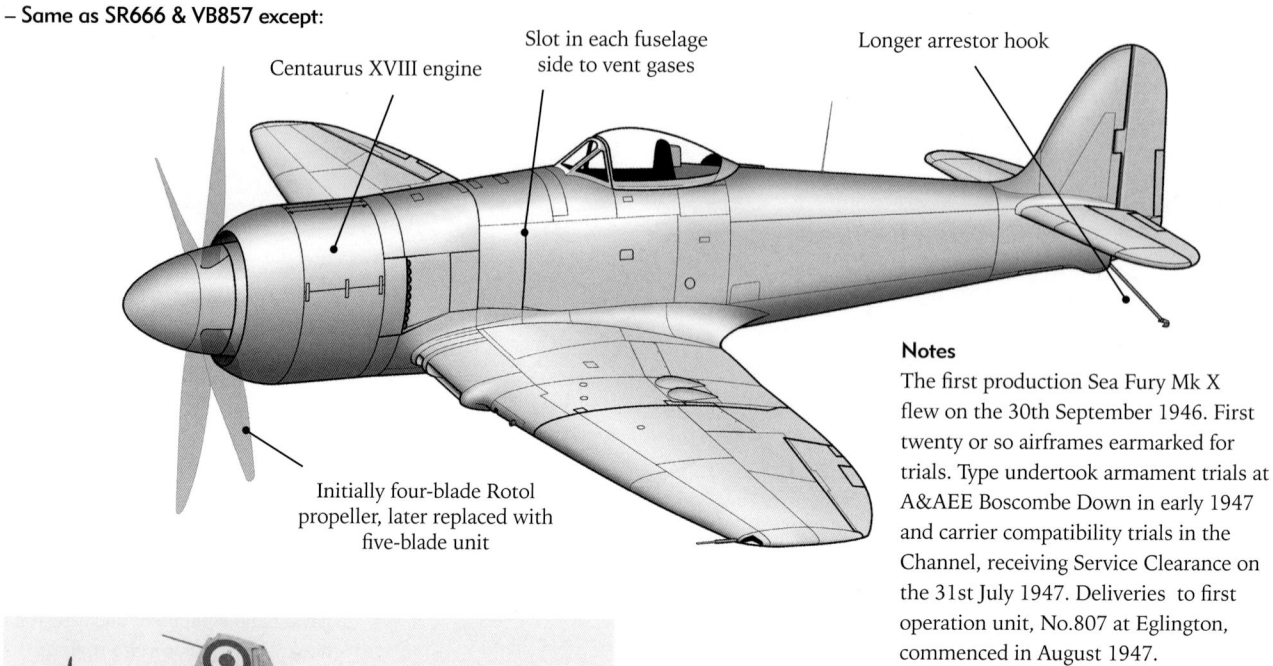

- Centaurus XVIII engine
- Slot in each fuselage side to vent gases
- Longer arrestor hook
- Initially four-blade Rotol propeller, later replaced with five-blade unit

Notes
The first production Sea Fury Mk X flew on the 30th September 1946. First twenty or so airframes earmarked for trials. Type undertook armament trials at A&AEE Boscombe Down in early 1947 and carrier compatibility trials in the Channel, receiving Service Clearance on the 31st July 1947. Deliveries to first operation unit, No.807 at Eglington, commenced in August 1947.

FB Mk 11 VR936 had previously been operated by Nos.807, 736, 738, 1831 and 700 Squadrons before going to Airwork for FRU duties. It is seen with Airwork here on the 2nd September 1957, it was SOC on the 27th June 1963 *(©R.J. Caruana Archive)*

The first production Sea Fury F Mk X TF895 is seen here in primer – note the short arrestor hook *(©Hawker Aircraft)*

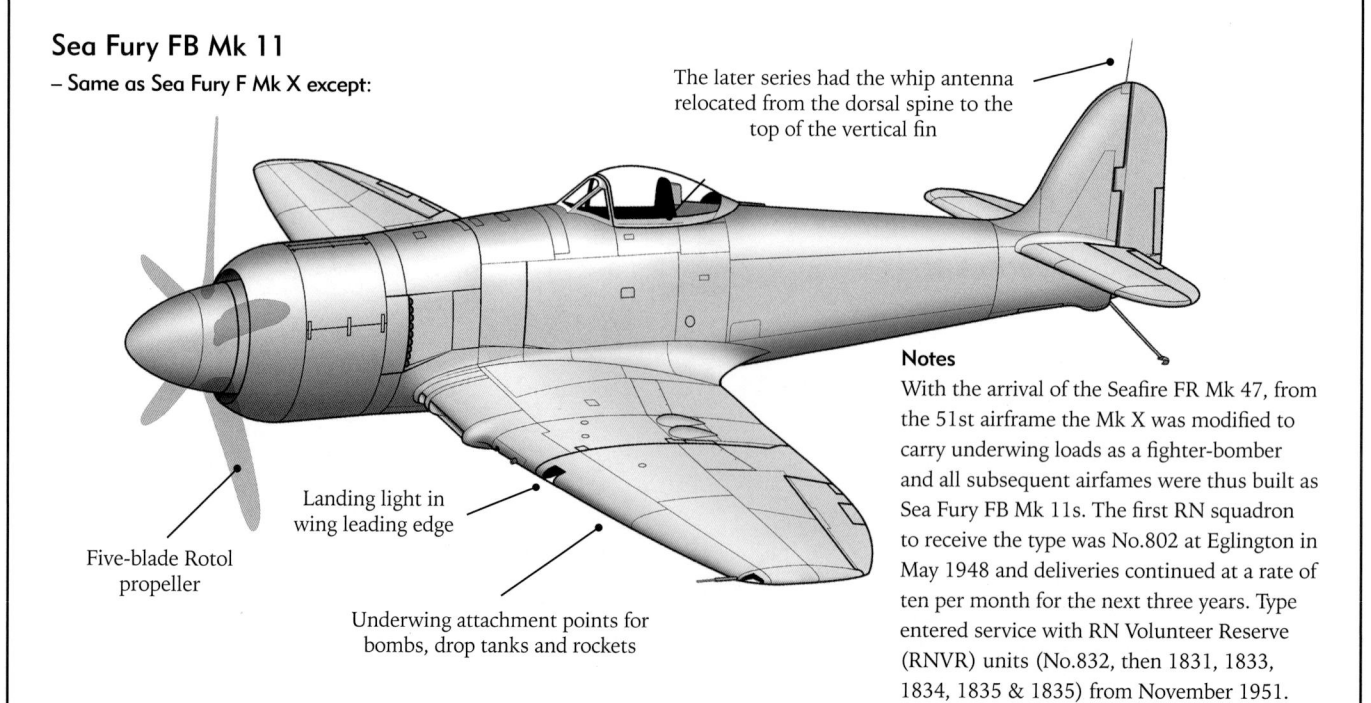

Sea Fury FB Mk 11
– Same as Sea Fury F Mk X except:

- The later series had the whip antenna relocated from the dorsal spine to the top of the vertical fin
- Five-blade Rotol propeller
- Landing light in wing leading edge
- Underwing attachment points for bombs, drop tanks and rockets

Notes
With the arrival of the Seafire FR Mk 47, from the 51st airframe the Mk X was modified to carry underwing loads as a fighter-bomber and all subsequent airfames were thus built as Sea Fury FB Mk 11s. The first RN squadron to receive the type was No.802 at Eglington in May 1948 and deliveries continued at a rate of ten per month for the next three years. Type entered service with RN Volunteer Reserve (RNVR) units (No.832, then 1831, 1833, 1834, 1835 & 1835) from November 1951.

Sea Fury Evolution
Production Versions

Sea Fury T Mk 20 prototype VX818
– Same as Sea Fury FB Mk 11 except:

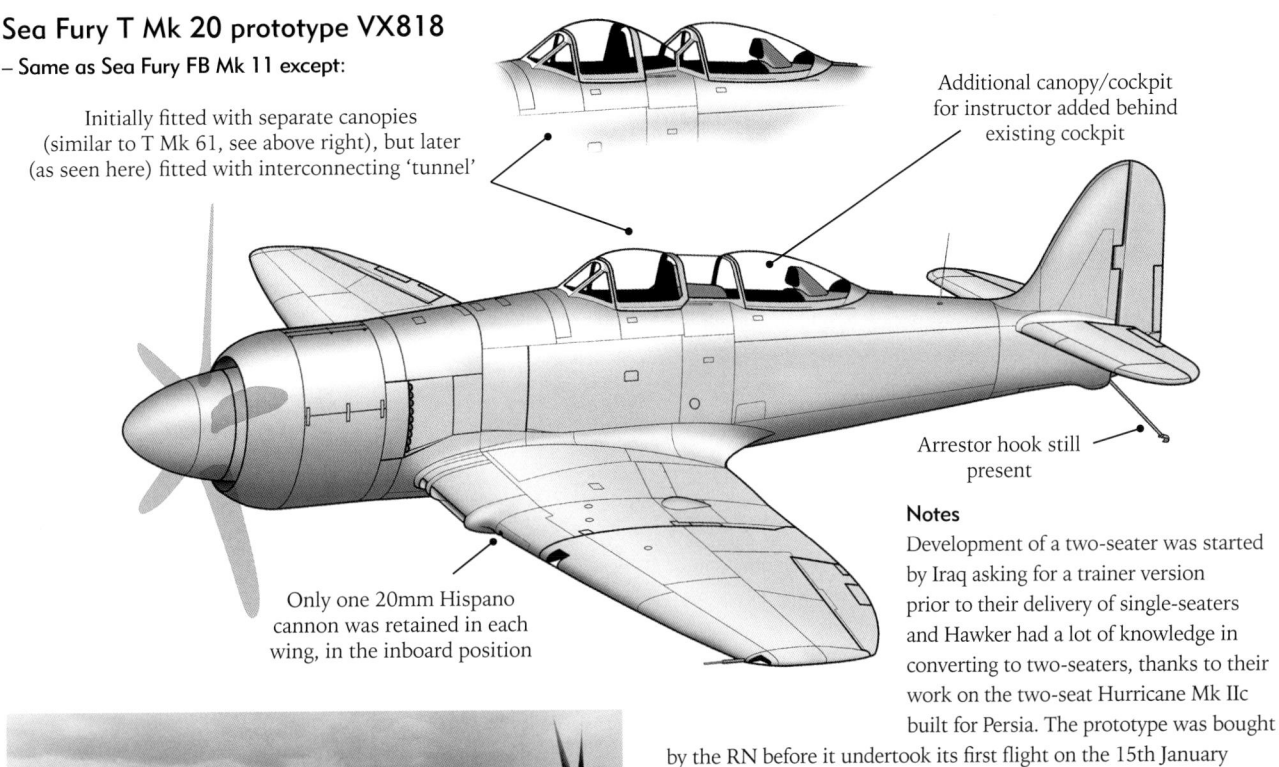

Initially fitted with separate canopies (similar to T Mk 61, see above right), but later (as seen here) fitted with interconnecting 'tunnel'

Additional canopy/cockpit for instructor added behind existing cockpit

Only one 20mm Hispano cannon was retained in each wing, in the inboard position

Arrestor hook still present

Notes
Development of a two-seater was started by Iraq asking for a trainer version prior to their delivery of single-seaters and Hawker had a lot of knowledge in converting to two-seaters, thanks to their work on the two-seat Hurricane Mk IIc built for Persia. The prototype was bought by the RN before it undertook its first flight on the 15th January 1948. Initially fitted with two separate cockpit canopies, however during trials at A&AEE Boscombe Down the rear one collapsed so a connecting 'tunnel' was fitted instead.

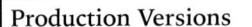

This image shows the first two-seat prototype, VX818 complete with arrestor hook although this is a later image (dated July 1948) as it has the 'tunnel' between the canopies installed when the original design failed in flight *(©MoS/British Official)*

This beautiful shot shows a production T Mk 20 in flight *(©MoS/Hawker Aircraft)*

Sea Fury T Mk 20
– Same as Sea Fury T Mk 20 prototype VX818 except:

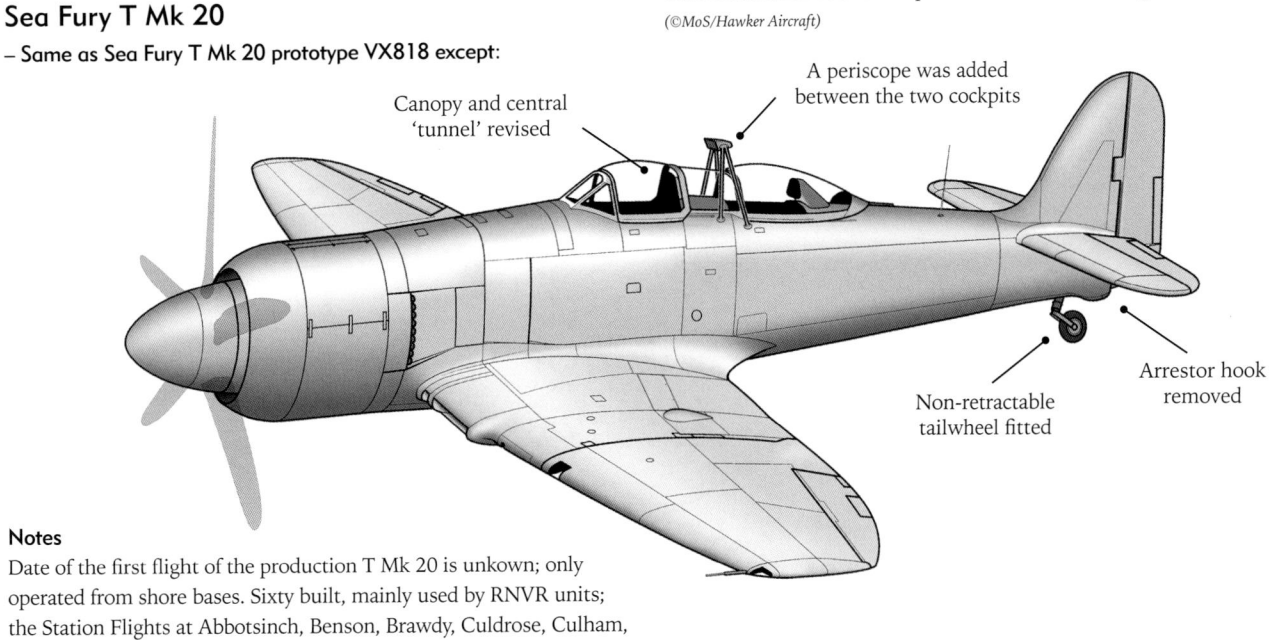

Canopy and central 'tunnel' revised

A periscope was added between the two cockpits

Non-retractable tailwheel fitted

Arrestor hook removed

Notes
Date of the first flight of the production T Mk 20 is unkown; only operated from shore bases. Sixty built, mainly used by RNVR units; the Station Flights at Abbotsinch, Benson, Brawdy, Culdrose, Culham, Donibristle, Lossiemouth, Stretton, Syerston and Yeovilton.

Sea Fury Evolution 2
Export Versions

Fury Demonstrator NX798/G-AKRY
– Same as Fury NX802 except:

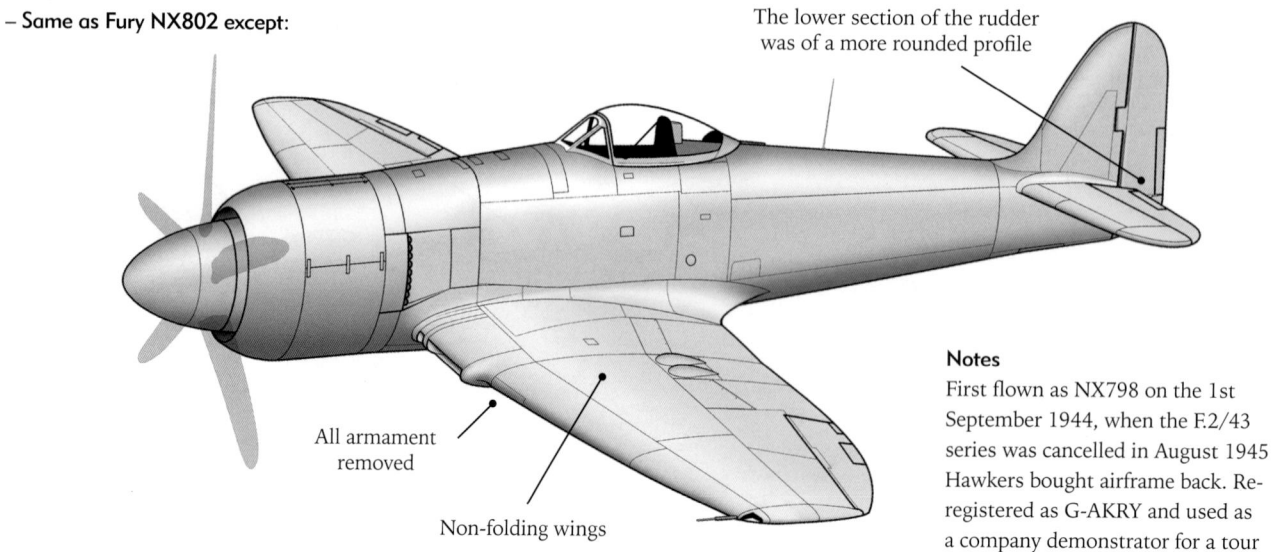

The lower section of the rudder was of a more rounded profile

All armament removed

Non-folding wings

Notes
First flown as NX798 on the 1st September 1944, when the F.2/43 series was cancelled in August 1945 Hawkers bought airframe back. Re-registered as G-AKRY and used as a company demonstrator for a tour of the Middle East. Was eventually given full military equipment and sold to Egypt.

Ex-NX798 the prototype Fury G-AKRY is seen here whilst on a company tour of the Middle East in the late 1940s
(©Author's collection via K. Darling)

Dutch-built machine 6•43 is seen here in the second scheme applied to Dutch machines and with the number repeated either side and under the nose, the latter only happening with Fokker-built machines (©Author's collection via K. Darling)

Sea Fury F Mk 50 (later FB Mk 50)
– Same as Sea Fury F Mk X

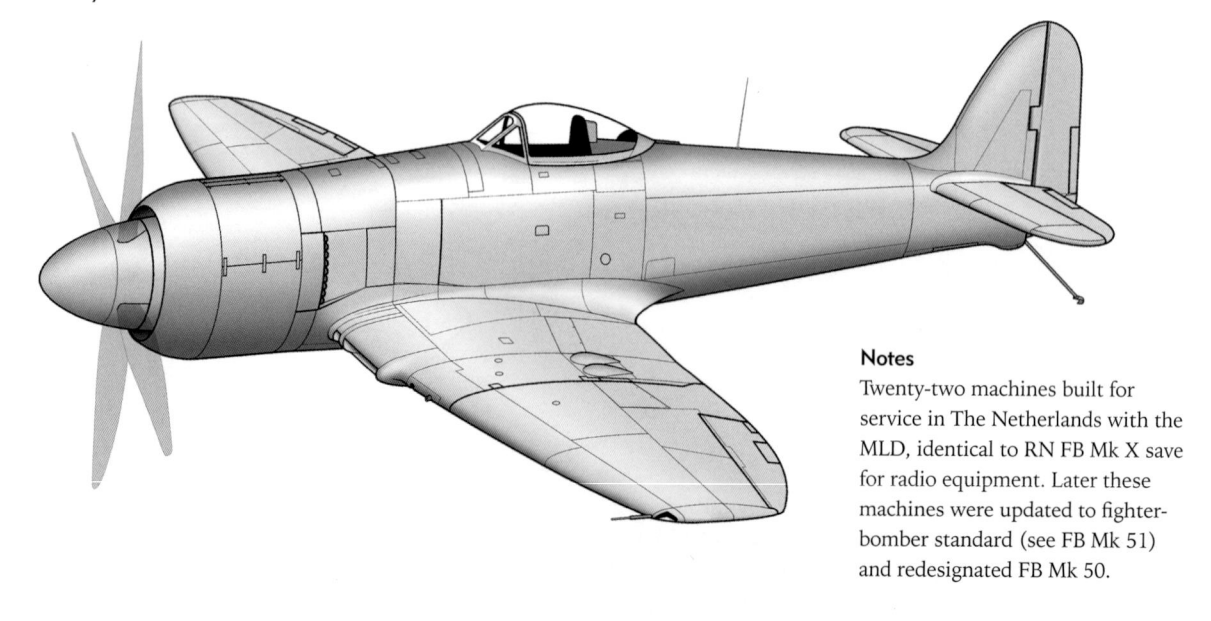

Notes
Twenty-two machines built for service in The Netherlands with the MLD, identical to RN FB Mk X save for radio equipment. Later these machines were updated to fighter-bomber standard (see FB Mk 51) and redesignated FB Mk 50.

Sea Fury FB Mk 51
– Same as Sea Fury FB Mk 11

Notes
Twenty-five machines were built under licence by Fokker for service in The Netherlands with the MLD, identical to RN FB Mk 11 except for radio equipment.

Pakistan Air Force machine L951 is seen here fitted with drop tanks prior, we presume, to delivery *(©Hawker Aircraft)*

Fury FB Mk 60
– Same as Sea Fury FB Mk 11 except:

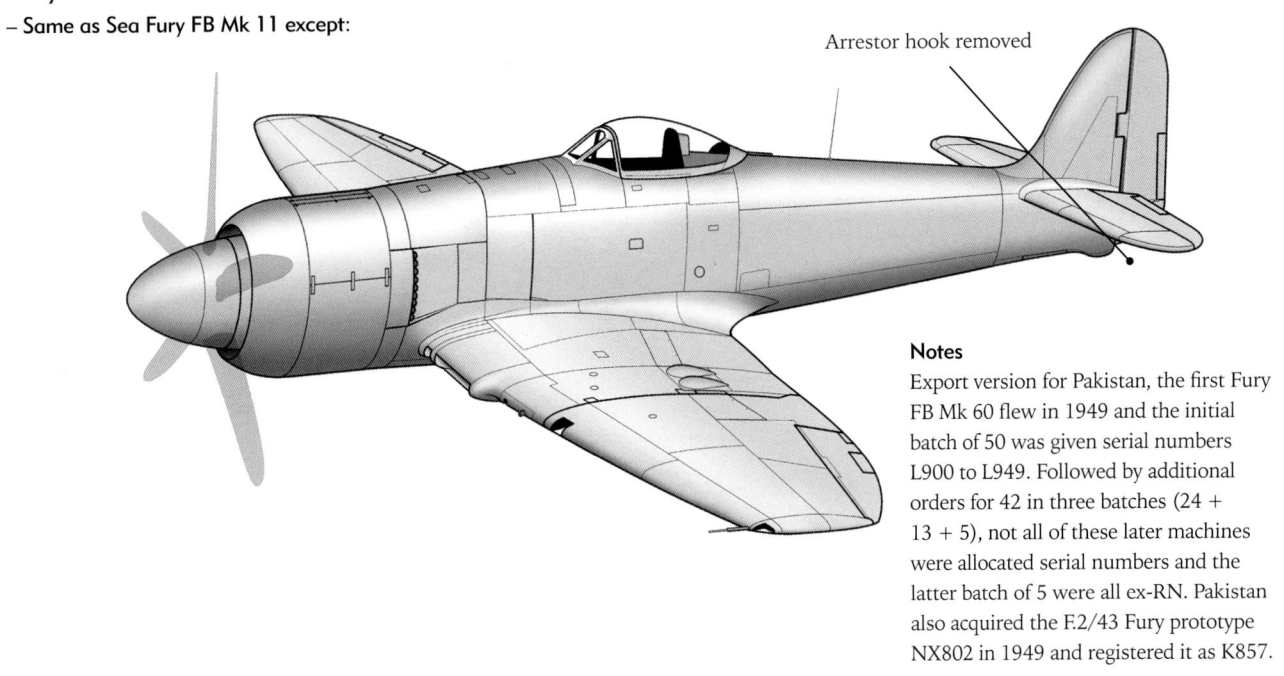

Arrestor hook removed

Notes
Export version for Pakistan, the first Fury FB Mk 60 flew in 1949 and the initial batch of 50 was given serial numbers L900 to L949. Followed by additional orders for 42 in three batches (24 + 13 + 5), not all of these later machines were allocated serial numbers and the latter batch of 5 were all ex-RN. Pakistan also acquired the F.2/43 Fury prototype NX802 in 1949 and registered it as K857.

Sea Fury Evolution 2
Export Versions

Fury T Mk 61
– Same as Fury FB Mk 60 except:

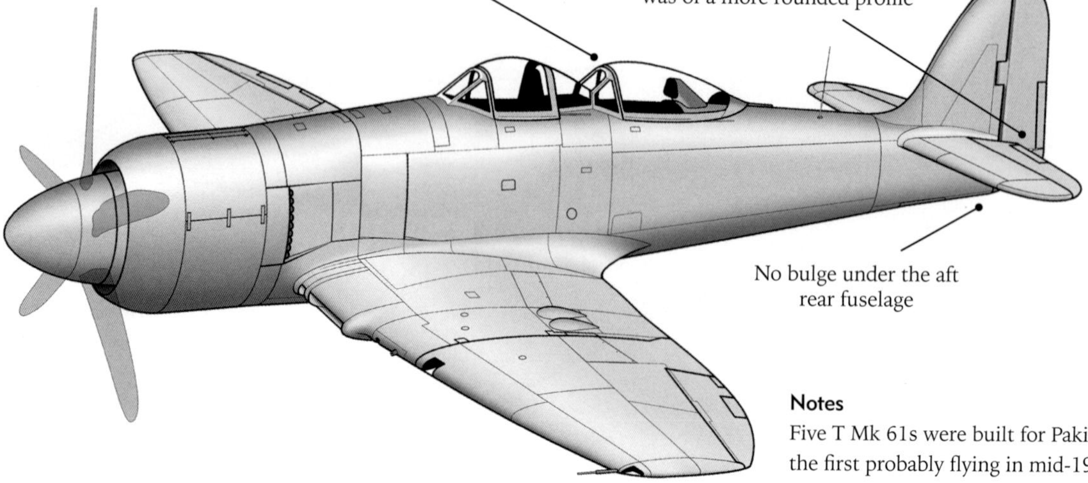

- Additional canopy/cockpit for instructor added behind existing cockpit
- The lower section of the rudder was of a more rounded profile
- No bulge under the aft rear fuselage

Notes
Five T Mk 61s were built for Pakistan, the first probably flying in mid-1949.

This T Mk 20, K850 is seen prior to delivery to Pakistan
(©Hawker Aircraft)

DLB-operated TT Mk 20 D-CAMI parked up after a sortie. The low sun does help to highlight the wires around the tail and rudder, just like those used on the Tempest TT Mk 5 (©T. Genth via K. Darling)

Sea Fury TT Mk 20
– Same as Sea Fury T Mk 20 except:

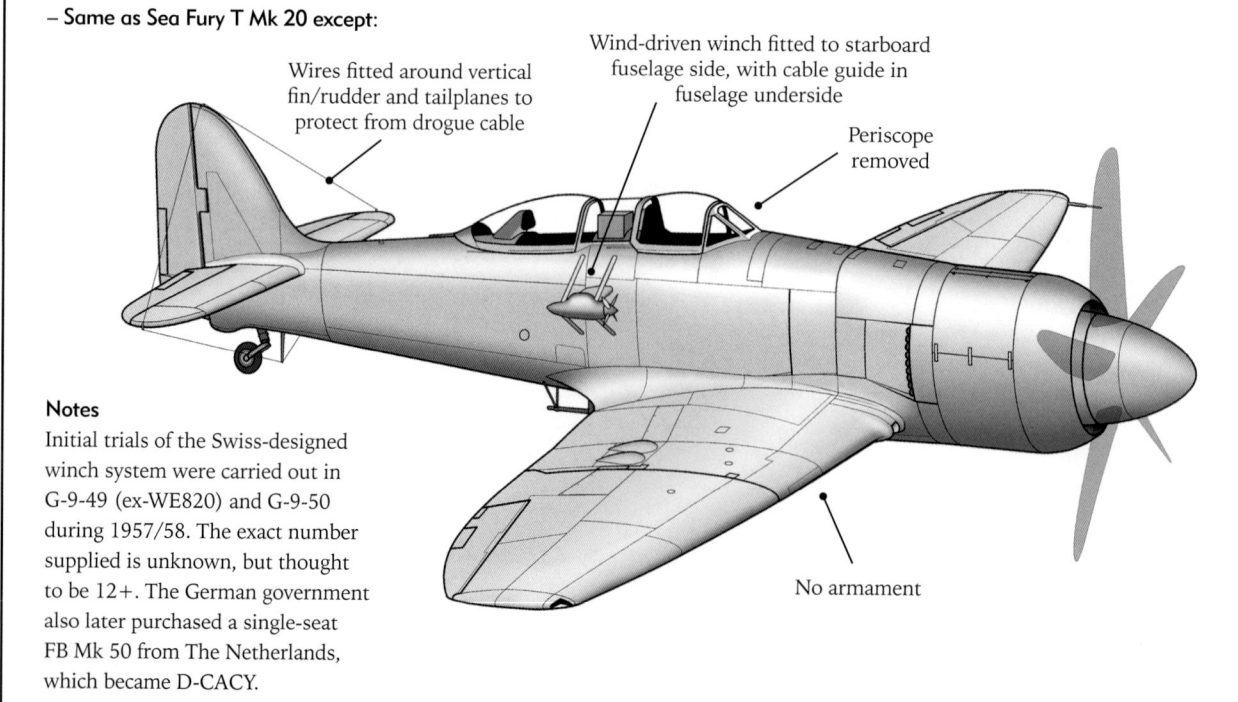

- Wires fitted around vertical fin/rudder and tailplanes to protect from drogue cable
- Wind-driven winch fitted to starboard fuselage side, with cable guide in fuselage underside
- Periscope removed
- No armament

Notes
Initial trials of the Swiss-designed winch system were carried out in G-9-49 (ex-WE820) and G-9-50 during 1957/58. The exact number supplied is unknown, but thought to be 12+. The German government also later purchased a single-seat FB Mk 50 from The Netherlands, which became D-CACY.

Camouflage & Markings

Fury I prototype LA610 with Sabre VII seen in June 1946, the film type used has turned the yellow 'P' marking and ring of the Type C1 roundel dark
(©MoS/British Official)

Let us first start by saying that nothing is certain when trying to deduce colours from old black and white photographs. The best you can make is an educated, and with luck intelligent, guess using both photographic and documentary evidence.

Fury & Sea Fury in the UK

The first Fury prototype, LA610, was built during wartime, so it exhibited the scheme then applied to all prototype fighters, although as initially intended for the RAF it had a day fighter scheme. This scheme comprised Dark Green and Dark Earth in a disruptive pattern on the upper surfaces, fuselage sides, vertical fin/rudder and tailplanes, while all undersurfaces were in yellow.

A nice shot of LA610 with its Sabre installation in flight, probably mid-1946. The yellow 'P' and Type C1 roundel on the fuselage, plus the Type C roundels on the upper wing can all be seen, as can the camouflage pattern (©R.J. Caruana Archive)

FB Mk 11 WE693 of No.810 NAS on HMS Centaur in 1954. The style, size and location of the '106' on either side of the fuselage is interesting, as it is not anywhere near the usual character style used
(©R.J. Caruana)

The markings comprised the Type C roundels above and below the wings, with a Type C1 roundel on either side of the fuselage, The prototype marking comprising a yellow 'P' in a yellow circle, was applied on each side of the fuselage, aft of the roundel and with the P pointing aft on the port side and forward on the starboard. A Type C fin flash was applied on either side of the vertical fin, with the aft edge lined up with the rudder hinge line. The only other marking was the serial (LA610) in 8in. high black characters aft of the prototype 'P' marking and forward of the tailplane leading edge; this marking was applied on a line that theoretically ran along the centre of each fuselage side. The spinner and propeller blades were black, with a slight sheen to them.

Throughout its service with the Royal Navy the Sea Fury F Mk X and FB Mk 11 only ever wore two camouflage schemes, and the only difference was in the colour demarcation. Both used Extra Dark Sea Grey over Sky, with the first pattern having the demarcation between these two colours low down on the fuselage side, probably using the 60° template system used by the RAF. The

F.2/43 prototype NX798 is seen here on a test flight. Note the Type B roundels on the upper wings, Type C1 on the fuselage and Type C fin flash (©Hawker Aircraft)

second scheme is the one probably best known and it uses the same colours but with the demarcation of the EDSG high up on the fuselage spine and with the entire vertical fin and rudder in Sky.

Colour Specifications
- Extra Dark Sea Grey BS381C 640 low gloss for early machines and high gloss for later ones
- Sky BS381C 210

With the first scheme the national insignia usually comprised the Type C1 roundel on each side of the fuselage and Type C roundels above and below each outer wing panel. A fin flash, if applied, was usually of the Type C version. The serial was now applied in smaller 6in black characters on the aft fuselage, but now below the theoretical centreline, as the title 'Royal Navy' was now applied above, again in 6in black characters. The serial number was repeated under each wing in 20in high black characters – that under the starboard wing faced the leading edge, whist those under the port faced the trailing edge. Each base, unit and carrier had

FB Mk 11, WG603 of No.738 NAS at RNAS Culdrose in 1953. Everything about the characters used for the '138' on the fuselage sides is at odds with the 'norm' for this marking! (©R.J. Caruana)

a call-sign that consisted of alphabetic characters (e.g. HMS Theseus = 'T', while RNAS Yeovilton = 'VL') and this marking was applied in white characters on the vertical fin. The size and style of these characters varied greatly, and if the fin flash was omitted they tended to be large, but if the fin flash was applied, they tended to be much smaller and applied directly above the flash. Each aircraft also had a fleet number, comprising three numbers, such as '120', '136' or '107' and these were applied in 20in high white characters aft of the fuselage roundel, both sides; again these were on the theoretical centreline. The spinner was

The Sea Fury prototype SR661 is seen here in flight whilst testing the five-blade propeller that would become standard for production machines. Note the application of the land-based temperate scheme (©MoS/British Official)

FB Mk 11 VR952 is seen here in service with No.807 NAS, Donibristle in September 1949 in the initial scheme. Note the thick style of the characters used for the fuselage and tail codes *(©R.J. Caruana Archives)*

often done in a colour, such as red, yellow or Sky, or in more than one (e.g. red/white).

With the later scheme the Type D roundel was used on both fuselage and wings and the fin flash was dispensed with on the tail. The high demarcation meant that a lack of contrast with white meant that both the fleet number and unit/carrier codes on the fuselage side and tail were now in black. Again, although the sizes seem quite consistent, the style of character used does not, with examples of a 'stencil' style being used for the fleet number, or a very 'square' character?

During the Korean War, the FB Mk 11 had identification stripes applied around the wings and aft fuselage, to stop confusion with Russian Yak fighters. These bands were equal bands of white/black/white/black/white and where they passed over the fleet number on the rear fuselage any area effected was applied in the contrasting colour, so that if the band passed straight through a '1', the half on the white was black, and vice versa. The bands under the wings either partially covered the serial number, or it was just not applied.

One thing you have to be careful with, is the application of 'exercise' markings, such as the black stripes around the aft fuselage and wings applied for a Home Waters exercise in 1952, as these look like the ID bands applied during the Korean War, but they were of different dimensions, location and only black was applied, no white. Temporary bands are also seen applied, such as the red/yellow ones applied to WE683 in 1953 (see photo below), as these went around the wings between the roundel and underside serial number, but went right over the top of the 'Royal Navy' legend and serial number on the rear fuselage.

The only other scheme applied to RN Sea Furies

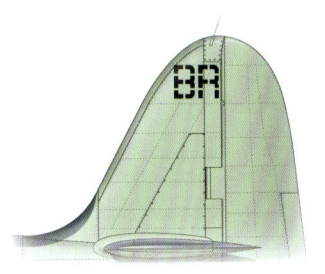

FB Mk 11, VW656 of No.1833 NAS, RNVR at RNAS Bramcote in 1954. Of note here is the use of a stencil style for the 'BR' on the vertical fin *(©R.J. Caruana)*

WE683 is seen here in service with No.1831 Sqn, RNVR at RNAS Stretton in 1953. The red/yellow tail bands are markings for an exercise *(©R.J. Caruana Archive)*

Camouflage & Markings 3
UK

VX652 is pictured here during its time either with No.736 or No.738 Squadron at Culdrose in 1950, because the '133' and 'CW' tail codes were used by both. Note the stencil style of the characters used for the '133' and 'CW' (©*Author's collection via K. Darling*)

relates to the T Mk 20 trainer. This machine was painted in line with the (then) current policy relating to training aircraft, therefore they were Speed Silver (aluminium, high gloss) overall with 24in wide yellow bands around the rear fuselage halfway between the rear/outer edge of the roundel and the leading edge of the tailplane. The yellow band was also repeated around each mainplane, again with its centreline halfway between the fuselage centreline and wingtip, putting it directly over the gun bays in the upper surfaces and cartridge ejector port in the underside. National insignia comprised 30in diameter Type D roundels in all six positions, those under the wings being positioned close to the tip to allow the serial number to be applied between it and the yellow band. This serial number was applied in 24in black characters under each outer wing panel, orientated so it could be read from the leading edge for the port wing, and trailing edge for starboard. The unit codes were applied in black characters at the top of each side of the vertical fin, and the 'Royal Navy' legend was applied either side of the aft fuselage, just slightly below the tailplane leading edge. Under this was the aircraft serial number in the same style/format. A fleet or unit coding system was usually applied aft of the fuselage roundel on each side and this would comprise a three-numeric code either in the 200 or 900 series applied in black characters of various styles and dimensions. The prototype T Mk 20 (VX818) carried a prototype 'P' marking in this position and had no unit code on the vertical fin. No other markings were usually carried on the T Mk 20, although it was not uncommon for the spinner to be painted a specific colour other than silver.

NB. Please note that although we have quoted dimensions for some of the markings there are many variations, especially in the size/style of the serial number under the wings and the fleet number on the fuselage.

T Mk 20 VX308 was operated by No.738 Squadron at RNAS Culdrose in 1951 and is seen here with rocket rails, not a usual fitment to trainers. Again the film used has turned the yellow bands into a dark shade (©*via R. Sturtivant*)

WZ643 was operated by the RAN and is seen here in the markings of No.805 Squadron based at Nowra. This scheme has the 'NAVY' legend and the Roodel applied *(©Author's collection via K. Darling)*

Royal Australian Navy

Australia was the second Commonwealth nation to order the Sea Fury. Initially the units formed at Eglinton in Northern Ireland and received ex-RN Sea Furies complete with the (then) current low demarcation scheme of Extra Dark Sea Grey and Sky. The national insignia would be standard RAF examples as this was the style used by the RAAF post-war, although photos prove that the fuselage ones had the yellow rim so were Type C1 – It is thus assumed that both under and upper wing ones were Type C? This initial scheme would also see the application of a Type C fin flash either side of the vertical fin. An aircraft three-digit number was applied in white aft of the fuselage roundel and a unit/carrier identification letter was applied to the top of the vertical fin, above the fin flash, in white.

When the RN adopted the later high-level demarcation scheme on the Sea Fury fleet the RAN followed suit and in line with the RN's changes, the RAN adopted black in place of white for all the legends and codes carried by their machines. Initially the layout remained as with the earlier scheme with the three-digit identification number aft of the roundel on each fuselage side, a carrier/unit identifying code on the top of the vertical fin and the 'RAN' and serial number on the aft fuselage. The only change from the original scheme was the deletion of the fin flash and the move to the Type D roundel of 36in diameter in all six positions. Oddly, even without the fin flash the size and location of the carrier/unit identifying code remained unchanged, so it looks to be floating at

F Mk X, TF952 of No. 805 Squadron at Eglinton in 1948 during their work-up. The small size and wide brush stroke of the characters used for the fuselage '106' is noteworthy *(©R.J. Caruana)*

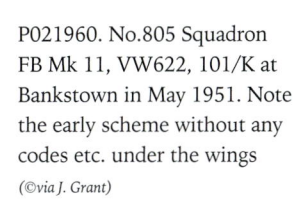

P021960. No.805 Squadron FB Mk 11, VW622, 101/K at Bankstown in May 1951. Note the early scheme without any codes etc. under the wings *(©via J. Grant)*

This shot of VW660, 120/K of No.805 Squadron at Bankstown in May 1951 is useful as it shows how close to the tip the underwing roundels were (©via J. Grant)

FB Mk 11, VW626, 105/K of No.805 Squadron after a landing accident on HMAS Sydney c.1950. An unusual angle, but it confirms the location of the roundels on the upper wing (©via J. Grant)

the top of the fin! This scheme was revised again in the early 1950s with the removal of the three-digit code and the application of a 'NAVY' legend aft of the fuselage roundel, on each side. This was applied in 24in high black characters, with the three-digit aircraft number now in front of the roundel, also in 24in black characters – this code was often placed well forward of the roundel directly below the mid-section of the canopy area. A unit/base or carrier identification code was applied in 18in high black characters either side of the vertical fin, positioned directly above the fillet for the tailplanes, although it should be noted that later this character was increased in size to 24in and moved down to be central on either side of the vertical fin.

The 'RAN' code was applied in 4in high white letters forward and below the leading edge of the tailplane, either side of the aft fuselage, with the aircraft serial number below it in the same 4in white characters. Again, it should be noted that often the serial number was split onto two lines, with the alphabetic element first (e.g. 'WZ') and the numeric bit (e.g. '652') below it. The serial number was repeated under each wing, applied in 21in high black characters, read from the trailing edge of the starboard and leading edge of the port wings. Looking at period photos the roundels under the wings were pushed right to the tips, positioned forward so that they

FB Mk 11 VX648, 112/K of No.805 Squadron is seen taxing out with its Korean War recognition stripes painted out in solid bands, Pearce, February 1952 (©via J. Grant)

A nice period colour photo of FB Mk 11, VW647, 127/K of No.805 Sqn in the later scheme with the 'NAVY' legend added to the fuselage. This machine is today preserved at Camden Aviation Museum (©via J. Grant)

FB Mk 11, VX730 of No. 805 NAS, Royal Australian Navy on HMAS Sydney, Korea, 1951. Here you can see the effect on the '109' that the identification stripes have on it, resulting in contrasting colours being used as the character passes over the white or black elements. This is how the RN also approached this problem (©R.J. Caruana)

did not overlap the ailerons, and are of smaller diameter than those on the fuselage. A good in-flight photo of the last Sea Fury delivered to the RAN (WN587) confirms that the upper wing roundels were also smaller, so these are all probably of 30in diameter. As most Sea Furies operated off HMAS Sydney, they often carried the ship's badge under the cockpit, below the windscreen/canopy break line, along with the pilot and ground crew names forward and below it in small white characters.

The last scheme to be applied to RAN Sea Furies was one of overall Oxford Blue, with the spinner and rear (sliding) element of the cockpit canopy framework done in white. Although some sources list the application of the 'Roodel' in about 1953 the RAAF/RAN officially revised its national insignia on the 2nd July 1956. This saw the replacement of the red dot in the centre of the roundel with a red Kangaroo 'in motion' and this Kangaroo always faced the front of an aircraft. This does of course mean that those on the wings also face forward, which makes them look like they are applied on their side! Again these roundels were of 36in diameter on the fuselage and 30in for those on the wings, with the upper wing ones positioned mid-span, whilst those underneath were right at the tip, and positioned forward so that they did not overlap the hinge line of the ailerons. The 'NAVY' legend was applied aft of the fuselage roundel in 24in high white characters, with the three-digit aircraft number in front of the roundel, also in 24in white characters – often placed well forward of the roundel. The unit/base or carrier identification code was applied in 18in high white characters either side of the vertical fin, while the 'RAN' code was applied in 4in high white letters forward and below the leading edge of the tailplane, either side of the aft fuselage, with the aircraft serial number below it in the same 4in white characters.

WH589 was last operated by No.724 Sqn at Nowra, whose markings it is seen in here. This machine survives and is currently in private hands, in this photo it shows the last scheme applied to RAN Sea Furies (©Author's collection via K. Darling)

Royal Canadian Navy

Now most people would state that the RCN also had two similar demarcation schemes for their Sea Furies, but there is a lot more to it than that. The overall schemes were as follows:

Uppersurfaces
- CMSA I to III = Extra Dark Sea Grey
- CMSA IV Early machines = Dark Grey 1-9 (similar to RAF Extra Dark Sea Grey)
- CMSA IV Later machines = Dark Grey 501-102

Undersides
- CMSA I to III = Sky
- CMSA IV Early machines = Light Grey 1-13 (close to FS16314/lighter version of Medium Sea Grey)
- CMSA IV Later machines = Light Grey 501-106

The RCN operated a system designated 'Camouflage Scheme and Markings Arrangements' (CSMAs), so we will follow this same system to identify the changes.

CMSA I
The initial machines received by the RCN in May 1948 had the then standard RN scheme of gloss Extra Dark Sea Grey on the upper surfaces, tail and wings, with Sky underneath with a low demarcation between them, and the spinner in black. RAF Type C roundels were applied above and below the wings, with a Type C1 on each fuselage side and a Type C fin flash on the vertical fin. The legend 'Royal Navy' and the serial number were applied in black characters, forward and below the leading edge of the tailplane on either side of the aft fuselage. The serial was repeated in black characters under each wing, with the starboard side facing the leading edge and the port facing the trailing edge. The two Mk Xs operated by the RCN (TF901 and TF909) were both in this scheme.

above: The codes on this FB Mk 11 TG120 are not those of No.803 Squadron, so our guess is that this is the CAG CO's machine and is seen here going out on a flight probably from Dartmouth. This is the early scheme used by RCN machines with the maple flag added to the RAF roundel
(©Author's collection via K. Darling)

This little close-up shows how the RAF roundel was made Canadian by the addition of a Maple leaf in black
(©British Official)

This scheme was later revised, with the spinner done in white and a Canadian maple leaf (in black) added to the red centre of the national insignia. The 'Royal Navy' legend was replaced by 'Royal Canadian Navy' and call-signs and individual aircraft letters were added fore and aft of the fuselage roundels. No.803 Squadron was allocated 'BC', while No.883 Squadron was 'AA'. The only known exception to this was the CO of the 19th CAG, whose aircraft carried the code B•CG (see photo above).

CSMA II
Most of the Sea Furies in the VW-prefixed range accepted by the RCN in February 1949 all had a significantly different scheme. The Extra Dark Sea Grey was restricted to the upper areas of the fuselage, as well as the wings, tailplanes and spinner, all the rest was Sky. The fin flash was gone and all the roundels were replaced with the Type D.

The black serial numbers under the wings remained, as did the 'Royal Navy' and serial numbers on the aft fuselage. This overall scheme was modified prior to squadron allocation, with the replacement of 'Royal Navy' with 'Royal Canadian Navy', radio call-letters in black either side of the fuselage roundel and maple leafs in the centre of the roundels. Unlike the RN, the RCN applied a Type C flash to either side of the fin and once again the CO of the 19th CAG had his machine coded 'BCG', with all of this aft of the fuselage roundel on both sides.

CSMA III
The third scheme used by RCN Sea Furies started to appear in the summer of 1950. This saw the replacement of the RAF Sky with a colour that was more greyish, although not the Light Grey seen in the later CSMA IV scheme. RCN roundels replaced the RAF Type D on the fuselage sides and upper wing surface. Both roundel and serial number were deleted from beneath each wing and replaced with a code (VG) under the starboard wing and a three-character squadron and individual aircraft code under the port wing. A Type C flash was applied to either side of the vertical fin, while occasionally the squadron crest was applied to either side of the nose cowling. This scheme also saw the extension of the Extra Dark Sea Grey to the fin root fillet, although this was not universal. The 'Royal Canadian Navy' legend was sometimes seen on one line, whilst on others it was split onto two with 'Royal' above the 'Canadian Navy'.

CSMA IV
The final scheme applied to RCN machines started to appear in the summer of 1952. The Sky was replaced with Light Grey, whilst the Extra Dark Sea Grey was replaced with Dark Grey. The roundels were reduced and the yellow seen up until this stage on the fuselage ones was deleted (this is not always the case, as VX692, AA•C seen

A nice line-up of the 19th CAG aircraft shows the massive variation in markings applied even with the early scheme (RCN)

in January 1952 still retains the yellow ring on the small diameter fuselage roundels). The roundels once again re-appeared under the wings, although these were now near the tip, in line with RN procedures of the day. The fuselage call-sign was now replaced with the word 'NAVY' to the left of the roundel with the three-digit radio call-sign to the right. This identification system was also applied to the underside of the wing, with the 'NAVY' under the port and the call-sign under the starboard. This last element was also repeated in small (4in) black characters

FB Mk 11 VX690 is seen here in the markings of No.803 Squadron at Dartmouth in 1951. The scheme is CMSA III (©Canadian Official)

to the lower lip of the front of the engine cowling. The radio call-sign numbers were usually in the 100-series, although there are exceptions including TF996, which was '294', whilst WZ636 was '364' and some VT 40 machines were coded in the 800-series, as this was usual for training aircraft. The CMSA IV scheme also saw the application of distinctive markings on the spinner as well as personal markings. The former was usually in the shape of a red star to the white spinner, although the exact shape/style of this star varied greatly with No. 870 Squadron machines having a white five-pointed star mounted on red and outlined in black, whilst VT 40 had the a red scalloped star on a white background.

Service records for TG129 don't show it with the markings it is seen with here. This is the CMSA IV scheme and probably relates to TG129's time on board HMCS Magnificent with No.871 Sqn in 1952 (©*Canadian Official*)

Here you can see the 'last three' added at the bottom of the chin cowl of CMSA IV machines

C&M does not always follow the regulations, as this shot of VW563 proves, nice CMSA IV scheme but the '100' is under the wrong wing, it should be under the port with 'NAVY' under the starboard! (©*Public Archives of Canada/RCN*)

F•16 and F•26 both from No.860 Sqn with the orange spinner associated with that squadron. F•26 was one of those built by Fokker
(©Burgerhout collection via L. Boerman)

The Netherlands

Marine Luchtvaartdienst (Royal Netherlands Naval Air Services)

The first batch of Sea Furies supplied to the MLD were in the initial scheme seen on RN examples, with the low demarcation on the fuselage between the Extra Dark Sea Grey and Sky. The national insignia of 36in diameter was applied above and below each wing (near the tip) and in a 30in format on either side of the fuselage. This initial batch had code numbers prefixed with a '10 (10-1 to 10-10), with this number applied in 32in white characters and orientated the same on both sides so that the 10 was aft of the fuselage roundel on the starboard side and forward on the port. The Dutch flag (12in x 18in) was applied as a small block mid-way up each side of the vertical fin, with its farthest aft edge on the hinge line. The only other marking was the 'KON. MARINE' legend in 4in high white characters on each rear fuselage side below the tailplanes, positioned just above the rear tailwheel, parallel to the panel line in that area.

The second batch received by the MLD (10-11 to 10-22) was supplied at a time when the RN had moved to the later high-level demarcation scheme, so all these machines were painted in this fashion. The roundels remained in the same style/location, the only changes were that the 10-prefixed code number was applied in black characters to contrast better with the Sky fuselage sides, although it remained orientated the same on both sides. The Dutch flag was again applied as a small block mid-way up each side of the vertical fin, with its farthest aft edge on the hinge line.

The 'KON.MARINE' legend was also applied in the same style/location, but it too was black to contrast with the Sky paint. It should be noted that all of the initial batch that remained in use at this time were also repainted in this 'later' demarcation scheme. At some later stage it can be seen that the practice of adding the last two of the code number to either side of the engine cowling became commonplace. This marking was in black characters, matching the style of those on the fuselage, but being approximately half the size/height. The position of this number was such that it fitted entirely on the forward engine cowl ring, with none extending back onto the main engine (removable) cowls

A Sea Fury fitted with an ex-FAA wing, this aircraft, built by Fokker, was fitted with a wing from British stock when its was damaged – not bad considering 6•43 was not built in the UK!
(©Geldhof collection via L. Boerman)

Camouflage & Markings 3 — The Netherlands

10•2 in the first scheme applied to Dutch Sea Furies (boundary pattern No.1)
(via L. Boerman)

– this number was also often repeated on the bottom edge of the front cowl ring as well. When Fokker started licence production of the type, these received codes prefixed with a '6' (6-23 to 6-47) but all other markings remained the same, although the code number (6-23 etc) was now applied in 24in black characters. The entire numbering system was revised in the 1950s and the '10' and '6' prefixes were all replaced with a 'J' for *Jachtvliegtuig* (fighter).

Of note is that for all the schemes the stencils on the type remained unchanged, with the DTD stamps on things like the rudder and vertical fin always applied in black, even on Extra Dark Sea Grey, and the emergency stencils like the canopy chop marks and canopy release ones in yellow, again on both schemes (fine on EDSG, but not that clear on Sky!). There are also a few exceptions with Dutch Sea Furies, the display team formed in No.860 Squadron painted the entire engine cowlings of their machines in the same orange as seen in the centre of the national insignia, and included the spinner. They also applied '860' in black 12in characters on either size of the cowling, but unlike the codes seen elsewhere, these were applied in a 45° stencil-style font and were on the removable cowling sections, not the forward ring cowl. 6-43 is odd in that during a visit to the UK it damaged the port outer wing, so received a replacement from stocks at Hawker, the problem was this was an RN example complete with Type D roundels top and bottom! The aircraft flew in this country like this, but on return to The Netherlands the roundels were replaced with Dutch ones. A photo of 10-9 in the earliest scheme also shows it with Type D roundels under the starboard wing, again the result of a replacement outer wing panel.

6•16 seen on final approach and with the boundary pattern No.2 for the camouflage
(©L. Boerman)

The demonstration team the 'Aerobats' of No.860 Squadron, RNeth Naval Air Service
(©Korbee collection via L. Boerman)

Camouflage & Markings 3
Pakistan / Iraq

Pakistan AF machine L982 is seen here prior to delivery
(©Author's collection via K. Darling)

Pakistan
The machines supplied to this nation adopted the Middle East RAF scheme of Dark Earth (BS450) and Mid Stone over Azure Blue with the demarcation of the upper and lower colours low down on the fuselage side and with the entire vertical fin and rudder in the upper colours. It should be noted that the spinner was usually in Mid Stone. Roundels of 36in diameter were applied either side of the fuselage and above the wings at mid-span. The roundel below the wing dispensed with the yellow rim so was only of 34in diameter and it was placed towards the tip, forward so it did not overlap the aileron hinge line. The national flag was applied in a 24in square block on either side of the vertical fin, with its aft edge on the hinge line. The serial numbers were applied in 8in black characters on the aft fuselage, forward and below the leading edge of the tailplane. This serial was repeated in 24in black characters under each out wing panel, inboard of the tip/roundel, with it reading from the trailing edge on the starboard and leading edge on the port sides.

Iraq
Iraq also had their machines supplied in the Middle East RAF scheme of Dark Earth (BS450) and Mid Stone over Azure Blue with the demarcation of the upper and lower colours low down on the fuselage side and with the entire vertical fin and rudder in the upper colours. The triangular-shaped national insignia was applied either side of the fuselage and above the wings at mid-span. The insignia below the wing was placed towards the tip, forward so it did not overlap the aileron hinge line. The four-bar fin flash was applied in a 24in square block (6x6x6x6in) on either side of the vertical fin, with its rearmost edge on the hinge line. The serial number was applied in large (24in?) Arabic characters aft of the fuselage insignia and under each outer wing panel with it parallel to the wing leading edge and read from the trailing edge on the starboard and leading edge on the port sides. When supplied, all stencils on these machines were in English and the two-seaters adopted the same overall scheme and markings.

Known as the 'Baghdad Fury', the Iraqi examples were de-navalised versions of the Sea Fury. The double-bubble canopies seen on this machine prior to delivery led to cavitation and damage, so later the fleet had the canopies replaced with those used on the Royal Naval T Mk 20
(©Hawker Aircraft Ltd via R.J. Caruana Archive)

A superb shot of an Iraqi Air Force Fury ISS en route to Baghdad
(©Author's collection via K. Darling)

The Burmese Air Force operated UB454 which is seen here in transit to that nation (©*Hawker Aircraft*)

Burma

Both single- and two-seat versions supplied to Burma were sprayed High Speed Silver (aluminium gloss) overall, including the spinner. The triangular-shaped national insignia was applied to each side of the fuselage and above and below the wings. Those above the wing were mid-span, whilst those underneath were nearer the tip to allow the serial number to be applied. The serial number was six character, comprising 'UB' with a three-figure numeric code in the 450-series. This serial was applied in black (24in?) characters aft of the fuselage roundel and under each wing. The large format and length of this number does mean that it overlapped the undercarriage doors. This serial was orientated under the wings so that it could be read from the trailing edge on the starboard and leading edge on the port sides. The fin flash was 24inx24in and was situated centrally on the vertical fin, not with its rearmost edge on the hinge line. The two-seaters were supplied at least with the 24in wide yellow bands around the aft fuselage and each wing. It should be noted that looking at period photos the only stencils applied were the emergency ones and these were all in English and black characters.

Cuba

Very little is known about the Cuban machines after the revolution. Initially the FAEC (*Fuerza Aerea del Ejercito del Cuba* [Cuban Army Air Force) machines would seem to have been either polished metal or High Speed Silver (aluminium gloss) overall with the upper decking immediately forward of the windscreen and stretching the entire length of the upper cowling in matt black. The forward cowling ring and spinner were painted yellow and the Cuban machines had the arrestor hooks removed. A three-digit numeric code in the 500-range was applied below the cockpit area on either side of the fuselage in black 24in high characters. The legend 'FAEC' and three-digit code were repeated on the vertical fin, again in black but of only 6in high characters. The entire rudder was painted in blue and white stripes of approximately 18in, with the red triangle at the hinge line containing the

The Burmese Air Force ordered the T Mk 20 as well as the single-seater and UB451 can be seen here prior to delivery (©*Hawker Aircraft*)

Camouflage & Markings
Cuba / Egypt

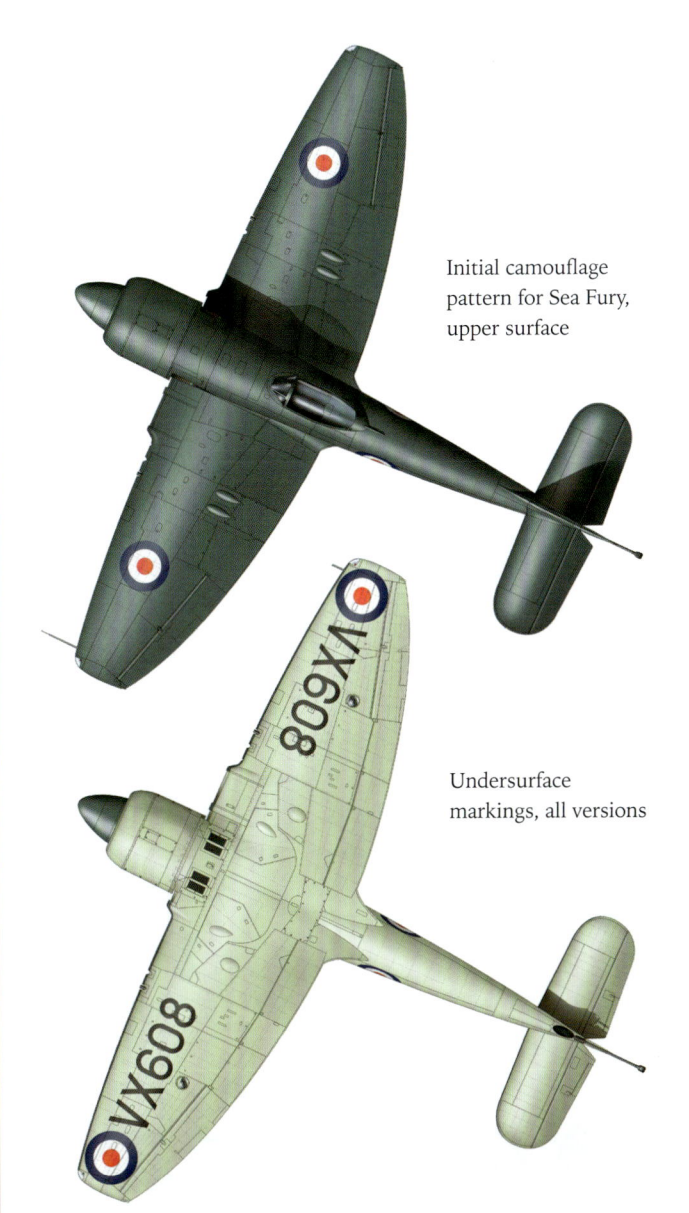

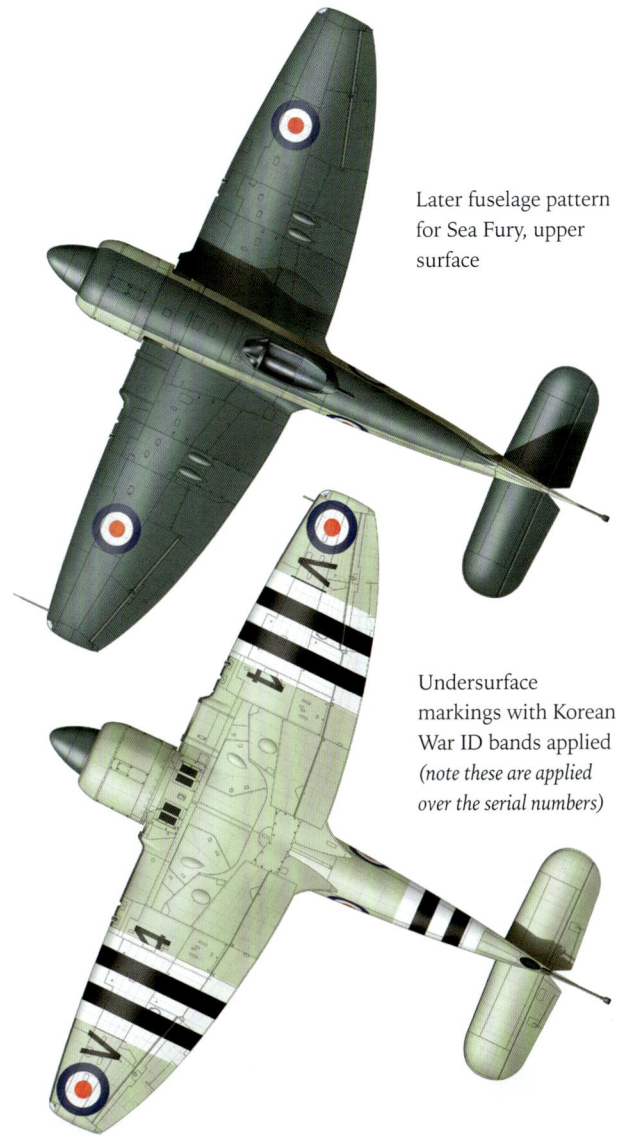

Initial camouflage pattern for Sea Fury, upper surface

Later fuselage pattern for Sea Fury, upper surface

Undersurface markings, all versions

Undersurface markings with Korean War ID bands applied (note these are applied over the serial numbers)

small white star. The national insignia star and bar was applied on either side of the fuselage and above the port and below the starboard wings. On the upper starboard and lower port wing 'FAEC' was again applied in 21in high black characters with both positioned parallel with the leading edge and read from the trailing edge.

There seems much confusion as to whether these machines once taken over by the FAR flew in their original scheme as recounted above, or in one of three schemes often quoted? The first of the three schemes is simply identified as Light Grey with the FAEC markings and codes (now with 'FAEC' changed to 'FAR') applied in black – these machines also had the cowling ring and spinner in either red or yellow. The second scheme, apparently applied in 1959, seems to show the machine in two shades of blue/grey, the upper one quite dark and the lower one a light blue. The new FAR roundel was applied to either side of the aft fuselage in what looks to be a 20-24in format and forward of it on either side is the aircraft serial number in 30in yellow numbers. The rudder remains in the blue/white stripes and there does not seem to be any roundels under the wings (we cannot confirm if they were carried on top?) – *Note that this scheme is only based on artwork, the sources for which are not quoted (Author)*. The final scheme is of Dark Olive Green overall with all the codes etc. in yellow now, albeit of much smaller sizes and different style to that seen in the original FAEC scheme. The aircraft number (e.g. FAR42) was carried in small (8in?) characters mid-way up the vertical fin. We suspect that the star and bar was applied above the port and below the starboard wings, with that aircraft number repeated below the port and above the starboard wings in small (12in?) yellow characters. It is often quoted that this green scheme is the one applied during the Bay of Pigs invasion, however for now this has to remain unconfirmed.

It should be noted that the Sea Fury today preserved in Cuba is painted in a much more modern scheme that is, as far as we know, not applicable to the type when in service.

Egypt
Little is known about the colour and markings applied to these machines, as few (if any) photos have ever appeared and the only information that we could find

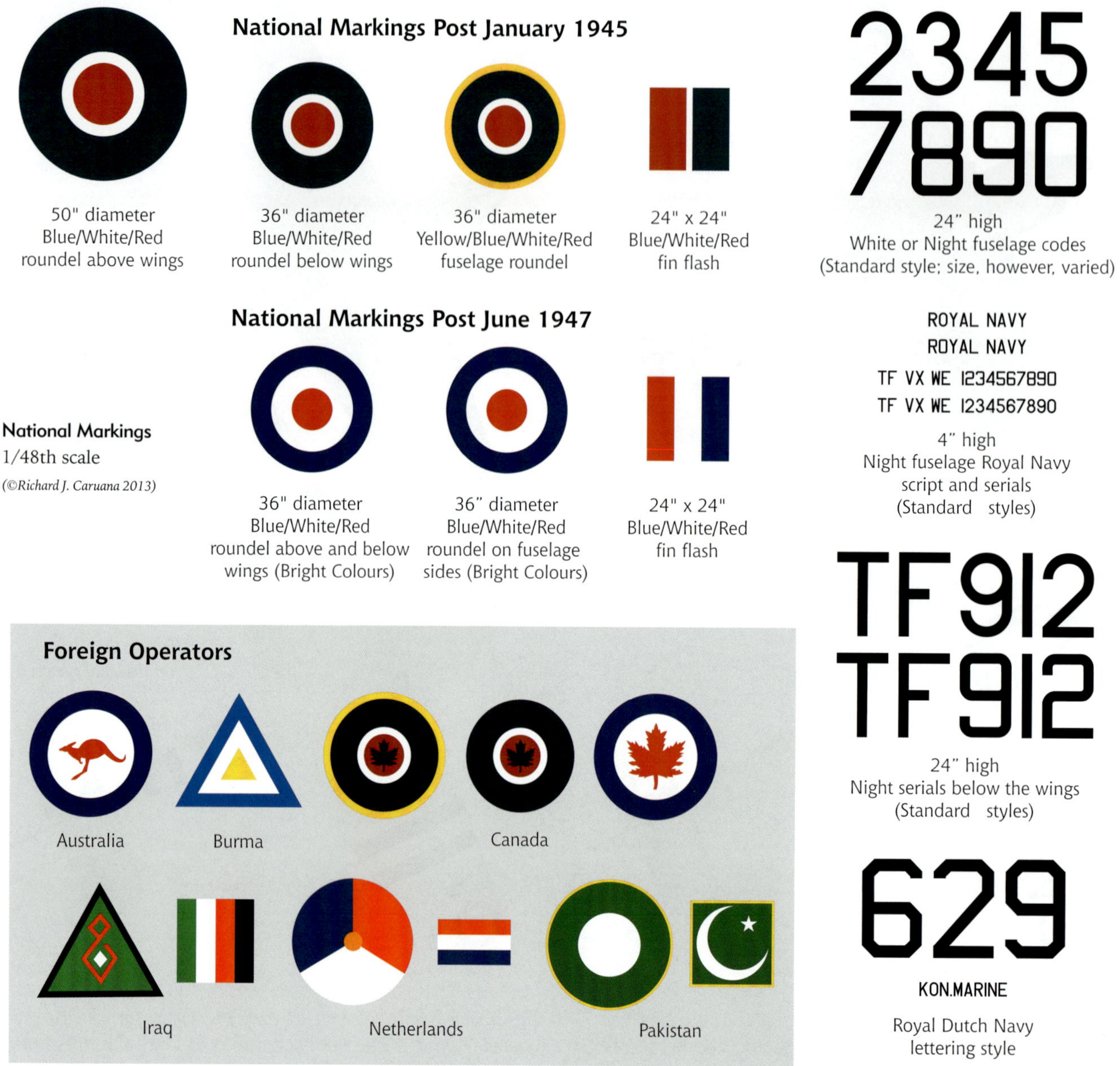

Camouflage & Markings 3
Egypt / Morocco

National Markings Post January 1945

- 50" diameter Blue/White/Red roundel above wings
- 36" diameter Blue/White/Red roundel below wings
- 36" diameter Yellow/Blue/White/Red fuselage roundel
- 24" x 24" Blue/White/Red fin flash

National Markings Post June 1947

National Markings 1/48th scale
(©Richard J. Caruana 2013)

- 36" diameter Blue/White/Red roundel above and below wings (Bright Colours)
- 36" diameter Blue/White/Red roundel on fuselage sides (Bright Colours)
- 24" x 24" Blue/White/Red fin flash

Foreign Operators

- Australia
- Burma
- Canada
- Iraq
- Netherlands
- Pakistan

2345 7890
24" high White or Night fuselage codes (Standard style; size, however, varied)

ROYAL NAVY
ROYAL NAVY
TF VX WE 1234567890
TF VX WE 1234567890
4" high Night fuselage Royal Navy script and serials (Standard styles)

TF912
TF912
24" high Night serials below the wings (Standard styles)

629
KON.MARINE
Royal Dutch Navy lettering style

---

was modern artwork, for which sources are not quoted, and Hobbycraft's 1:32 kit decals! Like those machines supplied to Burma, it would seem that those that went to Egypt also had the same scheme of High Speed Silver (aluminium gloss) overall, including the spinner. The Egyptian Air Force roundel was applied in (probably) 36in diameter on the fuselage sides. The aircraft construction number (700-series) was applied in small (8in?) black (*some say green*) characters behind the fuselage roundel and underneath two Arabic characters of a slightly larger format (12in?). Aft of this is a white band (18in?) running around the fuselage, which is edged with thin bands (2in?) of the same green used in the national insignia. An oblong (18inx24in) fin flash is applied to each side of the vertical fin. The white/green banding is also applied towards the tip around each wing, although this is shown as green/white/green/white/green, with the green bands being narrow and the white wider – our guess is 12in for the white and 2in for the green, but that is just a guess (*please note some sources show this as equal bands of each colour*). Inboard of these bands is another roundel, although this looks of smaller diameter (32in?).

As the type never operated post-1958 it never carried the later roundel adopted by Egypt after that year.

Morocco

As ex-Iraqi machines, they would most likely have retained their Iraqi Air Force scheme of Dark Earth and Mid Stone over Azure Blue. However, artwork exists (without quoting sources) that shows these machines to be in aluminium overall with red spinners. The Moroccan roundel is applied to each side of the fuselage in a small diameter we guess to be about 24in? There are no roundels shown above or below the wings. A red square is applied to either side of the top of the vertical fin with the five-pointed star in the centre created by letting the aluminium paint underneath show through.

Camouflage & Markings
West Germany

German TT Mk 20 D-CATA is seen here being refuelled at its Koln base prior to a sortie (©T. Genth via K. Darling)

below: The only single-seat Sea Fury operated by DLB in German for target-towing duties was this Dutch machine registered as D-CACY
(©Author's collection via K. Darling)

West Germany

As target-towing aircraft the TT Mk 20s operated on behalf of the Luftwaffe by *Deutsche Luftfahrt Beratungsdeinst* had to be in a high visibility scheme. Instead of the usual overall yellow scheme, though, these machines adopted an overall scarlet one. We have failed to find any official references for this colour, but being German we guess it will have an RAL code. The only markings carried comprised the civil registrations (e.g. D-CACY) in black 45cm characters on either side of the aft fuselage and above the starboard wing only. The German Democratic Republic flag surmounted on a white background was applied to either side of the tip of the vertical fin. Each aircraft also had another code number in the ES-prefixed range (e.g. ES3617), which was applied on either side of the rear fuselage, aft of the main registration and aft of the transit joint in that area (it was also seated on the prominent line of rivets in this area and probably of 15cm characters). All stencilling etc. was in German and either white or yellow? The only exception to this is D-CATA, which carried that marking in small (25cm?) black characters at the base of the vertical fin, its ES3503 number in an odd style font under each tailplane (probably 15cm) and the national flag on the top of the fin – otherwise it was devoid of markings.

The target-towing winch installed in the DLB machines was designed in Switzerland, and projected from starboard mid-fuselage as seen here on D-CATA (©T. Genth via K. Darling)

This DLB-operated TT Mk 20 D-CAMI confirms that the type never carried their registrations under the wings, as elsewhere you will see another shot of this machine showing the starboard wing also devoid of markings (©T. Genth via K. Darling)

Hawker Fury (Griffon) prototype LA610
Dark Earth/Dark Earth upper surfaces with yellow undersides; 'C1' type roundels on fuselage sides, 'C' type below wings, 'B' type above wings. Prototype marking on fuselage sides in yellow; propeller spinner and serial in black

Hawker Sea Fury F Mk X, TF912, 120/VL
No.799 Naval Air Squadron (NAS), RNAS Yeovilton. Extra Dark Sea Grey upper surfaces with Sky undersides; white codes, black serials. Yellow spinner; 'C' type roundels in four wing positions

Hawker Sea Fury FB Mk 11, VX608, 098-FD
No.703 NAS, RNAS Ford, 1953. Extra Dark Sea Grey upper surfaces with Sky undersides; black spinner, serials and codes. Roundels in six positions; unit crest ahead of windscreen

Hawker Sea Fury FB Mk 11, TF991, 102-JR
No.805 NAS, RNAS Eglinton, 1948. Extra Dark Sea Grey/Sky finish with white codes on fuselage and fin; remaining lettering in black. 'C1' roundels on fuselage sides, 'C' roundels in four wing positions. Spinners are believed to have been red

Hawker Sea Fury FB Mk 11, VR943, 105-R
No.801 NAS, HMS Glory, Korea, 1951. Extra Dark Sea Grey upper surfaces with Sky undersides; all lettering in black. Black/white bands around wings and rear fuselage; roundels in six positions

Camouflage & Markings 3
Profiles, Side 2

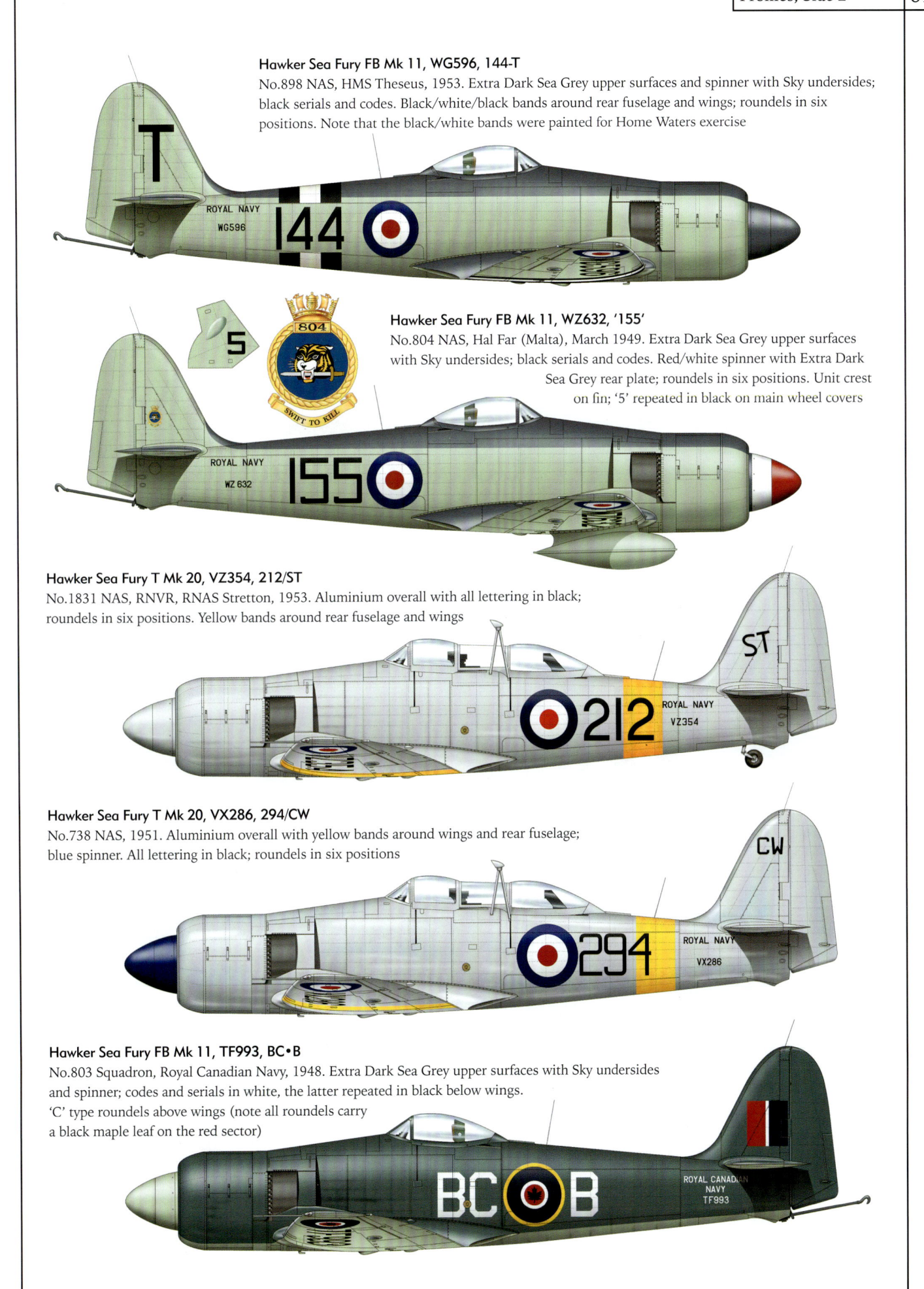

Hawker Sea Fury FB Mk 11, WG596, 144-T
No.898 NAS, HMS Theseus, 1953. Extra Dark Sea Grey upper surfaces and spinner with Sky undersides; black serials and codes. Black/white/black bands around rear fuselage and wings; roundels in six positions. Note that the black/white bands were painted for Home Waters exercise

Hawker Sea Fury FB Mk 11, WZ632, '155'
No.804 NAS, Hal Far (Malta), March 1949. Extra Dark Sea Grey upper surfaces with Sky undersides; black serials and codes. Red/white spinner with Extra Dark Sea Grey rear plate; roundels in six positions. Unit crest on fin; '5' repeated in black on main wheel covers

Hawker Sea Fury T Mk 20, VZ354, 212/ST
No.1831 NAS, RNVR, RNAS Stretton, 1953. Aluminium overall with all lettering in black; roundels in six positions. Yellow bands around rear fuselage and wings

Hawker Sea Fury T Mk 20, VX286, 294/CW
No.738 NAS, 1951. Aluminium overall with yellow bands around wings and rear fuselage; blue spinner. All lettering in black; roundels in six positions

Hawker Sea Fury FB Mk 11, TF993, BC•B
No.803 Squadron, Royal Canadian Navy, 1948. Extra Dark Sea Grey upper surfaces with Sky undersides and spinner; codes and serials in white, the latter repeated in black below wings. 'C' type roundels above wings (note all roundels carry a black maple leaf on the red sector)

Camouflage & Markings 3
Profiles, Side 3

©2013/2018 Richard J. Caruana

Hawker Sea Fury FB Mk 11, TG119/110
No.871 Squadron, Royal Canadian Navy, 1953. Dark Grey 1-9 (similar to Extra Dark Sea Grey) upper surfaces with Light Sea Grey undersides; all lettering in black. Blue/white roundels with red maple leaf in six positions; 'NAVY' in black below starboard wing, '110' below port, both reading from leading edge. Red/white spinner

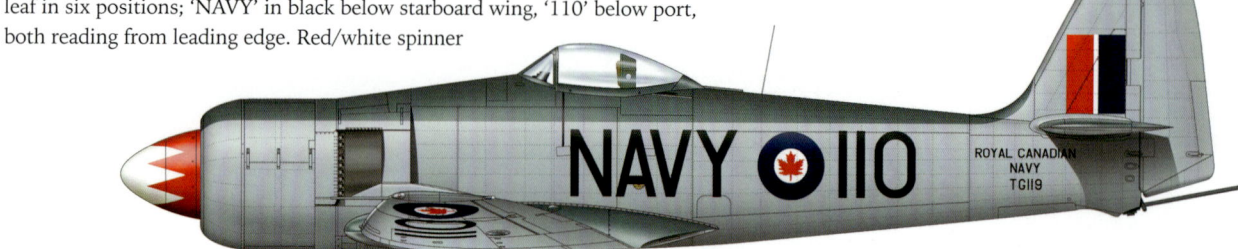

Hawker Sea Fury FB Mk 11, WZ645, 103/K
No.805 Squadron Royal Australian Navy. Extra Dark Sea Grey upper surfaces with Sky undersides; black lettering and red spinner

Hawker Sea Fury FB Mk 11, WE674, 105/K
No.805 Squadron Royal Australian Navy, HMAS Sydney, Korea, 1951. Extra Dark Sea Grey upper surfaces with Sky undersides and spinner; black lettering. Black/white bands around wings and rear fuselage; roundels in six positions. Lt (P) Clarkson (DFM) killed in this aircraft on 5th November 1951 whilst attacking enemy transports in the Han river area

Hawker Sea Fury FB Mk 11, WH589, 115/NW
No.805 Squadron, Royal Australian Navy (RAN), Bankstown, 1968. Oxford Blue overall with all lettering and spinner in white; national markings in six positions. Canopy frame unpainted

Hawker Sea Fury FB Mk 11, XV756/100
No.805 Squadron Aerobatic Team, Royal Australian Navy. Aluminium overall with red spinner, wingtips, fin leading edge, canopy frame and arrestor hook; black lettering. National markings in six positions

Camouflage & Markings 3
Profiles, Side 4

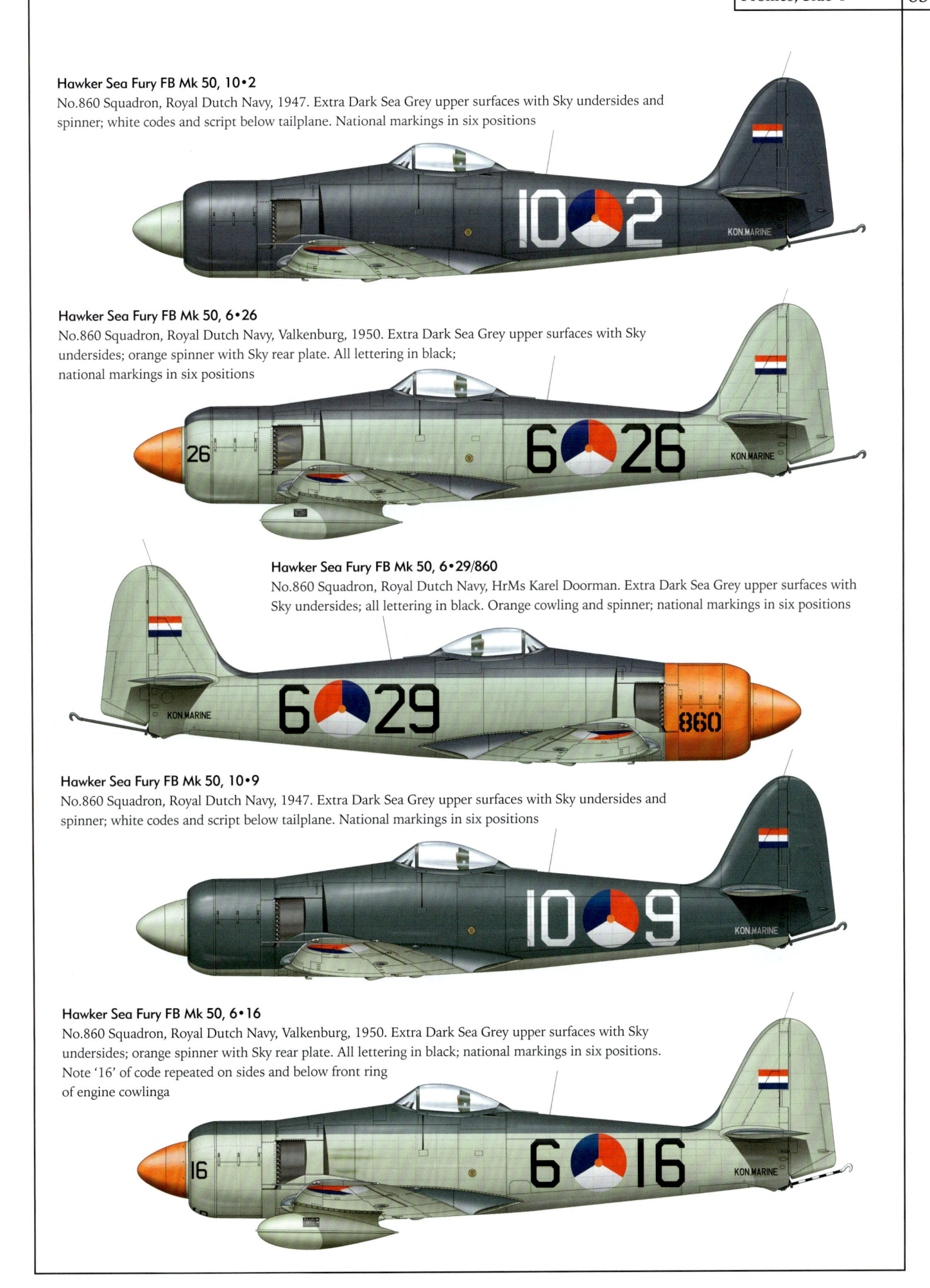

Hawker Sea Fury FB Mk 50, 10•2
No.860 Squadron, Royal Dutch Navy, 1947. Extra Dark Sea Grey upper surfaces with Sky undersides and spinner; white codes and script below tailplane. National markings in six positions

Hawker Sea Fury FB Mk 50, 6•26
No.860 Squadron, Royal Dutch Navy, Valkenburg, 1950. Extra Dark Sea Grey upper surfaces with Sky undersides; orange spinner with Sky rear plate. All lettering in black; national markings in six positions

Hawker Sea Fury FB Mk 50, 6•29/860
No.860 Squadron, Royal Dutch Navy, HrMs Karel Doorman. Extra Dark Sea Grey upper surfaces with Sky undersides; all lettering in black. Orange cowling and spinner; national markings in six positions

Hawker Sea Fury FB Mk 50, 10•9
No.860 Squadron, Royal Dutch Navy, 1947. Extra Dark Sea Grey upper surfaces with Sky undersides and spinner; white codes and script below tailplane. National markings in six positions

Hawker Sea Fury FB Mk 50, 6•16
No.860 Squadron, Royal Dutch Navy, Valkenburg, 1950. Extra Dark Sea Grey upper surfaces with Sky undersides; orange spinner with Sky rear plate. All lettering in black; national markings in six positions. Note '16' of code repeated on sides and below front ring of engine cowlinga

Hawker Sea Fury FB Mk 11, UB-471
Burmese Air Force. Natural metal overall with red spinner and red/white checks on rudder; national markings in six positions. Lettering in black

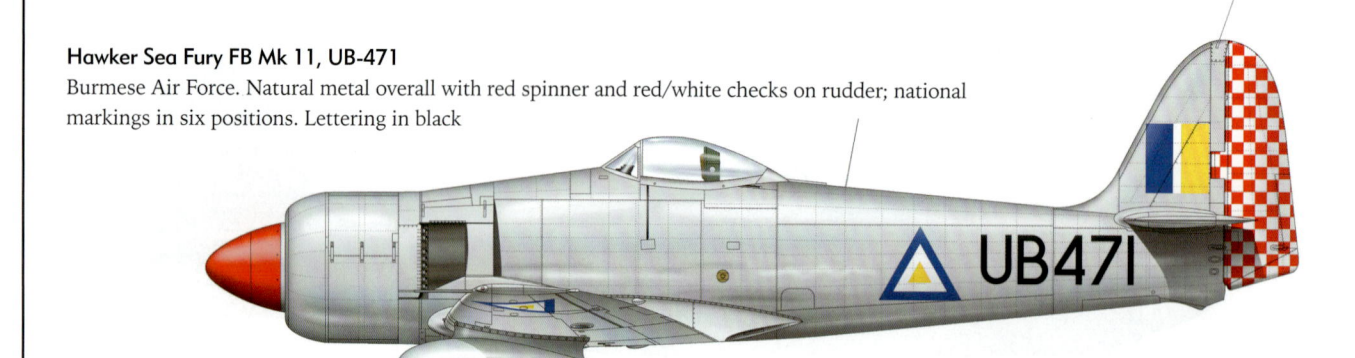

Hawker Sea Fury FB.Mk 11, FAR41
Cuban Air Force, post-1961 Bay of Pigs Invasion. Wrap-around olive green and dark green wavy camouflage pattern. National markings on fuselage sides, above port and below starboard wings. 'FAR41' in yellow on fin, repeated below port wing; '41' carried on main undercarriage doors

Hawker Fury ISS, 321
Royal Iraqi Air Force. Dark Earth and Mid Stone upper surfaces with Azure Blue undersides and spinner; white bands around wings and rear fuselage. National markings in six positions; serials in black, repeated below wings

Hawker Sea Fury FB Mk 60
Moroccan Air Force (ex-Iraqi Air Force), as preserved at Army HQ, Rabat, 1988. Light blue-grey overall with dark olive green wavy camouflage on upper surfaces. National markings in six positions; no serials or codes applied; undercarriage legs painted gloss black

Hawker Sea Fury FB Mk 60, L965
No.9 Squadron, Pakistan Air Force. Dark Earth/Mid Stone upper surfaces with Azure Blue undersides; red spinner, black serials. National markings in six positions (outlined in yellow); unit crest below windscreen

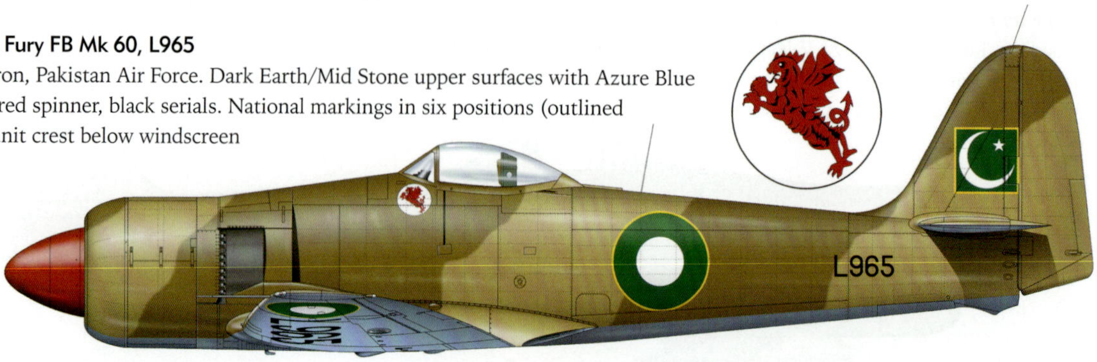

Camouflage & Markings
Profiles, Side 6

Hawker Sea Fury FB Mk 11, '703'
Royal Egyptian Air Force, 1960. Silver overall with white bands, edged in green, around wingtips (not overlapping onto ailerons) and rear fuselage; all lettering black. Roundels in six positions; serial in Arabic script repeated below wings

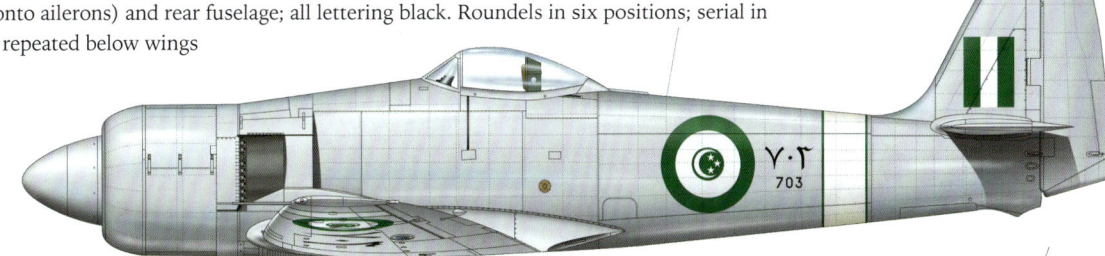

Hawker Sea Fury FB Mk 50, D-CACY/ES3617
Deutsche Luftfahrt Beratungsdienst. Scarlet overall with all lettering in black; note fin flash bordered in white. This ex-Dutch machine was the only single-seat version operated by DLB

Hawker Sea Fury TT Mk 20, D-CACU/ES3616
Deutsche Luftfahrt-Beratungsdienst. Scarlet overall with all lettering in black; note fin flash bordered in white

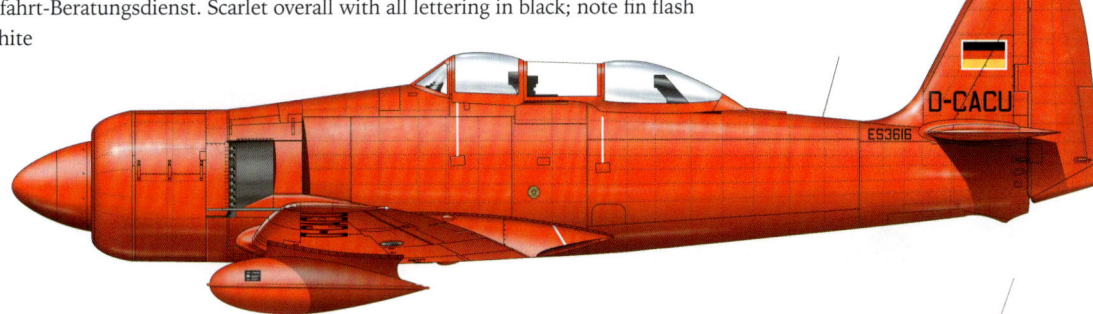

Sea Fury TT Mk 20, D-CAFO/ES8509
Deutsche Luftfahrt Beratungsdienst, 1974. Scarlet overall with orange spinner, rudder and wing tips. Fin flash bordered in white, registration in black on fuselage sides only

Sea Fury TT Mk 20, G-BCOV/ES3616
Deutsche Luftfahrt Beratungsdienst, 1974. Scarlet overall with orange spinner, rudder and wing tips. Fin flash bordered in white, registration in black on fuselage sides only

Not a huge number of kits of the Sea Fury have been produced over the years, but there are examples in all three of the major scales, however those in 1/72nd and 1/32nd are old and somewhat basic, so what follows are superb builds by Steve A. Evans of the new FB Mk 11 from Airfix and the two-seat T Mk 20 from AMG, both in 1/48th scale.

The classic Airfix look is now complete with the Adam Tooby art…superb!

Airfix 1/48th
Sea Fury FB Mk 11
by Steve A. Evans

Technical Specifications	
Scale: 1/48th	Manufacturer: Airfix
Kit No.: A06105	Material: IM
UK Price: £24.49	

Airfix have been threatening to do this one for a while, so when the test shots and a built pre-production kit appeared at the shows, there was understandably lots of interest. Now it's out and ready for sale, but what do you get? Well, the box is totally Airfix, you couldn't possibly mistake it for anyone else and as it's adorned with the masterful art of Adam Tooby, there's a lot to smile about. Inside it all looks pretty decent, with five sprues of their horrible light blue-coloured plastic and a single sprue of nicely clear transparent bits. The instructions are sixteen pages long, mostly taken up with CAD drawing of the construction stages, all 80 of them. There are three pages of very nice

The cockpit interior is reasonable; although you will need to supply seat belts, throttle handle and even a gunsight!

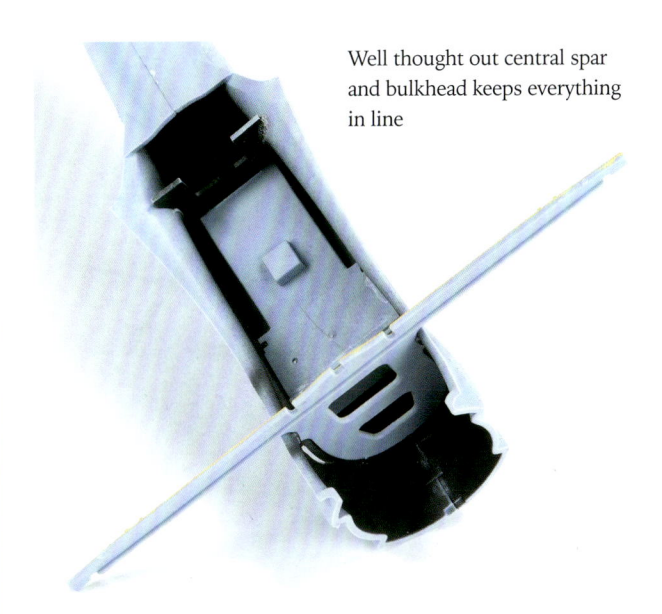

Hawker Sea Fury Models
1/48th FB Mk 11

Well thought out central spar and bulkhead keeps everything in line

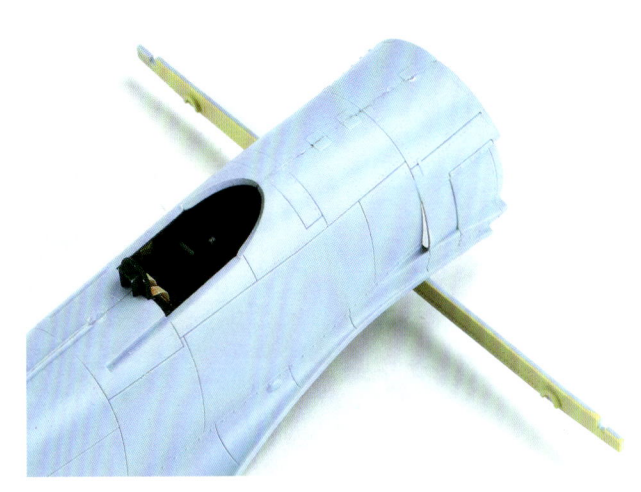

The fuselage joins nicely but you can see how limited the view into the interior is

The wing centre section is a busy place with inserts for the guns, oil cooler, carb intakes and of course the wheel bay

art for the markings and painting guide and the decal sheet is medium sized and beautifully printed by Cartograf. The plastic is nicely detailed, with recessed panel lines that are very accurately done and there are plenty of raised bits too for the larger fasteners and the dome-head rivets on the tail. Some of the bits are slide moulded, so you get stunning hollow exhausts. The box contains 123 parts with a big chunk of that given over to the armament, which includes bombs (two types) double rocket stacks, two sizes of drop tank and the strike camera pod as well. Other options in the box concern the wings, which can be built in the folded or open positions, as well as the fully poseable control surfaces, but sadly there are no dropped flaps. The markings are not to my taste I have to say. Option B is fine but option A is unutterably dull. I really cannot see the point of doing a Korean War Sea Fury without the theatre stripes, whoever in Airfix decided on that one needs a good talking to.

Construction
This starts with the dark and dingy cockpit, all black so nothing can be seen but it will need the seat belts and horror upon horror there is no gunsight in the kit! Seriously? What's going on back at Airfix HQ, they seem to have gone a bit daft? Apart from that, the fit of the parts is excellent, although there is an annoying amount of flash on some of the smaller parts, especially on sprue D for some reason. I especially like the interlocking construction of the bits and pieces to keep it all aligned and the right shape. Basic fit of all the parts is really good and when it comes to the options of the wing fold, it might be over-complicated but it works with a little TLC around the joints. I didn't use any filler on this one at all, apart from a little bit of cosmetic stuff around the lower wing/fuselage joint. The kit does have plenty of neat touches, with not only the control surfaces being poseable but there is also the RATOG pack to add, the hook is movable, the canopy open or closed, you get weighted tyres, the oil cooler radiator flap is a separate piece and you can even have it wheels up 'in flight' if you've got a suitable stand.

Colour & Markings
Paint-wise, if you're sticking to the British machines, then you have a limited choice, although they all look good. Airfix will of course be releasing a 'Commonwealth' box soon so the Canadian and Australian versions will become available. I opted to use Humbrol enamels for the main colours because they look gorgeous. I haven't found anyone else's paints to come up to scratch for a colour match. They may be considered old fashioned by some but that's fine by me. As you can see from the photographs, I elected to take a little bit of poetic licence with the kit markings and do a full set of stripes. Remember that if you do go down the stripey route, they can be positioned in a number of places so check your reference materials. I also ignored the black spinner and light underwing numbers bit as well because I have a picture of WJ236 from an old 1952 newsreel and it has an EDSG spinner and black serials, so that's what I followed.

The engine is beautifully simple because that's all you need. Check out the hollow injected exhausts and the neat detail on the cylinders

Hawker Sea Fury Models
1/48th FB Mk 11

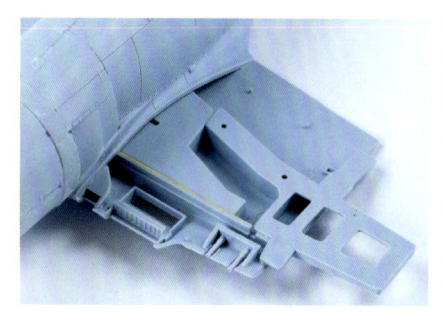

The wing structure for the open wing option is a neat touch

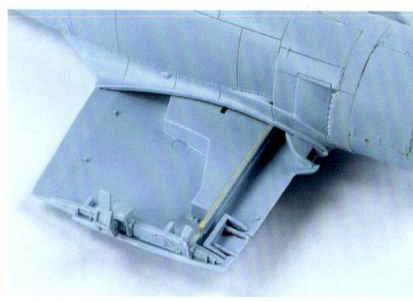

If you fancy the folded wings then there are the ribs and fold detail in the box for that too

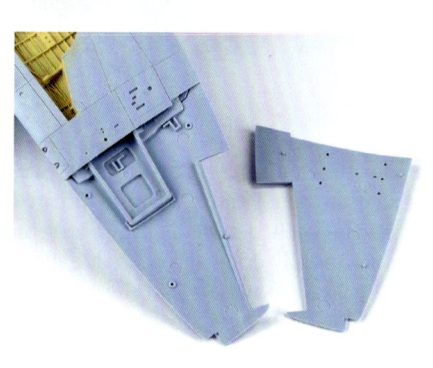

The outer wing panels have a very positive fit but it would have been much easier just to supply the wings in one section that you can cut if you want

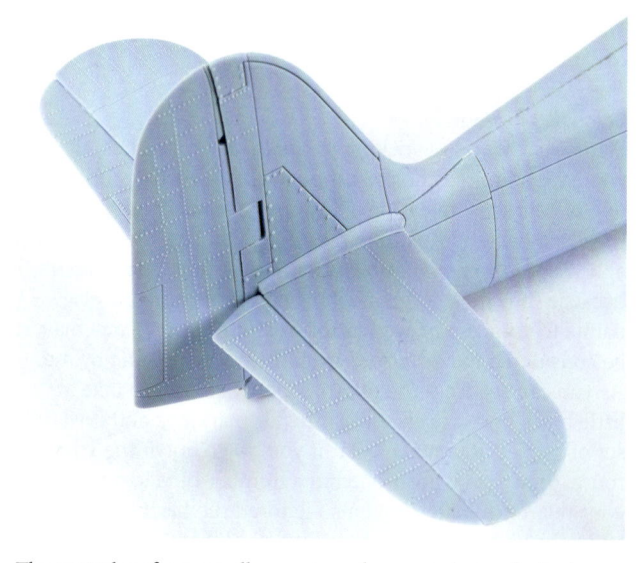

The control surfaces are all separate and you get plenty of raised detail for the rivets

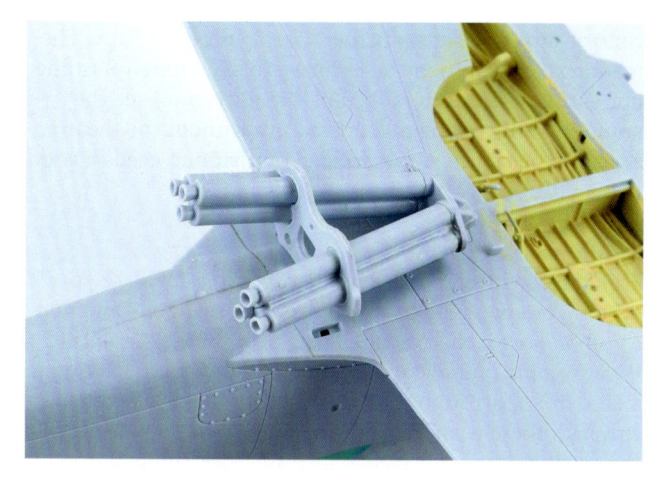

The Rocket Assisted Take-off Gear (RATOG) is a necessary bit of kit for when the steam catapult breaks...as it did for HMS Royal during its second tour in Korea

Weathering is kept to just the dirt and muck of operational life on board a wartime carrier with very little paint chipping, as that was almost instantly touched up to prevent the salty sea air getting in there and causing havoc with the metal. This was sealed in with Tamiya X-22 clear gloss and the decals were applied as per the instructions. The stencil placement diagram is excellent, as are both the full colour marking guides and the decals worked pretty well. Cartograf make some great stuff these days and even though these are done to the Airfix matt specification, they are still thin enough to work and look great once settled down. Softening solution will be needed over the larger panel lines and detail, though.

Final Details
After that it's down to the finishing touches and there are a lot of them to do. If you fit the rockets and RATOG then don't forget all the wiring will be needed or they'll look

Hawker Sea Fury
Models
1/48th FB Mk 11

4

EDSG, courtesy of Humbrol enamels. I have yet to find an alternative that looks quite as good

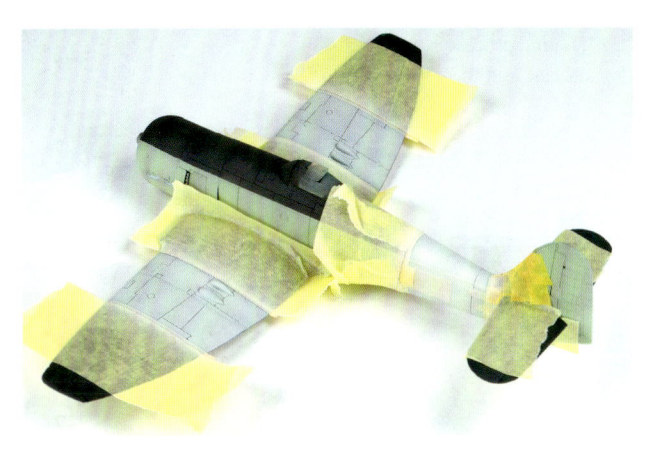

The Sky is also Humbrol but I take issue with the markings in the box being without ID stripes; what's the point of making it look so boring?

Now that is what a Korean vintage Sea Fury should look like!

This is obviously between hard-fought missions and is looking a little messy

Hawker Sea Fury Models
1/48th FB Mk 11

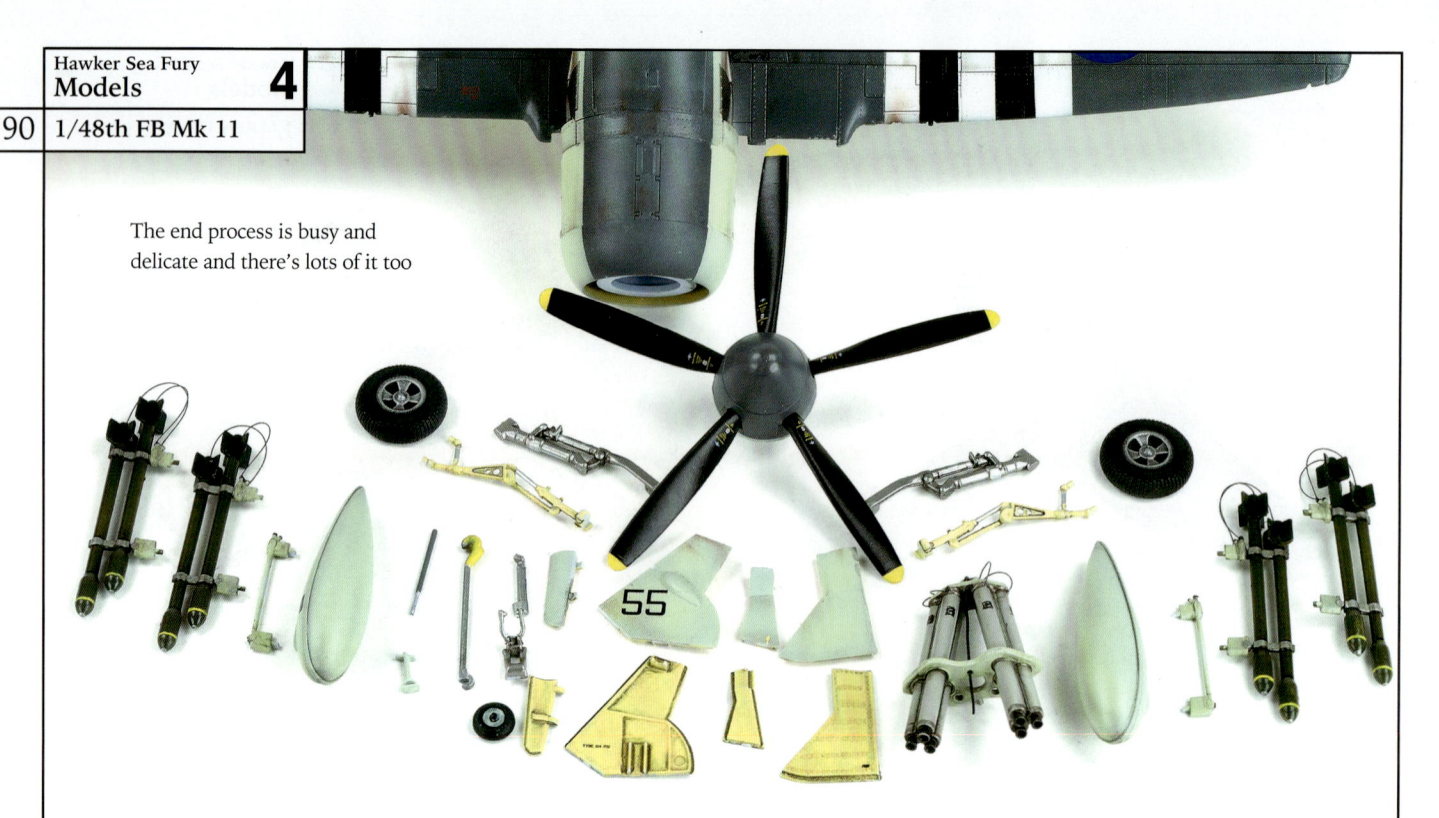

The end process is busy and delicate and there's lots of it too

bare, but there is a whole heap of other bits waiting to be fitted. Luckily it all goes together reasonably well so no great problems but a honourable mention must be made of the propeller assembly. Although I think the spinner could be a bit more refined in shape, the way it is constructed and slotted into place on the finished kit is a little bit of genius, that works beautifully and leaves you with a perfectly free-spinning prop. After which, the final finish of Alclad Matt Kote is applied, all the masking removed and this is one good-looking Sea Fury to sit on the shelf.

Verdict
The Fury/Sea Fury is one of my all-time favourite aircraft and Airfix have done a fine job of capturing the look of this amazing machine. The kit is easy enough to build and apart from the annoyances of the missing gunsight and the dull paint choice, it works as you would expect it to. It's not as easy to build as the P-51 but has lots of optional bits in the box to make it more interesting and even if it's not perfect, this is now the number one choice for this aircraft in this scale.

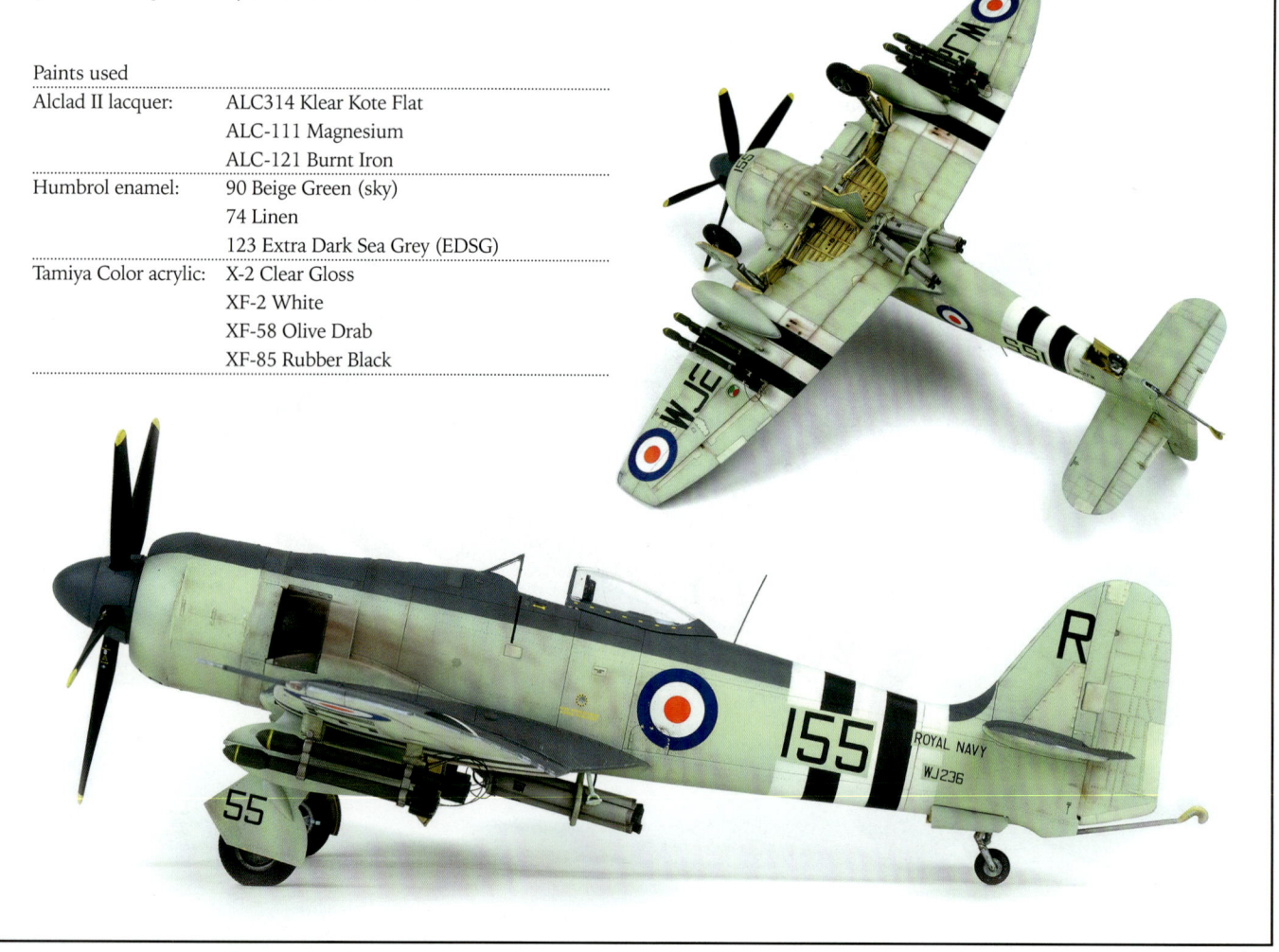

Paints used	
Alclad II lacquer:	ALC314 Klear Kote Flat
	ALC-111 Magnesium
	ALC-121 Burnt Iron
Humbrol enamel:	90 Beige Green (sky)
	74 Linen
	123 Extra Dark Sea Grey (EDSG)
Tamiya Color acrylic:	X-2 Clear Gloss
	XF-2 White
	XF-58 Olive Drab
	XF-85 Rubber Black

AMG 1/48th
Sea Fury T Mk 20 'Royal Navy'

by Steve A. Evans

Technical Specifications	
Scale: 1/48th	Manufacturer: Arsenal Model Group (AMG)
Kit No.: 48606	Material: IM, R, PE
UK Price: £45.99	

The Sea Fury is an amazing machine, as are all the last piston-engined fighters of course. Even in the two-seat trainer form seen here is was still a very capable aircraft, with 450mph performance and lots of guns and rockets to play with. This particular kit from AMG comes in a neat box with some good art on the lid and lots of stuff in the box. You get seven sprues of grey-coloured plastic, two of clear bits, two etched frets, vinyl masks, acetate sheet instruments and no fewer than four decal sheets in a little bag of their own. There is also a small bag of resin parts, including the gear bay and new horizontal tailplanes. The plastic is typical short-run stuff with lots of flash and mould lines to take care of. The external detail is gorgeous, with lots of neat recessed panel lines and delicate rivets. It's all very accurately mapped out as well, according to the plans I've got anyway. The resin stuff is dark grey-coloured and although the rivets on the tail aren't as delicate as the rest of the skinning, the wheel bay is beautifully cast. The etched frets are very comprehensive, with additions for most of the interior, including the instrument panels and seat belts front and back. This is good news for the interior because the plastic parts for this are basic in the extreme and suspiciously like the old Hobbycraft kit parts? The instructions are really where you get the feeling that all is not right with this kit because it's an A5 sized photocopied booklet of eight pages. The construction stages are chopped up into fourteen bits and they are extremely vague as to parts positioning and assembly. The parts in the drawing do not show what the plastic bits look like in reality and they just list the photo-etched parts without any indication as to where to actually fit them.

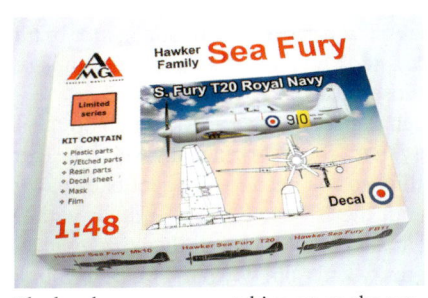

The fit of the plastic/resin parts is atrocious, with both the resin gear bay and the plastic wings needing to be massively thinned down

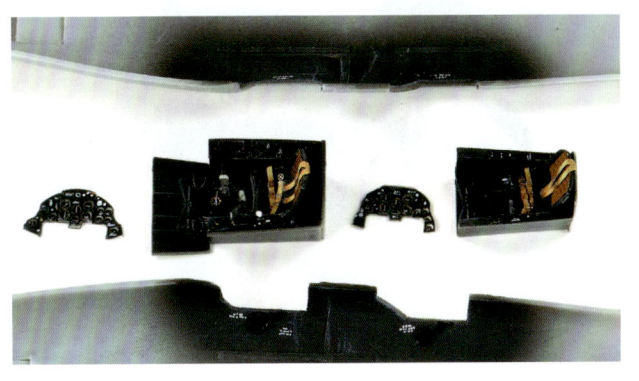

The box has some eye-catching art on the top and a neat design, which is always enticing

The interior is basic and poorly designed, looking very similar to the ancient Hobbycraft kit. You do get nice instrument panels, though

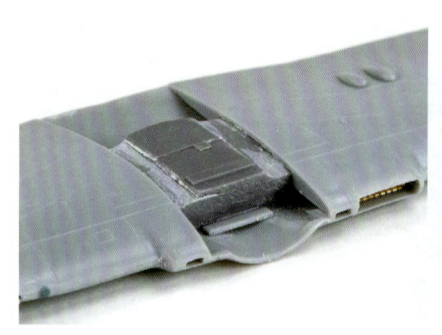

Here you can see the resin, now paper-thin, mated to the wings

Resin exhausts are poorly cast and the plastic and etched parts all need careful adjustment, trimming and sanding down

The cockpit is nearly invisible through the small openings, not to mention the very dark interior paint scheme

Construction

As far as the interior goes at least the etched instrument panels and seat belts are good so it's not all wasted. However, it doesn't get any better with absolutely no help at all with fitting the assembled cockpit tubs into the fuselage sides. There are no locating tabs to help the process so many trial fits and trimming will be required, especially as you need to thin down the fuselage sides to get them in. There is also an awful lot of trimming to do to get the resin wheel bay to fit in the wings. Basically you have to sand down the top of the bay until it is almost transparent and the same with the upper section of the wings. This continues with the fit of the fuselage on top of course, with trimming of both parts required. This process of trims and trial fits is needed for every single bit on this kit and some of it is tedious and could have been avoided with some better mouldings. For instance the exhaust heat shield inserts (parts D2 and 3 on the sprues) just don't fit, requiring lots of carful adjustment to get them anywhere near close and then it's out with the filler. Using filler on just about every single joint on the kit is disappointing, especially because the process of filling and sanding destroys a lot of the really nice exterior detail. But I'm afraid it's an absolute necessity with this kit.

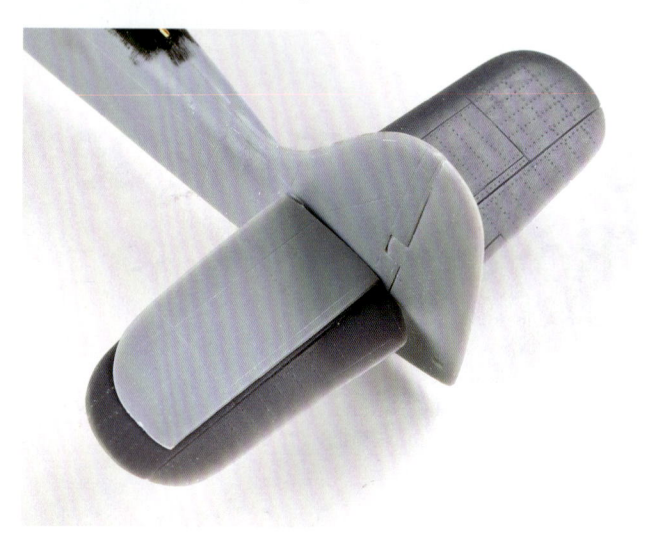

Colour & Markings

Never mind, at least the decals options are good. As I said earlier, there are four decal sheets in the box, one with national markings, one with stencils and two with the individual aircraft markings. The stencils and national markings are obviously generic sheets for all the Sea Fury variants that AMG offer because there are masses of Canadian and Australian markings on there. These will be welcome additions to the spares box.

The resin stabilisers are a good indication of how much bigger the tail was on the T Mk 20

Paint-wise, the British T Mk 20s all had the outer surfaces sprayed with High Speed Silver, so they are very plain, it's up to the markings to bring them to life. This does however mean that the paint process is remarkably quick. Alclad ALC-101 Aluminium is the main airframe colour, highlighted with a little ALC-102 Duralumin along the panel edges and some ALC-104 Pale Burnt Metal and ALC-121 Burnt Iron around the exhausts. The yellow stripes are Humbrol 24 Trainer Yellow, with the walkways done in Tamiya XF-69 NATO Black. Because the Alclad dries rock hard in a matter of minutes, the whole process took no more than a day to complete and it was on to those decals.

Although the decals look a little rough on the sheets, as they are very matt, they worked really well. The carrier film is extremely thin, so you need to take a lot of care with handling them but they settled down beautifully without a hint of silvering at all. I opted to brush them over with some grey pastel dust to try and calm down the bright colours of the roundels, after which they were sealed in with some Johnson's Klear and it was time for the finishing touches.

Nurse, get me the clamps! It needs all the help it can get to stay in the right shape

Hawker Sea Fury
Models
1/48th T Mk 20

Three-part canopy in place and it's ready for paint

Alclad always makes a beautiful surface; in this case it's a close match for the British High Speed Silver lacquer

The additional colours help to lift the plain scheme and note the very subdued panel accentuation but even this is way over the top compared to the real thing

Final Details

There is a lot to do with this one as all the delicate bits were left off until the end. There are plenty of the plastic parts that could really do with replacing as well because they are mostly over-scale, including the pitot, boarding step and tailwheel doors. The main doors get some photo-etched enhancements but they don't really work as supplied, so I added a bit more detail myself, and the rear cockpit periscope is supplied as a photo-etched part but this is too small and the wrong shape. I used the parts supplied because I was running out of time but to be honest a scratchbuilt item is really needed here.

After that the kit was dusted down with some Alclad ALC-313 Klear Kote Matte and the masking removed to call this one done.

Hawker Sea Fury Models
1/48th T Mk 20 — 4

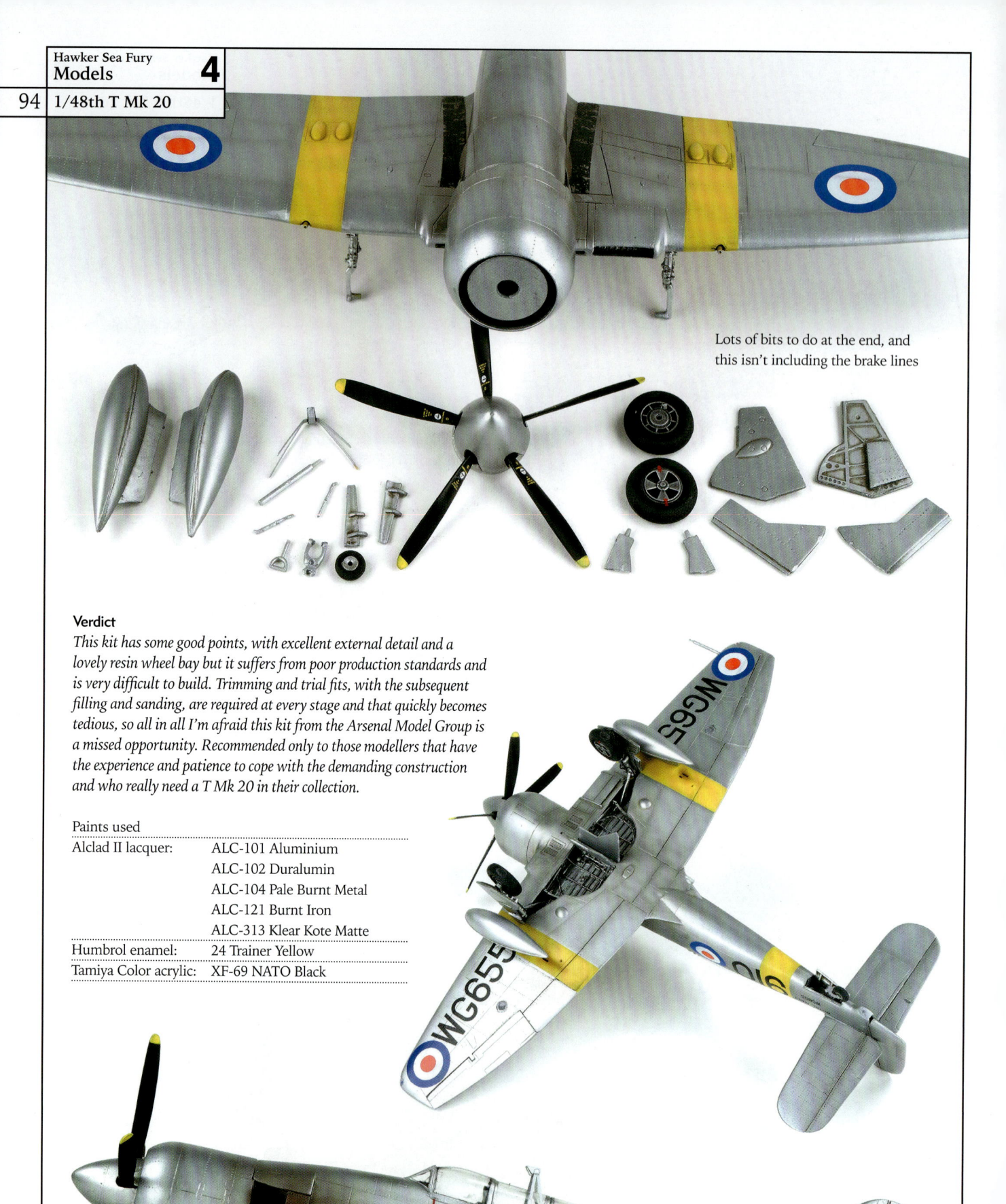

Lots of bits to do at the end, and this isn't including the brake lines

Verdict
This kit has some good points, with excellent external detail and a lovely resin wheel bay but it suffers from poor production standards and is very difficult to build. Trimming and trial fits, with the subsequent filling and sanding, are required at every stage and that quickly becomes tedious, so all in all I'm afraid this kit from the Arsenal Model Group is a missed opportunity. Recommended only to those modellers that have the experience and patience to cope with the demanding construction and who really need a T Mk 20 in their collection.

Paints used	
Alclad II lacquer:	ALC-101 Aluminium
	ALC-102 Duralumin
	ALC-104 Pale Burnt Metal
	ALC-121 Burnt Iron
	ALC-313 Klear Kote Matte
Humbrol enamel:	24 Trainer Yellow
Tamiya Color acrylic:	XF-69 NATO Black

Survivors

Probably the most famous Sea Fury there was, not just because it was the first production FB Mk 11, but that it had such a tragic demise. This photo taken by the author in the 1980s shows TF956 at its home base of Yeovilton during their annual air show.

Today numerous Sea Furies survive around the globe, so what follows is a brief(ish) history of all those we were aware of when compiling this title.

Please note that there is much confusion with the identities of many of these machines, especially those rebuilt as racers, as many airframes were broken down into component parts and these parts spread over a number of restoration projects, thus resulting in the construction serial numbers being quoted for more than one complete machine.

Those machines recovered from Iraq by Ed Jurist and David C. Tallichet in 1979 were broken down into component parts and stored, however when these were registered by Ed Jurist in August 1979 it seems that registrations were linked in a manner that did not reflect actual 'complete' airframes and thus when many were later sold, what was supplied under a civil registration was a mix-and-match collection of parts. VH-HFG is a good example, because although it is listed as C/No.37752 and ex-WJ298, only the rear fuselage of that machine is from that airframe, as it never went to Iraq and was still in service with No.776 FRU at Hurn in September 1958! We have tried to sort the resulting conflicting data out, but in many cases we have had to just add notes, because it is unlikely to ever be completely sorted.

UK

- **TF956**, built at Langley as the first production FB Mk 11 for the Royal Navy; first flew on 5th September 1947; delivered to RNAS Culdrose October 1947 and placed in store; moved to RNAS Stretton in July 1948; in August 1948 entered service as '108/JR' with No.805 Squadron, Royal Australian Navy, based at RNAS Eglinton (the unit was 'working up' in the UK before returning to

With the loss of TF956 the RNHF had their 'spares ship' VR930 rebuilt by BAE and it is seen here during a visit to Duxford

Sea Fury Survivors 5
UK

Seen during a display at Yeovilton in the 1990s, TG655 in her original form (©K. Darling)

Australia); from August 1949 used by No.799 NAS, RNAS Yeovilton; moved to RNAS Anthorn in January 1950 in readiness for voyage to Asia and ultimately Korea; loaded onto HMS Warrior and carried to Sembawang for re-assembly and testing; joined No.807 NAS on the 24th October 1950 as '123/T'; flew 213 hours in the Korean War conflict, and was hit by flak several times; returned to the UK aboard Theseus, and ferried to Fleetlands in May 1951' in 1952 noted in store at RNAS Anthorn; in May 1953 joined No.738 NAS at RNAS Culdrose as '125/CW'; from 1954 to early 1960 in store; in May 1960 transferred to the Fleet Requirements Unit at Hurn; SOC in November 1962 ; bought back by Hawker Aircraft in January 1963, and flown to Dunsfold and placed in store; a few years later the aircraft was placed on rebuild with the intention of it joining the Hawker Historic Flight alongside Hurricane PZ865; in 1971 it was decided to donate the partly restored airframe to the Navy; item received by the FAA at RNAS Yeovilton; restoration was completed by December 1971; the aircraft was test flown on the 16th January 1972 by Hawker's Chief Test Pilot Duncan Simpson; on the 21st January 1971 officially handed over to the RNHF; operated for seventeen years by the RNHF; aircraft lost in a flying accident on the 10th June 1989 shortly after taking off from RNAS Prestwick due to a hydraulic failure, as with one leg up and one down the order was given to point the aircraft to sea and abandon it, which Lt Cdr. John Beattie duly did; wreckage recovered and taken for investigation; presumed either scrapped (at Farnborough) or used as spares source for RNHF fleet.

○ **VR930**, construction number unknown; built as a FB Mk 11; first flight 23rd February 1948; delivered to the Royal Navy at RNAS Culham in March 1948 (brought on charge 8th March 1948); operated from May to December 1948 with No.802 NAS aboard HMS Vengeance and ashore at RNAS Eglinton; December 1948 to August 1953 held in reserve at various Aircraft Holding Units such as Anthorn, Abbotsinch, Sembawang and Fleetlands; undergoing a Category 4 repair at the Royal Naval Aircraft Yard Donibristle before returning to front-line service again with No.801 NAS; August 1953 to July 1954 flew a further 284 hours with the squadron before going to RNAY Fleetlands for reconditioning; airframe effectively returned to zero hours held in reserve at Anthorn and Lossiemouth; transferred to the Fleet Requirements Unit at Hurn (now Bournemouth Airport) in November 1959; flew a further 828 hours with this unit; put up for disposal in January 1961 with an absolute total of almost 1,280 flying hours; with Hawker-Siddeley Aircraft Ltd, Dunsfold from January 1963 until 15th January1965 (see engineless there in September 1964 – *See Aeroplane Monthly, March 1980*), when it moved to the regional collection at RAF Colerne; remained at Colerne until the unit closed on the 31st May 1976; passed to Royal Navy and stored at RNAS Yeovilton, RNAS Wroughton and Boscombe Down, being used as a spares source for the RNHF's original Sea Fury FB Mk 11 TF956; with the loss of TF956 in 1989 the decision was taken to rebuild VR930; moved to British Aerospace Brough for restoration to flying condition; moved by road to Brough 9th June 1994; rolled out marked as '110/O' at Brough in May 1997; sent by road from Brough to Yeovilton for completion on the 12th September 1997; first flight 1st March 2001; suffered engine failure at RNAS Yeovilton 21st August 2001; stored at RNAS Yeovilton 2002; returned to airworthy condition by 2006 – **AIRWORTHY**.

○ **VW589**, construction number unknown, built as an FB Mk 11, airframe salvaged from sea off Malta by Dave Pope, displayed for a while in Luqa; moved to and displayed at his home; sold to Peter Smith in UK (Hawkinge) at some stage before 2006 for use in his restoration project; remains stored there to this day.

○ **VX653**, built by Hawker Aircraft in 1949 as an FB Mk 11 to Contract No.2576/5/7/48; delivered to Royal Navy as VX653 and TOC at the Receipt and Despatch Unit, RNAS Anthorn 20th October 1949; allocated to No.736 Sqn, RNAS St. Merryn by January 1950; moved to Culdrose by 3rd February and combined with No.738 NAS to become No.1 Naval Air Fighting School/52nd Air Training Group; damaged during landing on 26th September 1951, repaired on site; to RNAY Donibristle (port mainplane was replaced) 20th August 1952; reconditioned and sent to RNAS Gosport, arriving 19th February 1953; transferred to RNAS Anthorn September 1953 to be prepared for allocation to No.811 NAS; transferred to No.811 NAS on HMS Warrior, 19th November 1953

For many years on display at Hendon, VX653 is slowly being restored to airworthiness by TFC at Duxford (©George Papadimitriou)

(code '112/J'); on board when carrier sailed to Malta 16th February 1954; broke tail oleo during landing 17th February 1954; taxied into WE722 at Hal Far, Malta GC 16th March 1954; SOC strength of No.811 NAS at Hal Far; remained with Aircraft Holding Unit, Hal Far; returned to RNAY Donibristle, probably abroad HMS Perseus, August 1954; in storage at RNAS Anthorn from 23rd November 1955 to 15th October 1957; transferred to Airwork Ltd at Bournemough 1957-1960 (coded '032'); transferred to RNAS Lossiemouth (HMS Fulmar) 31st March 1960; by May 1962 taken out of storage and used for static displays (e.g. seen outside on the 9th September 1967), eventually ended up on the main gates at Lossiemouth; SOC with the RN 6th August 1969 and earmarked for preservation; by mid-1970 moved to RNAY Fleetlands and then to RNAY Lee-on-Solent; to RNAS Yeovilton for display November 1970; when HAS decided to place its collection of historic aircraft with the RAF Museum it was mutually decided to pass their airworthy Sea Fury to Yeovilton in exchange for VX653; put on static display within the Sydney Camm Hall at the RAF Museum, Hendon from 23rd May 1972; swapped with The Fighter Collection, Duxford for restoration of the RAFM Tempest Mk II; arrived by road at TFC facility at Duxford, 24th November 1991; stored by TFC; registered with Patina Ltd/The Fighter Collection as G-BUCM 26th February 1992; displayed (complete) outside on the flightline at the Flying Legends airshow at Duxford, 15th July 1995; currently under restoration to airworthy condition by The Fighter Collection.

◯ **VX281**, construction number ES.3615 as a T Mk 20; to FAA as VX281 and served with Nos.736 and 738 NAS; to Hawker-Siddeley Aircraft at Langley from 1957 to 1963 as G-9-64; to Federal Republic of Germany as D-CACO, based at Bonn from 10th June 1963 to 1974; purchased by Doug Arnold/Warbirds of GB Ltd 11th October 1974 and registered as G-BCOW (in RN colours as '253'); ownership transferred to Spencer Flack from February 1977 to 1980; sold to

What was WE726 is now marked as WJ231 and displayed within the FAA Museum, Yeovilton (©George Papadimitriou)

Dale Clarke, Gardena, CA, July 1980 and registered as N8476W; flown at air races by Clarke as #40 'Nuthin Special" ownership transferred to Dale Clarke/Liberty Aero Corp., Gardena, CA June 1984 to 1988; transferred again to Liberty Aero Corp., Santa Monica, CA March 1988-1992 and registered as N281L, flown as 'Dragon of Mymru'; bought by Wally Fisk/Amjet Aircraft Corp., St. Paul, MN 16th September 1993 to 2000; registered to Zager Aircraft Corpo., Cupertino, CA from 2000 to 2002; in 2007 the civil registration N281L was cancelled; transported to the UK after purchase and registered as G-RNHF, based with the RN Historic Flight at RNAS Yeovilton; ownership changed on the 23rd February 2010 to Naval Aviation Ltd, still at RNAS Yeovilton; had to make an emergency (wheels up) landing at RNAS Culdrose on the 21st July 2014; repaired and returned to the air in September 2017 – **AIRWORTHY**.

The other member of the RNHF for many years was T Mk 20 WG655, which is again seen here at Yeovilton in the 1980s. This machine currently still flies with TFC at Duxford, although little of the original airframe remains in the rebuild after it hit two trees in a field near Castle Cary!

Sea Fury Survivors 5
UK

For a long time the Sea Fury displayed within the FAA Museum, Yeovilton carried the code WE726, as seen here during a rare trip outside
(©R.J. Caruana Archives)

● **VX309**, construction number ES.8501, built as a T Mk 20S; with Hawker-Siddeley Aircraft, Langley, 1957-58; to Federal Republic of Germany as D-FIBO, 29th August 1958; re-registered as D-CIBO in 1970; returned to UK (date unknown); used as spare parts source for RNHF at RNAS Yeovilton from 1976 to 1980; stored at both RNAS Wroughton and Yeovilton from 1980 to 1992; currently remains in storage.

● **VZ345**, construction number ES.8503, built as a T Mk 20; with Hawker-Siddeley, Langley 1957-58; to Deutsche Luftfahrt-Beratungsdienst based at Bonn from 16th September 1958 registered as D-FATA; re-registered as D-CATA in 1970; withdrawn from use and displayed ay Bonn-Kohn in 1974; presented to RAF as VZ345 in October 1974; flown by A&AEE Boscombe Down from 15th October 1974; operated marked as VZ345 'CH/22'; crashed at Boscombe Down 17th April 1985; wreckage stored at A&AEE 1985 to 1992; loaned to RNHF, Yeovilton 1992-2002; arrived dismantled at Yeovilton in November 1992; stored; sent by road to BAE Brough for use as spares source in rebuild of VR930, June 1994; returned to Yeovilton and stored from 1997 to 2002; currently stored by The Fighter Collection at Duxford for use in their restoration project (fuselage is twisted, so a complete rebuilt to airworthy seems unlikely).

● **WG655**, construction number 41H/636070 as a T Mk 20, to MoS Contract No: 6/Acft/5042/CB7(b) and built at Kingston with final assembly at Langley; first flight at Langley/ready for collection 28th September 1951; delivered to RNAS Anthorn 9th October 1951 and put in store; to No.781 Sqn, RNAS Lee-on Solent 7th December 1951; returned to RNAS Anthorn 13th February 1952; issued to RNAS Eglinton 8th March 1954, used by Station Maintenance Unit as '246/GN', then by Station Flight as '910/GN'; retired by RN in December 1955 and returned to Anthorn 17th December 1955; SOC 16th December 1956; bought by Hawker Aircraft 27th April 1957; by road from Chilbolton to Dunsfold 15th November 1960; converted to target-tug and flown as G-9-65 7th September 1962 (registration D-CACU reserved); sold to Federal West German Government; arrived at Bonn 7th August 1963; served with the Deutsche Luftfahrt-Beratungsdienst (DLB) of Wiesbaden and operated in Sigmaringen area based at München-Riem airport; registered as D-CACU/ES.3616 (E.S. stood for Ernst Seibert the DLB's main shareholder!); operator changed to Rhein Flugzeubau (RFB) from 1st January 1966 for operations in Todendorf-Putlos range and based at Lübeck; retired in 1975; undertook last flight of a German Sea Fury (Lübeck to Koln) 12th November 1975; registration cancelled 8th December 1975; noted at Koln 23rd June 1976; presented to RN by German government in 1976; left for UK

Another airworthy machine in the UK is G-CBEL, which is an ex-Iraqi machine (IAF315)

IAF 315, G-CBEL today flies marked as the Fury prototype SR661 and is seen here at Duxford (©Nigel Perry)

24th June 1976; initially seen at Colerne; to RNAS Yeovilton 29th June 1976; formally accepted by the RN Historic Flight on the 29th June 1976; operated for many years by RNHF although went to Fleetlands 15th May 1985 for refurbishment and was roaded to Boscombe Down for test flight(?) 14th May 1987; suffered engine failure during flight from Yeovilton to Silverstone on the 14th July 1980, crashed landed in field outside Bruton, Somerset and unfortunately struck two oak trees (the only objects in a 150 acre field!); wreckage stored at Yeovilton as deemed beyond repair; initially to Grant Beal in New Zealand, where parts were used in ZK-SFR; remains purchased by Chuck Greenhill, Kenosha, USA 17th August 1993; registered as N20MD (actually marked as 'NX20MD'); re-registered to Amphib Inc., Lake Zurich, Il 12th September 2002 (initial rebuild done here); final restoration by Sanders Aeronautics of aircraft that first flew on the 24th May 2005, albeit little of WG655 is present; appeared at Reno air races September 2007; sold via Provenance Fighter Sales to The Fighter Collection, Duxford in 2008; shipped in container to UK and arrived at Duxford 29th May 2009 marked as NX20MD; remained with TFC as N20MD; re-registered as G-CHFP 20th April 2014 – **AIRWORTHY**.

◉ **WJ231**, built as an FB Mk 11, with RNAS Anthorn in August 1965 displayed as 'WE726'; to FAA Museum, RNAS Yeovilton in 1972; initially displayed as WE726, later corrected to WJ231 marked as 115/O; currently on static display.

◉ **WJ244**, construction number 41H/642111, built as an FB Mk 11; at RNAS Lossiemouth, 19th May 1960 to 1963 in storage; to Hawker-Siddeley Aircraft Ltd, Dunsfold, 16th April 1963 (see engineless there in September 1964 – *See Aeroplane Monthly, March 1980*); sold to M.D.N. Fisher/Historic Aircraft Preservation Society, Biggin Hill, 1966; to Historic Aircraft Museum, Southend, 1971 in dismantled state; acquired by Spencer Flack, Elstree, 5th July 1978; restored to airworthy, first flight June 1980 and registered as G-FURY; crashed and destroyed, near Waddington, 2nd August 1981; wreckage acquired by Ted Sinclair, Milton Keynes in 1985; plans use in a composite restoration; current status unknown.

◉ **RNethN 6•18** construction number N/K, built as an FB Mk 50 by Fokker; delivered to Royal Netherlands Navy/Kon Marine; retired in mid-1950s and sold as scrap; forward fuselage and Centaurus engine recovered by the Fokker Heritage Trust in 2010; sent via road to Duxford 19th November 2010; presume remains in storage there (possible restoration or incorporation in the TFC's airworthy restoration project?).

◉ **IAF 315**, construction number 37539, built as an FB Mk 10; initially issued to RN but returned to Hawker-Siddeley for refurbishment prior to sale abroad; delivered to Iraqi A.F. as '315', delivered from Langley in 1953; recovered from Iraq by E. Jurist & D.C. Tallichet, Orlando, FL, 1979, stored in dismantled state; registered by Ed Jurist/Vintage Aircraft International/Nyack, NY, 27th August 1979 as N36SF; acquired by W.R. Laws/Coleman Warbird Museum, Coleman, TX, February 1988 and restored to airworthy at Coleman, TX with first flight, April 1991; shipped to UK in September. 1991 as acquired by John Bradshaw, Wroughton, UK, 2nd September 1991 (arriving at Wroughton 6th October 1991); marked as N36SF Dutch Navy/RCN/RAN 361 with John Bradshaw from 1991 to 2001; registered as G-CBEL(*), 6th August 2001 by John Bradshaw, Kemble; on loan to Bournemouth Aviation Museum, Hurn from 2004 to 2008; sold to Frederic Akary, Avignon, France October 2006 and registration F-AZXL reserved for it, but sale not completed and aircraft remained at Hurn during 2006 and 2007 in airworthy condition; Bournemouth Aviation Museum, Hurn closed 16th December 2007; aircraft flown from Hurn to Coventry 18th March 2008; registration D-FURI was reserved for sale to Germany, but not completed 5th February 2009; flown from Hurn to Bentwaters during September 2009 for crating and export; sold to new owner in Australia and struck off British Civil Register 7th October 2009; to Dave Warburton/Manekineko Pty Ltd. Moree, NSW and registered as VH-SFW 26th November 2009; stored whilst Centaurus engine was rebuilt, then test flown April 2016 and crated for export; returned to the UK and struck off Australian Civil Register 27th April 2016; registered to Graham Peacock/Anglia Aircraft Restorations Ltd. Sywell and re-registered again as G-CEBL 1st June 2016; refurbished and repainted by Air Leasing Ltd and painted as prototype SR661 (which was a modified Fury Mk II with a tail hook but no wing fold); currently based at North Weald Airfield – **AIRWORTHY**.
*Note – Some sources incorrectly list this as being previously registered as G-BCOW

◉ **IAF ???** construction number 623229, built as a Fury Mk 20; no other history known, found on concrete block as gate guardian at Shaibah AB, Iraq in 2003; seen on trailer at Shaibah in 2004 and reported shipped to UK as war prize; current location and condition unknown.

Sea Fury Survivors 5
Canada / USA

Canada

O TG119, construction number 41H/609977 as an FB Mk 11; delivered to Canada aboard HMCS Magnificent as TG119 and brought on RCN charge 24th May 1948; served with No.883 Squadron at HMCS Shearwater, Dartmouth, Nova Scotia; damaged in 1954 and repaired by Fairey Aviation Company (Canada Ltd); retired and struck off RCN charge 1956; purchased by Bancroft Industries, Montreal in 1956; stored by them at Fredericton, New Brunswick until 1963; donated by Bancroft Industries to the Canadian National Aeronautical Collection in 1963; restored by Fairey Aviation and a RCN unit at Eastern Passage, Nova Scotia between 1963 and 1964; moved to National Aviation Museum, Rockcliffe, Ontario in September 1982 (museum became the Canada Aviation & Space Museum in 2010); on display there ever since.

O WG565, construction number 41H/636292, built as an FB Mk 11; delivered to RCN as WG565 and brought on charge 28th August 1951; struck off RCN charge 18th April 1957; to Southern Alberta Institute of Technology, Calgary from April 1957 to 1966; with HMCS Tecumseh, Calgary from May 1966 to 1984, displayed as gate guardian (carried no markings, except roundels, or serial number); to Aero Space Museum of Calgary, Alberta, 1984-1988; to Naval Museum of Alberta/ HMCS Tecumseh, Canada, 1988-2003, displayed as WG565/AA•A; currently on display at the Calgary Military Museum.

USA

O TG114, construction number 41H/609972 as an FB Mk 10; delivered to RCN as TG114 24th May 1947; struck off RCN charge 2nd October 1956; registered as CY-OYF to Brian Baird November 1962 (ferry permit from Moncton to Ottawa 6th September 1962); registered as N4673T to Norman J. Magill, La Porte, IN 18th May 1964 (ferry permit from Pendleton ON to Le Porte, IN 8th May 1964); registered as N54M to J.W. Fornof, Houma, LA 11th July 1964; overturned on landing at Houma, LA 14th August 1964; passed to Brian Baird (now in USA) in 1969; wreckage stored at Mesa, AZ; restoration began using tail from VR918 and fuselage of VR919 in Phoenix, AZ; registered as N232J with Frank C. Sanders (1969-76); trucked to his home's garage at Tustin, CA in 1970; restoration completed, converted to two-seat configuration and first flew in 1971, in FAA markings as '232/O'; ownership passed to L.A. Hamilton, Santa Rosa, CA in 1980; sold to William E. Sims, Charleston, IL 1982-1987; sold to Ronald M. Runyan, Springdale, OH May 1988; leased to R.J. Lamplough 1988-1994, delivered by air to North Weald 24th April 1990; owned by Aces High Ltd, North Weald 13th June 1994 to 1995 (registered as G-BVOE); ownership transferred to Maruna Airplane Co., Akron, OH January 1995 (registered as N232J 25th January 1995); ownership transferred to Gallant Corp., Dover, DE 1st February 1995; owned by Michael Brown, Carson City 21st March 1996; registered to Michael Brown/ Sea Fury Ltd registered as N232MB from May 1997; restoration undertaken at Ione, CA 1996-1998; fitted with Wright R-3350 engine; first flight 1998; additional modifications done for racing, machine now called 'September Fury'; acquired by Rod Lewis/ Lewis Aeronautical LLC/Lewis Racing LLC/Lewis Air Legends, San Antonio, TX 2nd September 2017 (marked as FAEC 541, although their website states it is to be repainted shortly) – **AIRWORTHY**.
Note: during the restoration by Sander Aeronautics, parts were found on this airframe stencilled as 'WE723', 'TG114' and 'VR919'.

O VX300, construction number ES.8502, built as a T Mk 20; served with FAA as VX300, operated by Nos.736, 766 and 782 NAS; to Hawker-Siddeley Aircraft 1957-58 as G-9-24; moved to Federal Republic of Germany as D-FAMI, and based at Bonn from 29th August 1958; re-registered as D-CAMI in April 1959; purchased by D. Arnold/Warbirds of GB and registered as G-BCKH 9th August 1974 (arrived at Bitteswell that day); purchased by J.J. Stokes/ Warbirds of the World, San Marcos, TX September 1974; delivered by air via Prestwick to USA 20th October 1974 and registered as N62147L; purchased by Lloyd Hamilton and registered as N924G; contracted Frank Sanders/Sanders Aircraft to install F-102 wheels ands brakes; Frank Sanders/Sanders Aircraft purchased from Lloyd Hamilton in 1978; some sources state this aircraft was registered as N46690 by 1977; transferred ownership to Dennis and Brian Sanders/Sanders Aircraft, Chino, CA September 1989 to 1996; transferred to Dennis & Brian Sanders/Sanders Aircraft Technologies, Ione, CA from 1996 to 2002; aircraft underwent a complete rebuilt from 2002 and on the 27th June 2012 the Centaurus 18 engine was ground run for the first time in 15 years; aircraft entered in the National Championship Air Races in 2012; repainted by Arizona Aeropainting, Eloy, AZ in August 2013 in RN colours marked as '924' and carrying the serial number 'ES8502' – **AIRWORTHY**.

O VX715, built as an FB Mk 11; delivered to the Kon Marine and coded 6•14; used as instruction airframe at Gilze-Riijen AB by 1974; stored; purchased by L.A. Hamilton, Santa Rosa, CA in April 1974; rebuilt with parts from WH589 and repainted as that machine; currently on static display in the Pacific Coast Air Museum, Santa Rosa.

O VZ350, construction number ES.9505, built as a T Mk 20; with Hawker-Siddeley, Langley in 1957 (G-9-54); to Deutsche Luftfahrt-Beratungsdienst based at Bonn from 11th August 1959 registered as D-COCO; sold to J.J. Stokes, San Marcos, TX in 1978; ownership passed to Dr. William Harrison, Tulsa, Ok in 1978; registered as N20SF (this registration was later transferred to VZ368 – see elsewhere) and flown in FAA markings as '52'; owned by R.Z. Friedman/Everco Industries Inc., IL; crashed on take-off from Waukegan 16th December 1978 (killing Friedman); wreckage acquired by Sanders Aircraft, Chino, CA in 1979; parts used in rebuild of VZ368 (see elsewhere).

O VZ351, construction number 41H/63051, built as an FB Mk 11; with Hawker-Siddeley, Langley in 1957-58 (G-9-58); to Federal Republic of Germany on 11st August 1959, registered as D-CEDO; operated until 1972 then put in storage pending disposal; purchased by Eric Vormezeele, Antwerp, Belgium in 1975; reserved the registration OO-SFY, but never taken up; stored at Braaschaat from 1975 to 1985; owned by J. Hunt, Memphis, TX 1985 to 1987; owned by G.H. Baker/American Aero Services, New Smyrna beach, FL 1987-1990; owned by M. Brown/Fury Limited, Carson City, NV, 1997 to 2004, registered as NX233MB; restored at Ione, CA and fitted with Wright R-3350; first flight in 1997; raced as #911and named 'September Pops'; purchased by Rod Lewis 07/2012 and restored by Ezell Aviation, Breckenridge, TX in Cuban markings as 'FAEC 54' – **AIRWORTHY**.

O VZ365, construction number ES.3612, built as a T Mk 20; with Hawker-Siddeley, Langley in 1957 (G-9-61); to *Deutsche Luftfahrt-Beratungsdienst* at Bonn on 28th March 1963, registered as D-CACA; reported derelict at Cologne by April 1974; purchased by E. Vormeseele, Antwerp, Belgium in 1975; owned by J. Hunt, Memphis, TX from October 1985; owned by George H. Baker/ American Aero Service, FL from 1987 and used as a parts airframe in the restoration of IAF 325 (N30SF); with Utilco, Tifton, GA in 1990s (dates unconfirmed); owned by T-G Air Power Inc., Buffalo, NY from September 2000, registered as N1324 (*other sources list this as Iss11 an FB.10 also being restored by T-G Air Power but registered as N1324 and IAF 324 C/No.41H 623271 – see elsewhere*), undergoing restoration to fly at New Symrna Beach, Florida.

O VZ368, built as a T Mk 20, with Hawker-Siddeley, Langley in 1957; delivered to Burmese AF as UB-451; purchased by Frank. C. Sanders, Chino, CA in 1979 and stored dismantled; ownership transferred to Frank Sanders/Sanders Aircraft, Chino, CA from July 1983 to 1990; registered as N20SF and rebuilt as a SkyFury with P&W R-3460 engine using parts from VZ350; first flight 6th August 1983; adopted the identification of C/No.ES9505/VZ350; flown as race #8 and named 'Dreadnaught'; ownership transferred to Dennis & Brian Sanders/Sanders Aircraft, Chino, CA 13th August 1990; ownership transferred to Dennis & Brian Sanders/Sanders Aircraft Technologies, Ione, CA January 1996 – **AIRWORTHY**.

O WE820, construction number ES.8504, built as a T Mk 20; with Hawker-Siddeley, Langley 1957-58 (G-9-49); remanufactured as a target tug (T Mk 20S) in May 1958; to Federal Republic of Germany as D-FOTE at Bonn in September 1958; transferred to Deutsche Luftfahrt-Beratungsdienst at Bonn, registered as D-COTE from 1963 to 1972; owned by J.J. Stokes/Warbirds Of The World, San Marcos, TX, 1980, registered as N85SF; owned by E. Lorentzen, Caldwell, NJ, 1984-1987 and rebuilt as a modified racer with Wright R-3350 engine (other modifications included a square tailplane, clipped wings & low canopy); Race #88 'Blind Man's Bluff'; transferred ownership to E. Lorentzen/Window Majic Of Arizona Inc., Scottsdale, AZ in August 1987; owned by S.A. Bolan, Scottsdale, AZ from January 1988; owned by Bill Woods/Western Wings Aircraft Sales Co., Oakland, OR form October 1989, flew as race #90; damaged during wheels-up landing at Reno, NV in September 1990; owned by Thomas A. Dwelle, Auburn, CA, 1991; rebuilt to airworthy and first flown 4th September 1993; raced as #10 'Critical Mass'; damaged when high pressure bottle exploded in 1995 (Dwelle injured); repaired; raced for the last time during the 2003 National Championship Air Races at Reno, Nevada with Thomas Dwelle finishing third with a speed of 446.965mph, aircraft retired after the race; restoration and return to Sea Fury T.20 status by Sanders Aeronautics at Eagles Nest, California by 2011 (restored/returned fuselage to T.20 configuration, plus centre-section and outer wing panels, all rest will be done by owner's firm of Nella Oil, Auburn, CA); ownership transferred to Kenneth H. Dwelle of Auburn, CA 18th June 2014; 7th May 2016 first engine run in 13 years undertaken.

○ **WG567**, construction number 41H/636294, built as an FB Mk 11; delivered to RCN as WG567 and brought on charge 28th August 1951; struck off RCN charge on the 8th February 1957; purchased by R.P. Vanderveken, Pierrefords, Quebec 9th September 1961, registered as CF-VAN; owned by M. D. Carroll, Long Beach, CA, 1965-1969 registered as N878M; modified as a racer, military equipment removed, airframe lightened, outer wing panels clipped (removing 6.5ft in total), small bubble canopy installed; First race appearance at Reno in 1966, flown as race #87 'Signal Sea Fury' by Lyle Shelton; owned by Sherman Cooper, Merced, CA, 1969-1972, flew as #87 'Miss Merced'; nosed over during a forced landing after engine failure near Mojave, CA, 13th November 1971; wreck acquired by Frank C. Sanders, Chino, CA, 1980-1981; wreck sold to J.A. Mott, South Gate, CA, 1984-1999; rebuilt at Chino form 1984 to 1988; flew as #42 'Super Chief'; ownership and usage in the 1992 to 1999 period is unconfirmed; owned by St. Bolander and J. Michaels/J&S Aviation, Oconomowoc, WI from 24th March 1999 to 2002; airframe sent by road from Chino to Ione, CA for restoration, fitted with Wright R-3350 engine and additional racing modifications; First flight at Ione in March 2000 as #87 'Miss Merced'; owned by E. Woelbing, Franksville, WI from 21st July 2003, flown as #87/'Miss Merced' and based at Kenosha Airport, WI – **AIRWORTHY**.

○ **WH587**, construction number 41H/636334, built as an FB Mk 11; delivered to RAN and brought on charge 7th March 1952; struck off RAN charge (sold as scrap) 23rd September 1963; returned to Australia as deck cargo on HMAS Vengeance, March 1952; owned by G. Grieg, Sydney, 1963-1964; owned by Lord Tefgarne, Sydney, NSW, 1964 and delivered to Bankstown, NSW in November 1963 then shipped to USA in early 1964; owned by Grant Weaver, Pacific Air Academy, San Jose, CA, May 1965-1967 and registered as N260X, race #33; owned by Stan Booker, Fresno, CA, 1967; owned by J.R. Fugate, Aurora, OR, 1969; owned by S. Cooper, Merced, CA, 1971-1972; owned by Westernair of Albuquerque, Albuquerque, NM, 1972; owned by E. Getchell/Gretchell Aircraft Inc., San Jose, CA, 7th July 1975, flown as WH587 '105' in RAN colours; damaged during landing, at Midland, TX, 4th October 1997, repaired – **AIRWORTHY**.

○ **WH589***, construction number 41H/636336, built as an FB Mk 11; delivered to RAN and brought on charge 7th March 1952; collected from RNAS Sembawang, Singapore; arrived in Australia as deck cargo on carrier HMAS Sydney, March 1952; TOC by RAN 7th March 1952; transferred to Nowra NAS, withdrawn from use and delivered from Nowra NAS to Sydney-Bankstown for storage, 30th October 1961 (marked as '115/NW'); struck off RAN charge 23rd September 1963; to Fawcett Aviation, Sydney-Bankstown, NSW, 23rd September 1963; in open storage with Fawcett 1963-1969; Sold to Lord Trefgarne, London, UK, but not collected until November 1969; owned by Ormond Haydon-Baillie, Vancouver, BC, January 1969; shipped from Sydney to USA on USS Coral Sea, June 1970 and registered as CF-CHB; undercarriage collapsed on landing, Reading, PA, 14th June 1971 (flew marked as RAF WH589/O•HB); repaired as photographed as a complete aircraft at Abbottsford, BC by Bob McLeod in 1972; shipped from Vancouver to Southend, UK, 23rd November 1973; registered to Ormond Haydon-Baillie, Southend, 9th May 1974 and registered as G-AGHB; sold to Spencer R. Flack, Elstree, 1979; crashed during air test at Osnabruck, West Germany, 24th June 1979; Angus McVitie, Cranfield, UK, acquired wreckage 1979; moved by road to Cranfield for potential restoration, never undertaken; Craig Charleston, Colchester, UK, acquired wreckage in 1990; sold to L.A. Hamilton, Santa Rosa, CA, October 1983 and registered as N4434P; rebuilt as a modified racer, fitted with P&W R-4360 engine (this is a composite rebuild using parts from VX715, WJ290 & WH589*); after rebuild assumed identity of WH589 and flown as #15, 'Furias' (photographed at Reno in 1985 marked as such); sold to Joe Clancy Aviation, Camarillo, CA, 24th April 1997 and registered as N895HW; sold to B. Rodgers & D.V. Stolzer/R&S Aero Displays, Everett-Paine Field, WA, 19th July 2000 – **AIRWORTHY**.
Note – It is believed that only the rear fuselage of WH589 was used in the restoration project of what was mainly VX715 and as such other parts from WH589 have wound up in other restorations since. WH589 effectively ceased to exist in its original form circa.1983, but the adoption of this serial number by L.A. Hamilton means that it remains on the preserved listing even though VX715 is probably a better serial for this composite machine?

○ **WJ288**, construction number 41H/696792, built as an FB Mk 11; placed in storage at RNAS Lossiemouth, 9th May 1961; acquired by Hawker-Siddeley Aircraft Ltd, Dunsfold, 12th March 1963 and put in open storage (photographed there in September 1964 – *See Aeroplane Monthly, March 1980*); acquired by A.J. Osborne/Historic Aircraft Museum, Southend, September 1966, stored during 1966 and put on display in 1967 to 1983; acquired at auction for £34,000 by P. Luscombe, 10th May 1983; registered to P. Luscombe/British Air Reserve, Lympne/Duxford, 12th July 1983 and registered as G-SALY; restored to airworthiness; purchased by Doug Arnold/Warbirds of GB Ltd, Biggin Hill, 1988; sold to E. Stanley, Portland, OR, 1990 and shipped to Chino, CA, where it was registered as N15S in June 1991; acquired by D. W. Peeler, Memphis, TN, 28th December 1993; Restored to airworthy at Chino, CA, 1993-1994 & Wahpeton, ND, 1997; flown in RN markings as WJ288, '153/P'; owned by American Airpower Heritage Flying Museum, Midland, TX, 8th February 2006 (fitted with Wright Cyclone engine instead of original Bristol Centaurus); as of 2012 this machine was based at Richard Lloyd Jones Airport, Tulsa – **AIRWORTHY**.

○ **WJ290**, built as an FB Mk 11; with Hawker-Siddeley Aircraft Ltd, Dunsfold, 1957; in open storage there from 1960 marked as '38' and fitted with wings from WE717; delivered to Royal Netherlands Air Force in June 1964 and used as ground instruction airframe; at Delft Technical School, Holland by 1970s; acquired by L.A. Hamilton, Santa Rosa, CA, 1980 and used in the composite rebuild of WH539 (*see elsewhere*) using parts from this airframe and VX715.

○ **WJ293**, built as an FB Mk 11; delivered to Iraqi A.F. as '302'; recovered from Iraq by E. Jurist & D.C. Tallichet, Orlando, FL, 1979. Stored dismantled in Orlando, FL; registered to E. Jurist/Vintage Aircraft International, Nyack, NY, August 1979 as N39SF; acquired by H. Haigh/Haigh Industries, Howell, MI, December 1981; rebuilt at Breckenridge, TX and fitted with Wright R-3350 engine; first flight, 1990; owned by H-Trif Holdings Inc, Wilmington, DE, 30th April 1996; owned by J. Shackelford, Roanoke, TX, 18th April 2000 and based at Denton, TX – **AIRWORTHY**.

○ **WJ298**, construction number 37522, built as an FB Mk 11; delivered to Fleet Air Arm as WJ298; refurbished and delivered to Iraqi A.F. as '303' and brought on charge 9th July 1952; recovered from Iraq by E. Jurist & D.C. Tallichet, Orlando, FL, 1979; stored in

The true identity of the machine currently marked as VX730 in the Aircraft Hall of the Australian War Memorial in Canberra is open to speculation, but it is probable that the fuselage at least is from VX730!
(©P. Skulski)

a dismantled state in Orlando, FL; registered by Ed Jurist/Vintage Aircraft International, Nyack, NY, August 1979 as N26SF; owned by J.J. Dowd, Syracuse, KS, 28th Jan. 28 1988 and under restoration, at Breckenridge, TX; as of 2014 this machine was at Sonoma valley Airport, Schelleville, CA (presume still under restoration as current airworthiness class is 'unknown').
Note that the American civil registration N26SF is linked to at least two airframes, this being one, the other is C/No.37729 that was last seen at Breckenridge in 1993. Matters are confused further by this C/No. also being linked to VH-HFG/N97F (See C/No.37752 41H/65802).

● **WM483**, construction number 37721, built as an FB Mk 11; delivered to Iraqi A.F. as '304' in October 1952; recovered from Iraq by E. Jurist & D. C. Tallichet, Orlando, FL, 1979; stored in dismantled state in Orlando, FL; registered by Ed Jurist/Vintage Aircraft International, Nyack, NY, August 1979 as N42SF; owned by Richard Bertea, Irvine, CA, November 1990-; restored to airworthy at Chino, CA, 1992-1993, fitted with Wright R-3350 engine and four-blade propeller; first flight, December 1993 marked in RCN markings '14/B'; owned by B. Rheinschild/Unlimited Air LLC, Van Nuys, CA, 23rd September 1998, initially flown as #74, RCN '14/B', 'Bad Attitude' but later changed to #117, RCN '117/B' 'Bad Attitude' – AIRWORTHY.

● **WM484**, construction number 37755, built as an FB Mk 11; delivered to Iraqi A.F. as '305'; recovered from Iraq by E. Jurist & D.C. Tallichet, Orlando, FL, 1979, stored dismantled in Orlando. FL and registered as N59SF; owned by Ed Jurist/Vintage Aircraft International, Nyack, NY, August 1979; owned by Tom Reilly, Kissimmee, FL, February 1988; reported sold by Reilly as a restoration project in the early 1990s; as of April 2012 owned by DB Aero Inc., Wilmington, DE (airworthiness class = 'unknown')

● **WN480**, construction number 41H/656816, built as an FB Mk 11; delivered to Iraqi A.F.; recovered from Iraq by E. Jurist & D.C. Tallichet, Orlando, FL, 1979, stored in dismantled state in Orlando, FL; registered by E. Jurist/Vintage Aircraft International, Nyack, NY, August 1979 as N60SF; owned by J.D. Rodgers, St. Charles, IL, 1981 and restored in FAA markings as '757/JR'; acquired by D. Crowe/Crew Concepts Inc., Boise, ID, 13th February 1991; forced landing at Reno, NV, September 1993; by road to Victoria, BC where the Centaurus was replaced; acquired by D. Cowe/Lightfoot Aviation, Point Roberts, WA, 7th March 2000 flew in RCN markings as '181' 'Simply Magnificent'; sold to Gerald W. Yagen/Training Services Inc./Fighter Factory, Virginia Beach, VA 26th July 2005; initially stored at Suffolk Executive Airport, VA – AIRWORTHY.

● **WN482**, construction number 37528, built as an FB Mk 11; delivered to Iraqi A.F. in 1952 as '310'; recovered from Iraq by E. Jurist & D. C. Tallichet, Orlando, FL, 1979, stored in dismantled state in Orlando, FL; owned by John Williams, Tampa, FL; restored to airworthiness at Live Oak, FL registered as N19SF*, first flying 13th July 1979 masked as 'RCN 121'; crashed in the desert, Herlingen, TX 9th October 1981 (Williams killed).
This is the first use of N19SF, it was later used for the restoration of the composite aircraft that became 'Argonaut' and carried the serial TG114 (which already exists elsewhere to confuse matters further).

● **WN???**, construction number 41H/656803, built as an FB Mk 11; the history of this aircraft is unknown, but it is though to be an ex-RCN example; with Frank C. Sanders, China, CA from 1970 through to 1990 in store; registered to Brian Sanders/Sanders Aircraft Inc., China, CA and hulk used in composite airframe fitted with R-3350 engine, first flew 30th July 1994 marked as #19 'Argonaut'; registered as N19SF (previously used with WN482 lost in October 1981) to Denis and Brian Sanders/Sanders Aircraft Inc., Chino, CA; registered to Sanders Aeronautics, Ione, CA 20th July 1994 marked as #114, RCN TG 114/BC-L 'Argonaut'; fitted with P&W R-2800 instead of R-3350 at Ione, CA during 2010 – AIRWORTHY.

● **IAF 252** construction number 37727 (ISS22), built as an FB Mk 11; delivered to Iraqi A.F. as '252', 17th June 1948; recovered from Iraq by Ed Jurist & D.C. Tallichet, Orlando, FL, 1979, stored in dismantled state; registered by Ed Jurist/Vintage Aircraft International, Nyack, NY as N48SF 27th August 1979; this aircraft was struck off the American Civil Register on the 20th August 1985 as being sold to Australia, but this is due to the confusion with the true identity of VH-HFG; current status and location is therefore unknown.

● **IAF 254** construction number 37537 (ISS24), built as an FB Mk 10, first flown 16th September 1948; delivered to Iraqi A.F. as '254', November 1949; recovered from Iraq by E. Jurist & D.C. Tallichet, Orlando, FL, 1979, stored in dismantled state; registered to Ed Jurist/Vintage Aircraft International, Nyack, NY, 27th August 1979 as N35SF; acquired by Carl Scholl/Aero Trader, Chino, CA and stored in dismantled state in 1994; sold to Vernon C. McCallister, Del Norte, CO in 1994; being restored to fly at Chino, CA, later moved to Centennial, CO and fitted with Wright R-3350-26WD engine and F-102 wheels and brakes; registered to Heritage Hangar, South Fork, CO from 2007 to 2012; struck off the American Civil Register 20th June 2012; re-registered as N35SF by Heritage Hanger 11th March 2015; acquired by KKFG Aviation LLC, Huntersville, NC in 2017 – AIRWORTHY.

◉ **IAF 255** construction number 37536 (ISS25), built as an FB Mk 11; delivered to Iraqi A.F. as '255', in December 1949; recovered from Iraq by E. Jurist & D.C. Tallichet, Orlando, FL, 1979, stored in dismantled state; registered by Ed Jurist/Vintage Aircraft International, Nyack, NY, August 1979 as N34SF; acquired by H. Pardue/Breckenridge Aviation Museum, Breckenridge, TX, 1st Aprril 1986; owned by Breckenridge Aviation Museum, Breckenridge, TX, February 1988 and registered as N666HP; rebuilt with Wright R-3350 engine and flown as #66 'Fury'; struck Yak during air race at Reno, NV, 9th September 1997, but not damaged; re-registered as N13HP, April 2001 – AIRWORTHY.

◉ **IAF 253**, construction number 37703 (ISS23), built as an FB Mk 11; delivered to Iraqi A.F. via Blackbushe July 1953 (some sources state 21st November 1949); recovered from Iraq by Ed Jurist & D.C. Tallichet, Orlando, FL, 1979, stored in dismantled state; registered by Ed Jurist/Vintage Aircraft International, Nyack, NY as N40SF, 27th August 1979; acquired by Guido Zuccoli/Steelson Construction Pty Ltd, Darwin, NT in 1981; shipped to Australia, arrived by sea at Perth, WA 26th January 1982, then trucked to Darwin for restoration to fly; registered as VH-HFA to Steelcon Constructions Pty Ltd, Darwin, NT 25th January 1984; acquired by Ted Allen, Proserpine, QLD, 18th July 1984; initially incorrectly identified as WJ231; in RAN markings as '253/K', 'Magnificent Obsession'; acquired by John MacGuire, Abilene, TX, November 1988 and shipped to USA; shipped to Long Beach, CA and assembled at Chino, CA with first flight 19th May 1989; registered to John MacGuire/War Eagles Air Museum, Santa Teresa, NM, 13th February 1989, registered as N57JB; airframe displayed in museum as '253/K', 'Magnificent Obsession' and maintained in airworthy condition but not flown since 1989 – AIRWORTHY.

◉ **IAF 259** construction number ISS29, built as a Fury FB Mk 10; delivered to Iraqi A.F. as '259' in 1950s; delivered to Royal Moroccan A.F. 4th February 1960; in storage at Rabat, Morocco by 1978; with Amicale Jean Salis, La Ferte Alais, France; reported sold via a French broker to a customer in the USA; current status, location and full identity unknown.

◉ **IAF 308**, construction number 37522; delivered to Iraqi A.F. in 1952; recovered from Iraq by E. Jurist & D.C. Tallichet, Orlando, FL, 1979, stored in dismantled state; registered by Ed Jurist/Vintage Aircraft International/Nyack, NY, as N26SF* on the 27th August 1979; acquired by Guido Zuccoli/Steelson Constructions Pty Ltd, Darwin, NT, January 1982; shipped to Australia; registered as VH-HFG, 9th November 1983; restored to airworthiness in Darwin; first flight 14th November 1983, marked in RAN colours as '308/K'; damaged in forced landing at Leyburn, QLD 24th March 1984* (repaired and fitted with 'jump seat' behind pilot – *some state 1983?); registered to Lynette Zuccoli/Zuccoli Classic Aircraft Collection, Toowoomba, Queensland, Australia, June 1997; withdrawn from use in 1999; displayed at Toowoomba, 1999-2006 and maintained in airworthy condition; acquired by Dick Janitell/Pike Peak Aviation, CO, USA August 2006; departed Toowoomba in a shipping crate to USA via Brisbane, QLB 27th November 2006; struck off the Australian civil register 30th November 2006; arrived Sanders Aeronautics, Ione, CA 16th January 2007 for reassembly and flight-testing; registered by Pikes Peak Flyers, Colorado Springs, CO as N97SF 26th January 2007; purchased by Walter C. Bowe, Sonoma, CA 12th May 2014 – AIRWORTHY.
Note: This machine is often listed as C/No.37729, which actually applied to WJ298, however that machine never went to Iraq and was still in the UK with No.776 FRU at Hurn in September 1958. Only the rear fuselage of this machine is from WJ298. Other registration documents list this as C/No.37752 (41H/65802) or 37727, however here we have stayed with the original Hawker C/No. for the machine that became '308' with the Iraqi Air Force.

◉ **IAF 312**, construction number 37724, built as an FB Mk 10; initially issued to RN but returned to Hawker-Siddeley for refurbishment prior to sale abroad; delivered to Iraqi A.F. as '312' 23rd June 1953; recovered from Iraq by E. Jurist & D.C. Tallichet, Orlando, FL, 1979, stored in dismantled state; registered to Ed Jurist/Vintage Aircraft International/Nyack, NY as N45SF 27th August 1979; acquired by G. Perez/Sonoma Valley Aircraft Inc, Glen Ellen, CA, 10th June 1983; currently under restoration to airworthiness at Petaluma, CA.

◉ **IAF 313**, construction number 37517, built as an FB Mk 10; delivered to Iraqi A.F. as '313 in July 1953; recovered from Iraq by E. Jurist & D.C. Tallichet, Orlando, FL, 1979, stored in dismantled state; registered by E. Jurist/Vintage Aircraft International, Nyack, NY, August 1979 as N24SF; acquired by Sonoma Valley Aircraft Inc, Vineburg, CA, July 1988; owned by M.C. Leshe, Chandler, AZ, July 1989; restored to airworthiness at Breckenridge, TX, 1990-1992 and fitted with R-3350 engine as modified racer #8/CL-103; acquired by J.S. Dawson, McKinney, TX, 25th June 1996, registered as NX242SF and marked as #105, RAN 'SD/105/', 'Spirit Of Texas' – AIRWORTHY.

◉ **IAF 314**, construction number 37541, built as an FB Mk 10; initially issued to RN but returned to Hawker-Siddeley for refurbishment prior to sale abroad; delivered to Iraqi A.F. as '314' in 1953 (test flown Langley 3rd July 1953); recovered from Iraq by Ed Jurist & D.C. Tallichet, Orlando, FL, 1979, stored in dismantled state; registered by Ed Jurist/Vintage Aircraft International/Nyack, NY as N35SF, 27th August 1979; reported sold by Jurist as a restoration project in the 2002; to DB Aero Inc., Wilmington, DE 12th April 2011 and currently remains with them (status unknown).

◉ **IAF 318**, construction number 37726, built as an FB Mk 10; initially issued to RN but returned to Hawker-Siddeley for refurbishment prior to sale abroad; delivered to Iraqi A.F. as '318' 14th August 1953; recovered from Iraq by E. Jurist & D.C. Tallichet, Orlando, FL, 1979, stored in dismantled state; registered by Ed Jurist/Vintage Aircraft International, Nyack, NY as N46SF 27th August 1979; ownership between 2007 and 2011 is unknown; DB Aero Inc., Wilmington, DE 15th February 2011 to present.

◉ **IAF 325**, construction numbers 37525 and 41H/656823, built as an FB Mk 11; delivered to Iraqi A.F. in November 1953, recovered from Iraq by E. Jurist & D. C. Tallichet, Orlando, FL, 1979, stored in dismantled state and registered as N30SF; owned by Ed Jurist/Vintage Aircraft International, Nyack, NY, 1979; owned by G.H. Baker/American Aero Services, New Smyrna Beach, FL, November 1986; -1989; rebuilt as 'Sky Fury' fitted with P&W R-3350 engine and using parts from VZ365/D-CACA (see elsewhere); first flight 1990 as #71; owned by G.H. Baker, New Smyrna Beach, FL, September 1989 and registered as N71GB; damaged at Oshkosh, WI, August 1991 – repaired and flew as #76, RAN colours 'Southern Cross'; owned by J. K. Bagley, Rexburg, ID, 1998; owned by S. Patterson, Kansas City, MO, 2003, renamed 'Sawbones' in 2011 and 'Key Air' titles added either side of vertical fin; put up for sale and acquired by Dr Robin Crandall and kept at Anoka-Blaine airport (when raced it is flown by USAF Col. (ret) Curtiss L. Brown), 'Thomson Reuters' name and logo are applied across the vertical fin/rudder and plane marked as RCN '71' – AIRWORTHY.

◉ **IAF ???**, construction number 87954 (probably should be 37954?); initially issued to RN but returned to Hawker-Siddeley for refurbishment prior to sale abroad; delivered to Iraqi A.F. in late 1940s/early 1950s as spare airframe (hence, it may never have had an IAF serial number – used for spares?); recovered from Iraq by E. Jurist & D.C. Tallichet, Orlando, FL, 1979, stored in dismantled state; registered by Ed Jurist/Vintage Aircraft International/Nyack, NY as N63SF 27th August 1979; stored from 1979 to 2012; sold to Amphib Inc., Lake Zurich, IL 24th May 2012; presume currently stored by new owner.

◉ **IAF ???**, construction number 87953 (probably should be 37953?); initially issued to RN but returned to Hawker-Siddeley for refurbishment prior to sale abroad; delivered to Iraqi A.F. in late 1940s/early 1950s; recovered from Iraq by E. Jurist & D.C. Tallichet,

Sea Fury Survivors 5
USA / Australia

Orlando, FL, 1979, stored in dismantled state and registered as N62SF; owned by Ed Jurist/Vintage Aircraft International/Nyack, NY, August 1979; currently stored.

● **IAF ???**, construction number 41H/656822*, built as an FB Mk 10; delivered to Iraqi A.F. in 1950s; recovered from Iraq by E. Jurist & D. C. Tallichet, Orlando, FL, 1979, stored in dismantled state in Orlando, FL; owned by Ed Jurist/Vintage Aircraft International, Nyack, NY, August 1979; to Courtesy Aircraft, Rockford, IL, 1994; owned by Amjet Aircraft Corp, Anoka County, MN, 1994; remained stored there (unrestored) still wearing original Iraqi A.F. camouflage 1994-2002; purchased by Darryl Bond/Aero Classics, Chino, CA 2002; under restoration to airworthiness at Chino since 2006.
Some sources listed this as 41H/656803, but that is incorrect according to Amjet.

● **IAF ???** construction number N/K*, the early history of this machine is unknown (or at least is as yet unidentified positively); recovered from Iraq by E. Jurist & D.C. Tallichet, Orlando, FL, 1979, stored in dismantled state; with Ed Jurist/Vintage Aircraft International Inc., Nyack, NY August 1979 to 1987 (stored unrestored and for sale); to Charles D. Hillard, Fort Worth, TX, 1994; by road to Breckenridge, TX for restoration; fitted with Wright R-3350 engine and four-blade propeller; first flight at Breckenridge, TX as 'Lone Star Fury'; registered as N222CH (23rd February 1995); overturned during landing at Lakeland, FL, 16th April 1996 (Hillard killed); rebuilt, at New Smyrna Beach, FL during 1999; acquired by Joe Thibodeau, Denver, CO, August 2000, registered as N254SF and flown as #21 in an RCN scheme as 'Sea Fury'; damaged after ran off the runway on landing at Centennial, CO 25th May 2015 – **AIRWORTHY**.
US Civil Register lists as #37514, but it also has this number as relating to N21SF, also lists above machines type as "Charlie Hillard Hawker FB60"!

● **IAF ???**, construction number 41H 611317, built as an FB Mk 10; delivered to Iraqi A.F. in late 40s/early 50s; recovered from Iraq by E. Jurist & D. C. Tallichet, Orlando, FL, 1979, stored in dismantled state by Ed Jurist/Vintage Aircraft International, Nyack, NY from 1979 to 1992; with the MAPS (Military Aircraft Preservation Society) Air Museum, Canton-Akron, OH on loan, stored in dismantled state from 1992 to 2000 (fuselage arrived 12th April, wings on the 20th); current location/status/owner unknown, some sources state this is the aircraft being restored at Ione, CA in 2006 (which is where the C/No. quoted comes from, so this may turn out to be two separate airframes?).

● **ISS4** built as a Fury FB Mk 10; delivered to Iraqi A.F. as '234' in 1950s; delivered to Royal Moroccan A.F. 4th February 1960; in storage at Rabat, Morocco by 1978; reported sold via a French broker to a customer in the USA; current status, location and full identity unknown.

● **ISS11**, construction number ISS11, built as an FB Mk 10; delivered to Iraqi A.F. as '241' in 1950s; recovered from Iraq by Ed Jurist & D.C. Tallichet, Orlando, FL, 1979, stored in dismantled state; registered by Ed Jurist/Vintage Aircraft International, Nyack, NY as N64SF 27th August 1979; stored until 1987; current location/status/owner unknown.
Note: Some list this as N1324, but that is 36634/41H 623271 (IAF 324).

Australia

● **VW232** – See VX730.

● **VW623**, construction number 41H/61393, built as an FB Mk 11; delivered to RAN and brought on charge March 1949; returned to Australia as deck cargo on HMAS Sydney, 25th May 1949; used as a gate guardian at Nowra, NSW from 1965 to 1972 marked as '102/K'; moved to the Naval Aviation Museum at Nowra, NSW December 1974 and remained there until 1995 marked as '102/K'; moved to the RAN Historic Flight, Nowra, NSW in 1996 for restoration to airworthiness 1996-2001; registered as VH-NVS; not returned to the air, currently at the Australian Museum of Flight, Nowra although some state it is still being restored to airworthy condition?

● **VW647**, built as an FB Mk 11; delivered to RAN and brought on charge in March 1949; struck off RAN charge 15th November 1949; returned to Australia as deck cargo on HMAS Sydney, arriving 25th May 1949; to National Building Technology Centre, Sydney 15th January 1959 and remained there until 1969 (*used as a wind generator to test building strength!*); to Skyservice Aviation, Camden June 1969; to Camden Museum of Aviation first at Camden and later at Narellan, NSW from October 1969 to 2002; during time with CMA the airframe was restored as VW647 marked as '127/K' and the engine was run in October 1976; currently remains on static display at the Camden Museum of Aviation, NSW.

● **VX730**, *Note: there is much confusion as to the true identity of the aircraft now painted as 'VX730' at the AWM, as it is believed to be the fuselage of VX730 with the centre wing section of VW232 and outer wings and tail/stern post of TF925, so what follows is details of VX730's history with additional info on VW232 and TF925 in italics at the end:* built as an FB Mk 11, operated by RN then purchased by RAN and shipped to Australia; first official records show aircraft with the 21st Carrier Air Group on HMAS Sydney in 1950; served with RAN during Korean War, suffered damage on landing, HMAS Sydney 10th Sept 1951, repaired; received at least three bullet strikes during operations over Korea in November-December 1951; repaired at Iwakuni after third strike on 17th December 1951; returned to Australia; rejoined No.805 Sqn on HMAS Sydney; later operated by No.808 Sqn on HMAS Vengeance; damaged in landing accident, to Bankstown for repair, then to NSW Nowra; rejoined No.805 Sqn 25th November 1955; suffered a forced landing due to engine failure 18th June 1957; sold to NSW Department of Technical Education as a training airframe 9th March 1959; anecdotal evidence seems to indicate this airframe was accidentally cut up for scrap when the RAN disposed of their Sea Fury fleet in 1959, also states another machine (TF925 or VW232) was given the number 'VX730' in haste to cover the loss of this combat veteran!; airframe used/stored at various locations in the next 34 years including, displayed at Museum of Applied Arts and Sciences, Sydney (1966-1974); Camden Museum of Aviation (1974-77); sold to the Australian War Memorial (1983); RAAF Fairbairn (1984); loaned to RAN Historic Flight, NSW Nowra (August 1987 along with WG630), returning to the Australian War Memorial in 1993 (some state 1991); initial study of both airframes (VX730 and WG630) held by AWM in December 1998 to determine which was best option for restoration – VX730 chosen; conservation commenced in the Treloar large technology conservation workshop in January 1999; conservation continued for 14 months; rolled-out after conservation and put on display as part of the 'Air Power in the Pacific' display within the Aircraft Hall at the Australian War Memorial from April 2000, remained there ever since.
Author's Note – It is my guess that in 1959 when the RAN was disposing of their Sea Furies the airframes were all in one place and were broken down into component parts prior to sale/scrapping, this resulted in engine, fuselage, tail, wing centre sections and outer wing panels (these latter two may have remained joined as one, as may the fuselage/engine). Then the real VX730 was partially destroyed with the wings and tail being scrapped, but the fuselage (and possible engine) remained. Realising the mistake, the wings and tail of another machine were substituted onto the fuselage of VX730 along with that machine's tail – this was 'VW232', but in fact the outer wing panels and tail were all off TF925, which had been used to repair VW232 in the early 1950s. This is probably why the fuselage cockpit area shows signs of a Korean War operational tally, while the wings and tail show signs of both serials for TF925 and VW232! This is all speculation I know, but it seems a likely scenario until such time as someone either strips VX730 completely to uncover all the paint and markings, or technology allows a non-invasive method of looking through all the paint, layer by layer!

● **WG599**, construction number ES.3617, built as an FB Mk 11; delivered to the RN in 1954; operated by the Deutsche Luftfahrt-Beratungsdienst at Bonn from 1964 to 1972 registered as D-CACY; displayed at the Luftwaffemuseum at Uetersen AB, Germany from 5th June 1973 to 1990; to Old Flying Machine Co., Duxford 26th

May 1995; registered as G-BWOL 18th March 1996; not restored, often on display statically at Duxford, civil registration cancelled 4th January 2001; exported to Australia, with Precision Aerospace Productions at Wangaratta for restoration (VH-SFY); as of 2012 aircraft was up for sale (listed by Platinum Fighter Sales); current condition/location/owner unknown.

○ **WG630**, built as an FB Mk 11; delivered to RAN and brought on charge in March 1952; struck off RAN charge 15th November 1959; to Experimental Building Station, Ryde, NSW in November 1959 (Used as wind generator to test building materials); to Australian War Memorial, Canberra, ACT, August 1986; to Naval Aviation Museum, Nowra NAS, NSW, 1987-1991; used as spares source by Australian War Memorial in the restoration of VX730 in 1998; sold to RAN in 1998; currently under restoration to airworthiness with RAN Historic Flight, Nowra.

○ **WJ232** – See IAF 326.

○ **IAF 326**, construction number 41H/643827 and 37723 as an FB Mk 10; supplied to RN (WJ232) but later returned to Hawker-Siddeley for refurbishment prior to sale abroad; delivered to Iraqi A.F. as '326', December 1953; recovered by E. Jurist & D. C. Tallichet, Orlando, FL, 1979, stored in dismantled state; registered by Ed Jurist/Vintage Aircraft International, Nyack, NY as N43SF 27th August 1979; acquired by Grant Biel, Robbie Booth & John Greenstreet/New Zealand Sea Fury Syndicate, Ardmore, 1986; registered as ZK-SFR, 11th February 1987; airfreighted to NZ by RNZAF C-130 and rebuilt at Ardmore; first flight, 12th March 1988, marked as WJ232/O and fitted with wing-folding mechanism from WG655 (ex-RNHF T Mk 20 that crashed in July 1980) in 1991; acquired by Flightwatch Services Ltd., Ardmore, 30th August 1993; acquired by Steve Hart/Unlimited Aerobatics/Hart's Flying Fighter Museum, Brisbane, Queensland, Australia, September 2000; operated by Hart's Flying Fighters Pty. Ltd., Brisbane, Queensland, Australia from 31st May 2001, registered as VH-SHF and flown in FAA colours as WJ232, '114/O'; aircraft was impounded in hangar at Archerfield by Government due to owner's tax liability 18th April 2006 – **AIRWORTHY**.

Europe

○ **VX302**, construction number ES.3613, built as a T Mk 20; to FAA as VX302 but no operational use; to Hawker-Siddeley Aircraft 1957-63 as G-9-62; moved to Federal Republic of Germany as D-CACE, and based at Bonn from 5th April 1963 to 1974; purchased by D. Arnold/Warbirds of GB and registered as G-BCOV (9th August 1974) October 1974 to 1976; arrived from Germany 11th October 1974; owned by Mike Stow, Blackbushe, September 1976 to 1985; owned by R.S. Drury, Goleta, CA, June 1985 to 1987 registered as N613RD and flown in RN markings called 'Iron Angel'; ; owned by J.C. Janes & Associates Inc., Rockford, IL, August 1987 to 1994 registered as N51SF; rebuilt with a Wright R-3350 engine and flown as racer #20 'Cottonmouth'; owned by S. Misick/Musick Aircraft Corp., Brownwood, TX, December 1994 to 1995; owned by J.Diley/Fort Wayne Air Service, Fort Wayne, IN from 4th February 1997 to 2000; owned by P.Z. Besterveld, Van Nuys, CA, 21st December 2000 to 2002 marked as RAN '103'; to Stuart Aviation Inc., Wilmington, DE, 28th January 2004 to 2006, flown as 'Conch Fury' still in RAN markings; purchased by Cavanaugh Flight Museum, Galverston, TX in 2006; badly damaged in a forced landing in August 2008; being restored to airworthy condition by Meier Motors, Bremgarten in Germany with the fuselage restoration undertaken by Sander Aeronautics in USA (returned to original T.20 configuration).

○ **WG652**, construction number ES.8509, built as a T Mk 20; to RN as WG652, served with No.759 Sqn; Station Flights at RNAS Culdrose & St. Merryn; with Hawker-Siddeley Aircraft Ltd, Langley, 1957 (G-9-57); to Federal Republic of Germany, registered as D-CAFO, at Bonn, 23rd May 1960 (remained in use until 1974); bought by Doug Arnold/Warbirds of GB Ltd, 30th July 1974 and registered as G-BCKG (arrived at Bitteswell 15th August 1974); registration cancelled 30th September 1974; owned by Dr. M.D. Schulke, Orlando, FL, September 1974 and registered as N62143; delivered to Schulke, 13th October 1974; owned by J.J. Stokes/Warbirds Of The World, San Marcos, TX, September 1974; owned by L.A. Hamilton, Santa Rosa, CA, May 1977; converted to single-seat configuration in 1979; owned by J.R. McMillan, Breckenridge, TX, 1984; owned by A.W. McDonnell, Mojave, CA, May 1984, flew as #106 (JR-106); badly damaged in hanger fire at Shafter, CA in July 1988; owned by M.E. Keenum/Aileron Inc., Forest Park, IL, 28th July 1995, rebuilt with Wright R-3350 engine; first flight in 1995 and initially flown as 'Wright Up Front' but later changed to #99 'Riff Raff'; registered to Ailerons Inc., Forest Park, IL with c/no.N62143 5th March 1997; registered to Michael E. Keenum (Trustee), Palopark, IL, 15th July 1998; to Aileron Inc., Kankakee, IL 24th June 2010; to Aircraft Guaranty Corp. (Trustee), Onalaska, TX 18th August 2011; currently based at Mnichovo Hradiste, Central Bohemia, Czech Republic – **AIRWORTHY**.

○ **WH588**, construction number 41H/636335, built as an FB Mk 11; delivered to RAN and brought on charge 7th March 1952; returned to Australia as deck cargo on HMAS Sydney, March 1952; struck off RAN charge 23rd September 1963; owned by Lord Tefgarne, Sydney-Bankstown, NSW, November 1963; owned by Fawcett Aviation, Bankstown, NSW, 1963-1969 and registered as VH-BOU by November 1965 (modified as a target tug); owned by A.J. Glass, Sydney, NSW, 1971-1972; owned by L.A. Hamilton, Santa Rosa, CA, April 1972, registered as N588; damaged in a forced landing near Santa Rosa, 5th May 1974 – repaired (flew as #16, WH588, '16/K', 'Baby Gorilla'); owned by P. Morgan/Ilmore Engineering Ltd, UK, 1997, was delivered from Santa Rosa, CA to Galveston, TX, 15th July 1997, then shipped to UK; transferred ownership to Paul J. Morgan, Sywell, UK, December 1997 to 2002, registered as G-EEMV, retained RAN markings (WH588/16/K/ Baby Gorilla); overturned on landing at Sywell, 12th May 2001 (Morgan fatally injured); owned by Dan Borgström, Karlskoga, Sweden, 2006 and undergoing restoration to airworthiness.

○ **IAF 249**, construction number 37731(ISS19), built as an FB Mk 10; delivered to Iraqi A.F. as '249' 23rd September 1949; recovered from Iraq by Ed Jurist & David C. Tallichet, Orlando, FL, 1979, stored in dismantled state; registered by Ed Jurist/Vintage Aircraft International, Nyack, NY as N54SF 27th August 1979; acquired by Rob Poynton, Australia, 1981; registration VH-HFR was reserved by Rob Poynton, Toodyay, WA but not taken up; shipped to Australia from Florida, arriving in Perth 26th January 1982; restoration initially began on his farm, but then the airframe was stored; by road from Cunderdin, WA to Perth-Jandakot, WA in 1992; registered as '249' to Rob H. Poynton/Panama Jacks Vintage Aircraft Co., Perth-Jandakot, WA, 15th September 1992, restored to airworthy at Perth-Jandakot from 1994 to 2002; airframe stored at Perth-Jandakot 2002-2010; sold to Frederic Vormezeele, Brasschat, Belgium 2010; packed at Perth-Jandakot and shipped to Antwerp in 2010; under assembly at Antwerp-Deurne February 2011; first engine run at Antwerp-Deurne 29th March 2014; purchased by K. Van den Bergh/Vintage Fighter Aircraft BVBA, Antwerp and registration OO-ISS reserved for it 6th December 2013 – **AIRWORTHY**.

Note – This construction number for this machine is often quoted as 37729, but that is incorrect, as that relates to the machine that was for a while registered as N26SF and last seen at Breckenridge in 1993.

○ **IAF 316** construction number 37733, built as a Fury ISS (FB Mk 10, TF987); delivered to Iraqi A.F. as '316', November 1949; later converted to a T Mk 20 for the Iraqi AF; recovered from Iraq by E. Jurist & D.C. Tallichet, Orlando, FL, 1979, stored in dismantled state and registered as N56SF; owned by Ed Jurist/Vintage Aircraft International, Nyack, NY, August 1979; restored as an FB Mk 11; first flight 1995; destroyed in fatal crash at Sarina International Airshow, Ontario, Canada 9th July 2001; completely rebuilt and fitted with Wright R-3350-26WD engine by Sanders Aeronautics in USA (also fitted with Sanders wing-tip smoke generators); first engine run 17th March 2009; first flight 2nd June 2009, marked as RAN WH589, '115/NW', currently owned by C. Jaguard and registered as F-AZKXI in France – **AIRWORTHY**.

Sea Fury Survivors 4
Europe / RoW

○ **IAF 324**, construction number 37734 and 41H 623271, built as an FB Mk 10; initially issued to RN but returned to Hawker-Siddeley for refurbishment prior to sale abroad; delivered to Iraqi A.F. as '324' in late 1940s/early 1950s (as a two-seater); recovered from Iraq by E. Jurist & D.C. Tallichet, Orlando, FL, 1979, stored in dismantled state; registered by Ed Jurist/Vintage Aircraft International/Nyack, NY as N58SF 27th August 1979; acquired by Weeks Air Museum, Tamiami, FL, 1980; damaged in hanger fire, at Rockford, IL, 19th July 1989; acquired by Buddy Bryan/Utilco Inc, Tifton, GA, July 1990 and registered as N1324(*), restored using many other Sea Fury components and fitted with Wright R-3350 engine 1990-1993; acquired by Neil J. McClain, Salt Lake City, UT, 5th November 1993 and restoration continued (completed in 1997); purchased by Sandy Thomson, Hamilton, Ontario, Canada, 2000; to T-G Air Power Inc, Buffalo, NY, 4th January 2001; registration C-GGAT reserved for it by T-G Air Power in 2004; struck off the American Civil Register 14th September 2005; registered to Sandy Thompson/Cinema Sixteen Inc., Hamilton, ONT as CF-GAT September 2005; registered as C-FGAT with Cinema Sixteen Inc., Hamilton, ONT 16th September 2005 until 2011; operated by Canadian Warplane Heritage, Hamilton, ONT 2005-2011; undercarriage collapsed on landing at Breckenridge, TX 20th October 2010, repaired on site during 2010/2011; sold to new owner in Czech Republic; registered as N1954H by Aircraft Guaranty Corp., TX (as trustee) 4th October 2011; shipped from USA to Czech Republic 2011-2017 – **AIRWORTHY**.
Note – there is much confusion about N1324, as it is listed for two other machines being restored by T-G Air Power (See VZ365 & ISS11 elsewhere) while the US Civil Register has N1324 as being Construction Number 41H 623282 (N1954H), but it is also reported as being mostly D-CACA!

○ **RNethN 10•43** construction number 6310, built as an FB Mk 50 by Fokker in 1951; delivered to Royal Netherlands Navy/Kon Marine in 1952; serial was later changed to 6-43; served with Nos.3 and 960 Squadrons; to Delft Technical University, Delft, Netherlands by 1956; to Aviodome Museum, Amsterdam-Schiphol, Netherlands in 1971; loaned to the Militaire Luchtvaart Museum, Kamp Van Zeist from 1993 to 2014; ownership changed to the Aviodome Museum, Lelystad airfield in 2004-2005; moved to the Nationaal Militair Museum, Soesterberg AB, Netherlands in February 2014 for display; remains on display there suspended from the roof with a Sea Hawk.

Rest of World

○ **541** built as an FB Mk 11, supplied to RN but returned to Hawker for refurbishment and sale to Cuba in 1958; currently displayed at Bahia de Cochinos (Bay of Pigs) Museum, Playa Giron, Cuba (marked as 'FAR-541').

○ **542** built as an FB Mk 11, supplied to RN but returned to Hawker for refurbishment and sale to Cuba in 1958; currently displayed at the Museo de la Revolucion (Museum of the Peoples' Revolution), Havana, Cuba (marked as 'FAR 542').

○ **ISS28** built as an FB Mk 10; delivered from Langley to Iraqi Air Force 24th March 1950 (operated as '258'); last known in 2003 used as a derelict airfield decoy at Shaibah AB, Basra, Iraq.

○ **IAF 250** construction number 37514 (ISS20), built as an FB Mk 11, first flight 10th June 1948; delivered to Iraqi A.F. as '250', November 1949; recovered from Iraq by E. Jurist & D.C. Tallichet, Orlando, FL, 1979, stored in dismantled state; owned by Ed Jurist/Vintage Aircraft International, Nyack, NY, 28th August 1979 and registered as N21SF; acquired by Michael H. Mock & Robert del Valle/International Ship Repair Service, Tampa, FL, March 1980 and restored in RAN colours as '369/DM'; acquired by Russ Francis, Wallingford, VT, July 1986; acquired by Wiley C. Sanders/Sander Truck Lines, Troy, AL, October 1988; damaged during a wheels-up landing at Troy, AL. 7th July 1990; rebuilt with P&W R-3350 engine and extra seat in cockpit at Breckenridge, TX; acquired by Stuart Davidson, Port Elizabeth, South Africa in July 2000 and shipped from USA to Port Elizabeth arriving in May 2001; the registration ZS-ORF was reserved in 2000 but never used; registered by Stuart D. Davidson, Port Elizabeth, South Africa as ZU-WOW on the 1st June 2001, retains RAN markings of '369, but tail letters now 'SD'; sold to Frederic Akary, Avignon, France September 2007; registered as F-AZXL to Frederick Akary 9th June 2008; sold to Jan Roozen, Cannes-Mandelieu – **AIRWORTHY**.

○ **IAF 243**, construction number 37534 (ISS13), built as an FB Mk 10; delivered to Iraqi A.F. as '243', 23rd September 1949; recovered from Iraq by E. Jurist & D. C. Tallichet, Orlando, FL, 1979, stored in dismantled state and registered as N28SF; owned by Ed Jurist/Vintage Aircraft International, Nyack, NY, Aug. 1979; acquired by G. Zuccoli, Darwin, NT, 1981; registered as VH-HFX, 22nd April 1985; owned by B. Andrews, Melbourne, Victoria, November 1985, flew marked in RAN colours as WH589, '115/NW'; acquired by Ray Hanna/The Old Flying Machine Company, Duxford, 25th July 1991 and registered as G-BTTA; marked in RNethN colours as '115', although it later carried IAF markings as '243; and FAA markings PR772, '107/Q' & VW238, '107/Q'; flew with pseudo Luftwaffe markings for TV movie 'Fall from Grace' in 1994 and with RAF roundels and Iraqi desert scheme in 1999; acquired by John Sayers, Johannesburg, South Africa, 2000 as ZU-SEA and shipped from UK to USA then to South Africa; registered to Flying Ducks Inc., Wilmington, DE, November 2000, registered as N103FD, then to John Sayers/Jayesse Trust/Balding Eagles Historic Association, Johannesburg-Lanseria, RSA, 12th April 2001-2002 and in RN colours as '105/R'; sold to Gus Larard in Australia in 2002 and packed and shipped to Precision Aerospace Productions hangar at Wangaratta, where it was unpacked, re-assembled, a passenger seat added behind the pilot with original instruments replacing the modern equipment fitted; as of 2014 this machine was still crated at Wangaratta waiting to be shipped to France for new owner (Jan Roozen?) – **AIRWORTHY**.
Note: Various documents quote the construction number for this machine as 37234, 37524 or 37762!

○ **UB466** built as an FB Mk 11, initially with RN but returned to Hawker and refurbished for sale to Burma; delivered to Union of Burma AF via Bahrein 12th April 1958; displayed as a wreck diorama (using parts from Spitfire UB431) at Defence Services Museum, Yangon, Burma, 1996 to present.

○ **UB471** built as an FB Mk 11, previous identifications G-9-21 and WH585, currently displayed at Service Defence Museum, Yangon, Myanmar, Burma.

○ **IAF ???** construction number N/K, built as a Fury FB Mk 10; delivered to Iraqi A.F. in 1960; in storage at Rabat, Morocco by 1978; with Amicale Jean Salis, La Ferte Alais, France; currently being restored by Pierre Dague, La Ferte Alais, France.

○ **IAF ???** construction number N/K, built as a Fury FB Mk 10; delivered to Iraqi A.F. in 1960; by 2006 this aircraft was displayed mounted on poles at Rabat, Morocco.

○ **IAF ???** construction number N/K, built as a Fury FB Mk 10; delivered to Iraqi A.F. in 1960; by 2006 this aircraft was displayed on the ground at Rabat, Morocco.

○ **IAF ???** construction number N/K, built as a Fury FB Mk 10; no other history known, found derelict as airfield decoy at Shaibah AB, Iraq in 2003; current location and condition unknown.

○ **IAF ???** construction number N/K, built as a Fury Mk 20; no other history known, found derelict as airfield decoy at Shaibah AB, Iraq in 2003 (wrecked cockpit area and inner wing sections only).

○ **IAF ???** construction number N/K, built as a Fury FB Mk 10; no other history known, displayed at the Military Museum of Iraq, Baghdad from 1970 to 1996; displayed at Al-Abied Race Circuit, Baghdad 1996 to 2012; current location/condition unknown.

○ **Fury ISS** construction number N/K; as of 1998 this was stripped for restoration at Amicale Jean Salis, La Ferte Alais, France, still there 2002; current status is unknown.

Fury & Sea Fury
Kits
Appendix I

Airfix #A02045

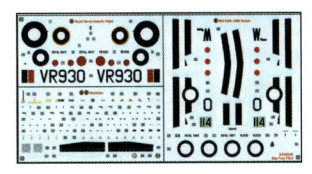

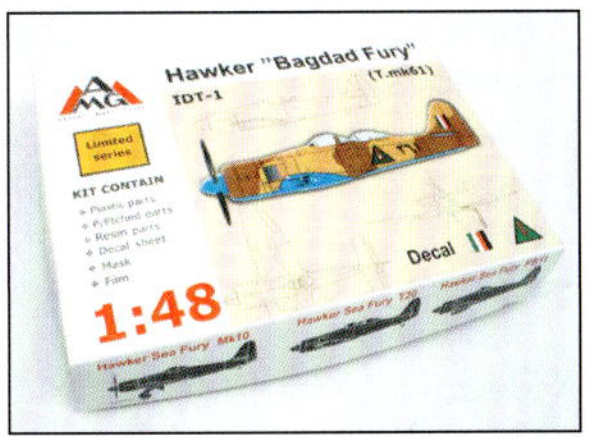

AMG #48602

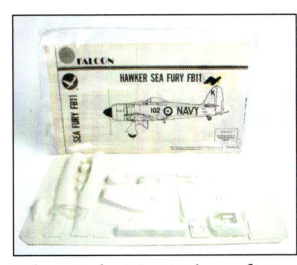

Falcon Industries 48th vac-form

Frog #F221F

AMG #48607

Hobbycraft #HC1532

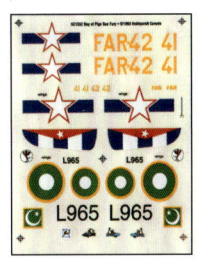

Hobbycraft #HC1583

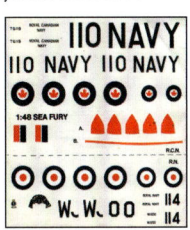

Frog #154P

Below is a list of all static scale construction kits produced to date of the Fury and Sea Fury series. This list is as comprehensive as possible, but if there are amendments or additions, please contact the author via the Valiant Wings Publishing address shown at the front of this title.

- **Airfix** (ex-PM) 1/72nd Sea Fury FB.11 #A02045 (2008)
- **Airfix** 1/48th Sea Fury FB Mk 11 #A06105 (2018)
- **Airfix** 1/48th Sea Fury FB Mk 11 'Export Edition' #A06106 – *Due 2018*
- **Aki Products**, Japan [res] 1/72nd Sea Fury FB.11 #AP.4 (2007)
- **AMG** 1/48th Hawker Sea Fury Mk X 'FAA' #48601 (2017)
- **AMG** 1/48th Hawker Sea Fury 'Baghdad Fury' (T Mk 61) #48602 (2017)
- **AMG** 1/48th Hawker Sea Fury 'Baghdad Fury' (single-seat) #48603 (2017)
- **AMG** 1/48th Hawker Sea Fury 'T.61 Pakistan Air Force' #48604 (2017)
- **AMG** 1/48th Hawker Sea Fury T Mk 20 'Royal Navy' #48606 (2017)
- **AMG** 1/48th Hawker Sea Fury T Mk 20 'Burma Air Force' #48614 (2017)
- **Bienengraber**, West Germany (ex-Frog) 1/72nd Sea Fury FB Mk 11 #F211F (1969-74)
- **Classic Plane**, Germany [ltd inj] 1/72nd Hawker Sea Fury Mk 50 Target Tug #CPI028 (1997->)
- **Combat Models**, USA [vac] 1/32nd Hawker Sea Fury #32-038
- **Elliott Models** [vac] 1/72nd Sea Fury FB Mk 11 #N/K
- **Falcon Industries** [vac] 1/48th FB Mk 11 #N/K (mid-1980s)
- **Fine Molds** – See 'Unlimited Air Models'
- **Fisher Model & Pattern**, USA [res] 1/32nd FB Mk 11 #3204 (2007)
- **Fisher Model & Pattern**, USA [res] 1/32nd Sea Fury Unlimited Racer #N/K (2009) – *Markings for 'Signal' and 'Miss Mercedes'*
- **Frog** 1/72nd Hawker Sea Fury F.10* #154P (1963-1965) – *Was in fact an FB Mk 11* – Renumbered #F154 (1965-1969), #F221F (1968-1974), proposed as a Spin-a-Prop kit #F249 in 1971 but never fully modified (a new propeller was created with the blades moulded to the spinner), back as #F154 (1974-1977)
- **Frog** 1/72nd 'The Sea Wolves!' Gift Set inc. Sea Fury, Wessex & HMS Exeter & HMS Torquay #F149 (1965-1968)
- **Hema**, The Netherlands (ex-Frog) 1/72nd Hawker Sea Fury – *Offered as part of the group kit set* (early 80s)
- **High Planes Models**, Australia [ltd inj/mtl/vac] 1/72nd Hawker Sea Fury #72033 (late 2000)
- **High Planes Models**, Australia [ltd inj/mtl/vac] 1/72nd Sea Fury Racer 'Critical Mass' #RACE 002 (1998) – *'Taco Bell' and 'Critical Mass' markings* – Modified and reissued in 2004 marked as 'Critical Mass 1999/2000' [vertical tail reduced in height]
- **High Planes Models**, Australia [ltd inj/mtl/vac] 1/72nd Sea Fury 'Furias' Unlimited Racer (2000) #Racer 006 (2000)
- **High Planes Models**, Australia [ltd inj/mtl/vac] 1/72nd Sea Fury Racer 'Miss Merced 1975' #Racer 018 (2001)
- **High Planes Models**, Australia [ltd inj/mtl/vac] 1/72nd 'Signal Sea Fury' Unlimited Racer #Racer 019 (2001)
- **High Planes Models**, Australia [ltd inj/mtl/vac] 1/72nd Sea Fury Racer 'Furias' #Racer 020 (2001)

Hobbycraft #HC1531

Kitech #O8M-3314H

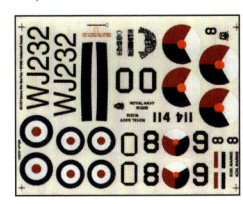

Notes
- inj – Injection Moulded Plastic
- ltd inj – Limited-run Injection Moulded Plastic
- mtl – White-metal (including Pewter)
- pe – Photo-etched metal
- res – Resin
- vac – Vacuum-formed Plastic
- (1999) – Denotes date the kit was released
- (1994->) – Date/s denote start/finish of firm's activities, the exact date of release of this kit is however unknown
- ex- – Denotes the tooling originated with another firm, the original tool maker is noted after the '-'

Fury & Sea Fury Kits
Appendix I

- **High Planes Models**, Australia [ltd inj/mtl/vac] 1/72nd Sea Fury Racer 'Blind Mans Bluff' #Race 7226 (2011)
- **High Planes Models**, Australia [ltd inj/mtl/vac] 1/48th Sea Fury Unlimited Racer 'Critical Mass' #N/K (1999)
- **High Planes Models**, Australia [ltd inj/mtl/vac] 1/48th Sea Fury Unlimited Racer 'Critical Mass' #N/K (2000)
- **High Planes Models**, Hong Kong [ltd inj/mtl/vac] 1/72nd Sea Fury Racer 'Furias Reno 1983' #N/K
- **High Planes Models**, Hong Kong [ltd inj/mtl/vac] 1/72nd Sea Fury Racer 'Signal.Miss Merced Reno 1966-1971' #N/K
- **High Planes Models**, Hong Kong [ltd inj/mtl/vac] 1/72nd Sea Fury Racer 'Furias Reno 2000' #N/K
- **High Planes Models**, Hong Kong [ltd inj/mtl/vac] 1/72nd Sea Fury Racer 'Critical Mass Reno 1997' #N/K
- **High Planes Models**s, Hong Kong [ltd inj/mtl/vac] 1/72nd Sea Fury Racer 'Critical Mass Reno 1999-2000' #N/K
- **High Planes Models**, Hong Kong [ltd inj/mtl/vac] 1/72nd Sea Fury Fb Mk 11'RN, RCN & RAN' #HPK072033
- **Hobbycraft** 1/48th Sea Fury FB Mk 11 #HC1531 (1989) – Reissued, same number, 1995
- **Hobbycraft** 1/48th Sea Fury 'Bay of Pigs' #HC1532 (1995)
- **Hobbycraft** 1/48th Sea Fury 'Korean War Sea Fury' #HC1541 (1995)
- **Hobbycraft** 1/48th Sea Fury FB.11 'RCAF' #HC1583
- **Hobbycraft** 1/48th Sea Fury 'Prop Perfection' #HC1454 (2001)
- **Hobbycraft** 1/48th Sea Fury 'Elite series' #HC9583
- **Hobbycraft** 1/32nd Sea Fury 'Cold War Warrior' #HC1716 (2008)
- **Hornet**, CZ [res] 1/144th Hawker Sea Fury FB Mk 11 #009 (2009) – Released in their 'Miniwings' series
- **ID Models** [vac] 1/32nd Hawker Sea Fury #3268 (1978-1999)
- **Kitech**, China [inj] 1/48th Hawker Sea Fury #N/K (2003->) – Same as the Hobbycraft kit/or copy?
- **Matchbox** (ex-PM) 1/72nd Sea Fury T.20 #40148 (1995)
- **Minicraft**, USA (ex-Frog) 1/72nd Hawker Sea Fury FB Mk 11 #221 (1972)
- **Miniwings** – **See Hornet**
- **Model Master** [res] 1/48th Hawker Sea Fury FB Mk 11 #N/K (1988)
- **Novo** (ex-Frog) 1/72nd Hawker Sea Fury FB Mk 11 #78103 (1980) – Although a few samples reached the shops this kit was never generally available under the Novo label as the firm was liquidated in 1980 – instructions also carry original Frog item number #F154
- **OzMods**, Australia [ltd inj] 1/144th Hawker Sea Fury #N/K – Announced for 2002, not released to date
- **Pioneer 2**, UK (ex-PM Model) 1/72nd Sea Fury FB Mk II #4002 (1992)
- **Pioneer 2**, UK (ex-PM Model) 1/72nd Sea Fury T.20 #4014 (late 1991)
- **Platz**, Japan [inj] 1/72nd Sea Fury Racer 'Critical Mass' #KR-3 (2002/3)
- **PM Model**, Turkey 1/72nd Sea Fury FB.11 #PM-211 (1992->)
- **PM Model**, Turkey 1/72nd Sea Fury T.20 #PM-212 (1992->)
- **PM Model**, Turkey 1/72nd Baghdad Fury Sea Fury T.61 #PM-214 (1992->)
- **Special Hobby**, CZ [ltd inj] 1/72nd Hawker Sea Fury FB Mk 11 #SH72073 (2004)
- **Special Hobby**, CZ [ltd inj] 1/72nd Sea Fury T.61 'Baghdad Trainer Fury' #SH72121 (2006)
- **Special Hobby**, CZ [ltd inj] 1/72nd Sea Fury T.20 #SH72124 (2011)
- **Special Hobby**, CZ [ltd inj] 1/72nd Sea Fury 'TT Mk 20 DLB' #None (2009) – Special edition in co-operation with IPMS Deutschland using SH72121 with new resin parts and decals, only 150 produced
- **Special Hobby**, CZ [ltd inj] 1/72nd Sea Fury Mk 11 'FAEC' #SH72282
- **Tashigrushka**, Russia (ex-Frog) 1/72nd Hawker Sea Fury #169-TG (early 80s) Also #N-16-TG
- **Touchdown Models**, UK [vac/res/mtl] 1/32nd Hawker Sea Fury FB Mk 11 #N/K (1991) – Subscription only and very limited edition, the series only remained in production until 1992
- **Trumpeter** 1/72nd Sea Fury FB.11 #01631 (2007)
- **Trumpeter** 1/48th Sea Fury FB.11 #02844 (2008)
- **Unlimited Air Models**, Japan [res] 1/72nd Sea Fury Racer 'Critical Mass' #FU-02 (2006)
- **Welsh Models**, UK [inj] 1/144th Hawker Sea Fury #PJW54/I – Release not confirmed

PM-211

PM-214

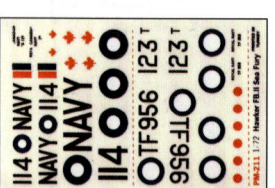

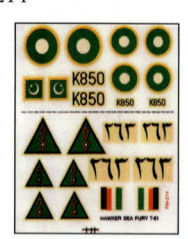

Special Hobby #SH72073

Special Hobby #SH72124

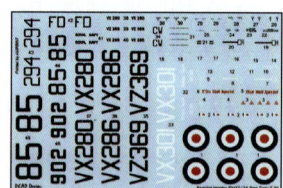

Special Hobby #SH72121

Novo #78103

Trumpeter #01631

Trumpeter #02844

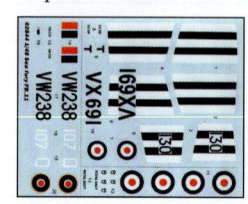

Fury & Sea Fury
Accessories
Appendix II

Below is a list of all accessories for static scale construction kits produced to date for the Fury & Sea Fury series. This list is as comprehensive as possible, but if there are amendments or additions, please contact the author via the Valiant Wings Publishing address shown at the front of this title.

1/72nd
- **Aeroclub** [mtl] Sea Fury FB Mk 11 propeller #P121 {Trumpeter}
- **Aeroclub** [mtl] Sea Fury undercarriage #V106
- **Airwaves** [pe] Sea Fury detail set #AC72-015 {PM}
- **Airwaves** [pe] Sea Fury wing fold #AC72-219 {Frog, Novo or PM}
- **Eduard** [ma] Sea Fury FB Mk 11 canopy & wheel masks [Kabuki Tape] #CX199 {Trumpeter}
- **Eduard** [pe] Hawker Sea Fury FB Mk 11 detail set [Pre-painted/SA] #72-283 {Trumpeter}
- **Eduard** [pe] Hawker Sea Fury FB Mk 11 interior detail set 'Zoom' series [pre-painted/SA] #SS283 {Trumpeter}
- **Engines & Things** [res] Bristol Centaurus engine #N/K
- **Falcon** [vac] Fleet Air Arm canopy set {inc. Sea Fury FB Mk 11} #Set 19 {PM/Pioneer}
- **Master Models** [br] Hispano Mk V cannon barrel tips and pitot tube #AM-72-121
- **Pavla Models** [res] Hawker Sea Fury FB Mk 11 cockpit set #C72062 {Trumpeter}
- **Pavla Models** [res] Hawker Sea Fury FB Mk 11 pilot's seat #S72045 {Trumpeter}
- **Pavla Models** [res] Hawker Sea Fury FB Mk 11 propeller blades & backplate #U72-85 {Trumpeter}

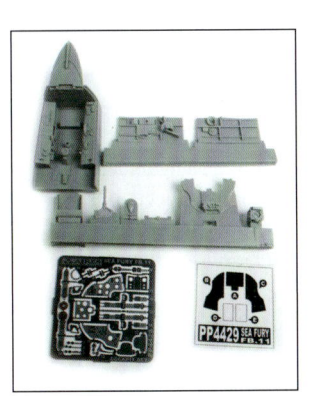

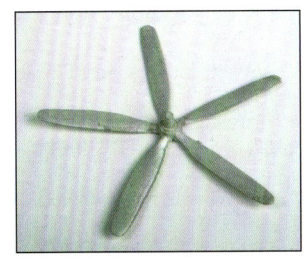

Aeroclub #P121

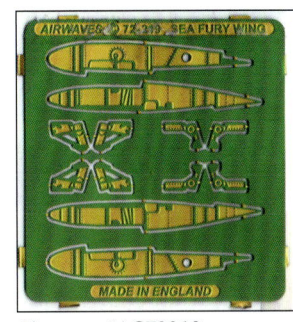

Airwaves #AC72219

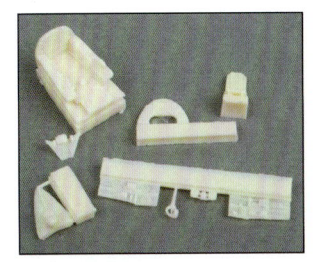

Pavla #C72062

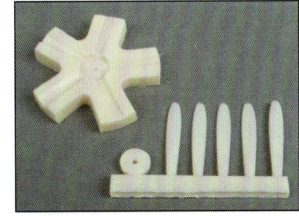

Pavla #U72-85

1/48th
- **Aeroclub** [vac] FB Mk 11 canopy #C045 {Hobbycraft/Academy}
- **Aeroclub** [mtl] Sea Fury Prop blades #V007
- **Aeroclub** [mtl] Sea Fury main legs, tailwheel, hook #V020
- **Aires** [res/pe] Sea Fury FB Mk 11 cockpit set #4429 {Trumpeter}
- **Aires** [res/pe] Sea Fury FB Mk 11 wheel bays #4452 {Trumpeter}
- **Airwaves** [pe] FB Mk 11 detail set #AEC48001 {Hobbycraft}
- **Airwaves** [pe] FB Mk 11 wing fold #AEC48103 {Hobbycraft}
- **BarracudaCast** [res] Hawker Sea Fury main and tail wheels #BC48006 {Hobbycraft or Trumpeter}
- **BarracudaCast** [res] Hawker Sea Fury 90 gallon drop tanks #BC48007 {Hobbycraft or Trumpeter}
- **Cooper Detail** [res] Sea Fury FB Mk 11 main & tail wheels #CD4850 {Trumpeter}
- **Cooper Detail** [res] Sea Fury FB Mk 11 90 gallon drop tanks #CD4851 {Trumpeter}
- **Eduard** [pe] Sea Fury FB Mk 11 'Big ED' detail and mask set #BIG4907 {Trumpeter}
- **Eduard** [pe] Sea Fury FB Mk 11 landing flaps #48-944 {Airfix}
- **Eduard** [pe] Sea Fury FB Mk 11 exterior detail set #48-946 {Airfix}
- **Eduard** [pe] Sea Fury FB Mk 11 exterior set #48-602 {Trumpeter}
- **Eduard** [pe] Sea Fury FB Mk 11 cockpit detail set #49-423 {Trumpeter}
- **Eduard** [pe] Sea Fury FB Mk 11 interior detail set #49-878 {Airfix}
- **Eduard** [ma] Sea Fury FB Mk 11 canopy & wheel masks [Kabuki Tape] #EX253 {Trumpeter}
- **Eduard** [ma] Sea Fury FB Mk 11 canopy & wheel masks [Kabuki Tape] #EX573 {Airfix}
- **Eduard** [pe] Sea Fury FB Mk 11 interior detail set 'zoom' #FE423 {Trumpeter}
- **Eduard** [pe] Sea Fury FB Mk 11 seat belts - steel 'zoom' #FE879 {Airfix}

Aires #4429

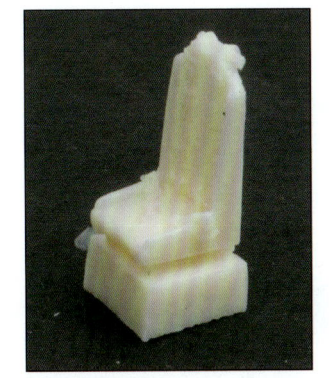

Pavla #S72045

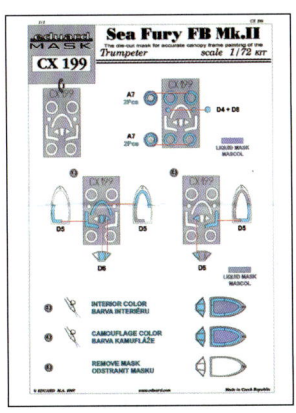

Eduard #CX199

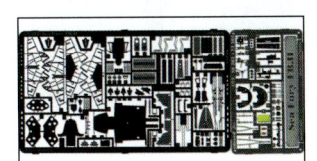

Eduard #73-283

Eduard #SS283

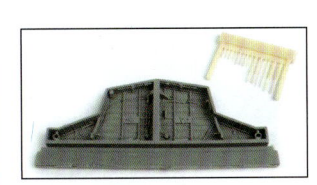

Aires #4452

Cooper Details #CD4851

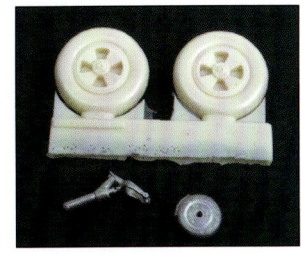

Cooper Details #CD4850

Notes
ma – Die-cut Self-adhesive Paint Masks [tape]
mtl – White-metal (including Pewter)
pe – Photo-etched Brass
res – Resin
SA – Self-adhesive
vac – Vacuum-formed Plastic
vma – Vinyl Self-adhesive Paint Masks
{Academy} – Denotes the kit for which the set is intended

Fury & Sea Fury
Accessories
Appendix II

- **Eduard** [pe] Sea Fury FB Mk 11 BIG ED detail set #BIG4907 {Trumpeter}
- **Falcon** [vac] RAF Fighters WWII canopy set {inc. Sea Fury FB Mk 11{ #Set 31 {Hobbycraft}
- **Final Connections** [res] Bristol Centaurus engine #48-003
- **Flightpath** (ex-PP Aeroparts) [res/mtl/pe] Sea Fury FB Mk 11 detail set #48051 {Hobbycraft}
- **Master Models** [br] Hispano Mk V cannon barrel tips and pitot tube #AM-48-134
- **PP Aeroparts** [res/mtl/pe] Sea Fury FB Mk 11 detail set #AK002 {Hobbycraft}
- **Scale Aircraft Conversions** [mtl] Sea Fury FB Mk 11 landing gear #48096 {Trumpeter}
- **Squadron** [vac] Sea Fury FB Mk 11 canopy #9511 {Hobbycraft}
- **True Details** [vac] Sea Fury FB Mk 11 wheels #48041 {Hobbycraft}

1/32nd

- **Fisher Model & Pattern** [res] Sea Fury FB Mk 11 cockpit detail set #AHC1 {Hobbycraft}
- **Fisher Model & Pattern** [res] Sea Fury FB Mk 11 propeller #AHC3 {Hobbycraft}
- **Fisher Model & Pattern** [res] Sea Fury FB Mk 11 wheel well detail set #AHC2 {Hobbycraft}
- **Master Models** [br] Hispano Mk V cannon barrel tips and pitot tube #AM-32-096

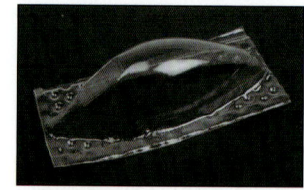

Aeroclub #C045

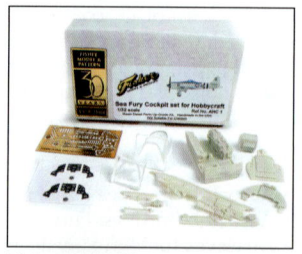

PP Aeroparts #AK002

Fisher #AHC1

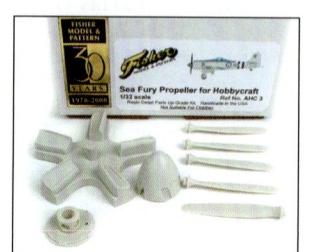

Fisher #AHC3

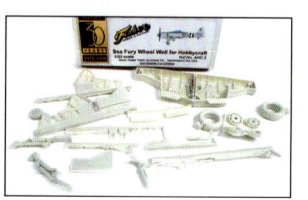

Fisher #AHC2

Four No.805 Sqn Sea Fury FB Mk 11s being refuelled by a Vacuum Oil fuel tanker at Bankstown circa 1955
(©via J. Grant)

The second Sea Fury delivered to The Netherlands 10•2 is seen here at Hawker's Langley base prior to delivery. It sports the first scheme applied to the MLD Sea Fury fleet (©Hawker Aircraft)

Fury & Sea Fury
Decals
Appendix III

There seem to have been few decal sheets produced to date for the Fury and Sea Fury, so below is a short list of those that we could find. This list is as comprehensive as possible, but there are bound to be omissions so if there are amendments or additions, please contact the author via the Valiant Wings Publishing address shown at the front of this title.

Aeromaster

1/48th #48-215 Sea Fury Collection
- WJ232, '114/O', No.802 NAS, HMS Ocean, flown by Lt Peter Carmichael, Korea, 1952
- FB.11, TF996, BC•F, No.803 Sqn, Royal Canadian Navy, 1949
- WH589, '115/NW', Royal Australian Navy
- FB.11 WG578, '140' Canadian Navy, 1953

1/48th #48-702 Sea Fury Pt.I
- WJ232, '114/O', No.802 NAS, HMS Ocean, flown by Lt Peter Carmichael, Korea, 1952
- 6•31, Royal Netherlands Navy, 1952
- '541', FAEC 541, Cuban Army Air Force, 1957

1/48th #48-703 Sea Fury Pt.II
- WX730, '109/K', No.805 Sqn, RAN, HMAS Sydney
- WH589, '115/NW', Royal Australian Navy
- 10•2, No.860 Sqn, Royal Netherlands Navy, 1950

1/48th #48-712 Sea Fury Pt.III
- FB.11 WG578, '140/R' Canadian Navy, 1953
- FB.11, VX691, '130/T', No. 807 NAS, HMS Theseus, 1951
- Mk 60, '254', Royal Iraqi Air Force

1/48th #48-713 Sea Fury Pt.IV
- FB.11, TF996, BC•F, No.803 Sqn, Royal Canadian Navy, 1949
- FB.11, VX726, '101/K', RAN, HMAS Sydney, 1952
- FB.11, UB455, Burmese Air Force, 1960

Aims

1/72nd 72D015 UK & Commonwealth in Korea
- Inc: Hawker Sea Fury FB Mk 11, VX730, '109/K', No.805 Sqn RAN, HMAS Sydney, 1951

Almark

1/48th A48-12 Hawker Sea Fury FB.11
- TF956, '123/T', Royal Navy/RN Historic Flight 1978
- WJ232, '114/O', No.802 NAS, HMS Ocean, flown by Lt Carmichael, Korea, 1952
- VX639, '136/CW', No.738 NAS

Aussie Decals

1/72nd #A72008
- VW632, '108/K', No.805 Sqn, Royal Australian Navy, 1950
- VX730, '109/K', No.805 Sqn, RAN, HMAS Sidney, Korea, 1951
- WH587, '105/K', No.805 Sqn, Royal Australian Navy
- WH588, '114/NW', No.724 Sqn, Royal Australian Navy
- WH589, '115/NW', No.724 Sqn, Royal Australian Navy
- '253/K' 'Magnificent Obsession' warbird airworthy in Australia
- '308/K', owned by Guido Zuccoli, Australia, 1993

1/48th #A48005
- VW632, '108/K', No.805 Sqn, Royal Australian Navy, 1950
- VX730, '109/K', No.805 Sqn, Royal Australian Navy, HMAS Sidney, Korea, 1951
- WH587, '105/K', No.805 Sqn, Royal Australian Navy
- WH588, '114/NW', No.724 Sqn, Royal Australian Navy
- WH589, '115/NW', No.724 Sqn, Royal Australian Navy
- '253/K' 'Magnificent Obsession' warbird airworthy in Australia
- '308/K', owned by Guido Zuccoli, Australia, 1993

Aeromaster #48-215

Aeromaster #48-702

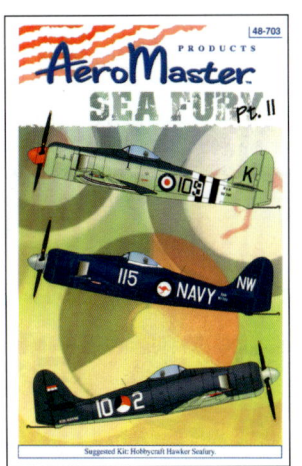

Aeromaster #48-703

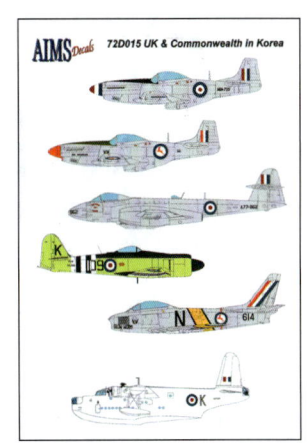

AIMS #72D015

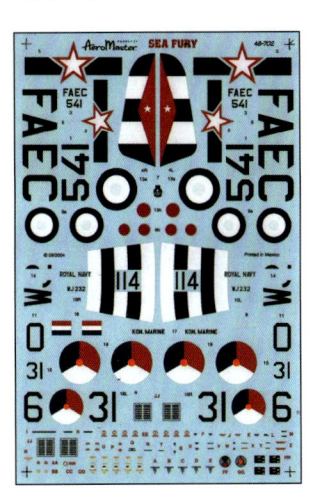

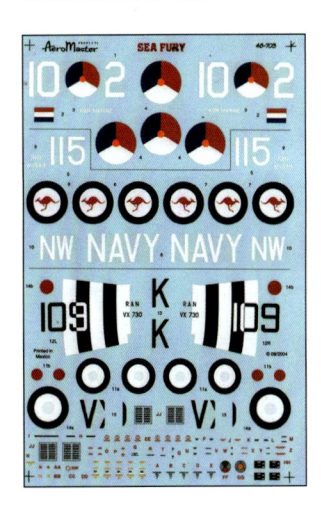

Fury & Sea Fury
Decals
Appendix III

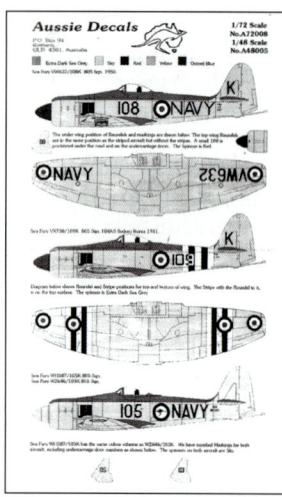

Aussie Decals #A48005

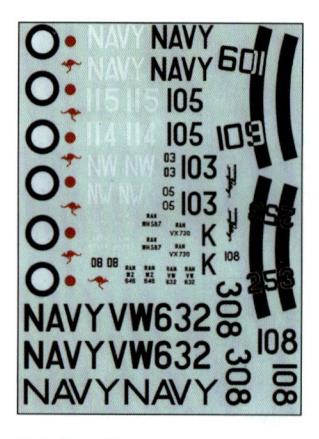

Belcher Bits #BD17

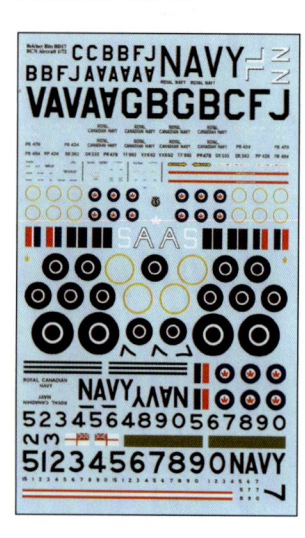

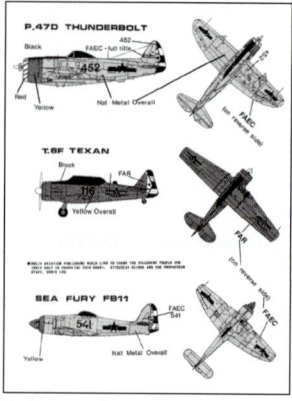

Delta Decals #72-002

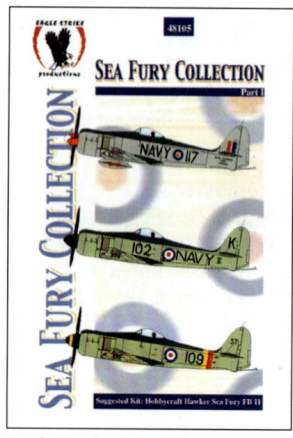

Eagle Strike #48105

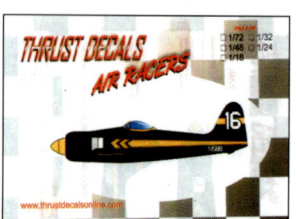

Trust Decals #041

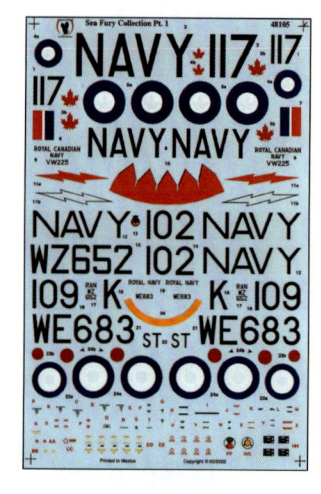

Belcher Bits
1/72nd #BD17 Seafire, Firefly, Sea Fury & Tracker Inc.
- TF993, BC•A, No.870 Sqn, Royal Canadian Navy, 1952
- VX692, AA•C, No.871 Sqn, Royal Candian Navy, 1952

Dutch Decals
1/32nd #32022 Inc.
- Sea Fury FB Mk 50, '10-7', VSQ4, Royal Neth Naval Air Services, MVK Valkenburg, 1948
- Sea Fury FB Mk 50, '10-9', VSQ4, Royal Neth Naval Air Services, MVK Valkenburg, 1948

Eagle Strike
1/48th #48105 Sea Fury Collection
- VW225, '117', No.870 Sqn, Royal Canadian Navy
- WZ652, '102', No.805 Sqn, RAN, HMAS Sydney, 1956
- WE683, '109/ST', No.1831 Sqn RNVR, RNAS Stretton

Fündekals
1/48th Hawker Sea Fury of the RCN
- FB Mk 11, TG113, No.803 Squadron, RCN, HMCS Shearwater, Nova Scotia, summer 1948
- FB Mk 11, TF999, No.803 Squadron, RCN, HMCS Shearwater, Nova Scotia, 1949
- FB Mk 11, VW571, No.803 Squadron, RCN, HMCS Shearwater, Nova Scotia, 1950
- FB Mk 11, VX695, No.883 Squadron, RCN, HMCS Shearwater, Nova Scotia, 1950-51
- FB Mk 11, WG566, VF870, RCN, HMCS Magnificent, 1952
- FB Mk 11, TG124, VF870, RCN, HMCS Magnificent, 1951
- FB Mk 11, TG114, VF870, RCN, HMCS Shearwater, Nova Scotia, 1952
- FB Mk 11, TG118, VF870, RCN, HMCS Shearwater, Nova Scotia, September 1952
- FB Mk 11, WG569, VF870, RCN, HMCS Magnificent, November 1952
- FB Mk 11, TG117, Winter Experimental Establishment, RCAF Edmonton, Alberta, 1950

Mike Grant Decals
1/72nd MG72-049 Royal Canadian Navy Sea Furies
- TG113, BC•K, No.803 Sqn, RCN, September 1948
- TG118, '108', No.870 Sqn, RCN, mid-1952
- VX695, AA•S, No.883 Sqn, RCN, 1950-51
- TG114, BC•F, No.870 Sqn, RCN
- TG122, BC•H, No.870 Sqn, RCN, 1951
- TG117, ZZ•A, Winter Experimental Establishment, 1948
- VW563, '100', No.871 Sqn, RCN

1/48th MG48-049 Royal Canadian Navy Sea Furies
- TG113, BC•K, No.803 Sqn, RCN, September 1948
- TG118, '108', No.870 Sqn, RCN, mid-1952
- VX695, AA•S, No.883 Sqn, RCN, 1950-51
- TG114, BC•F, No.870 Sqn, RCN
- TG122, BC•H, No.870 Sqn, RCN, 1951
- TG117, ZZ•A, Winter Experimental Establishment, 1948
- VW563, '100', No.871 Sqn, RCN

Print Scale
1/72nd #72-165 Hawker Sea Fury
- WJ222, '114/O', No.807 Sqn FAA, HMS Ocean, August 1952
- FB Mk X, VW236, '107/Q', No.802 Sqn FAA, HMS Vengeance, December 1948
- FB Mk 11, TG113, BC•K, No.803 Sqn RCN, 1948
- VW225, '117', No.817 Sqn RCN, June 1953
- T Mk 20, VX301 used by Ferranti for trial purposes
- FB Mk 60, serial unknown, Moroccan Air Force, Rabat-Sale, October 1976

Fury & Sea Fury
Decals
Appendix III

1/48th •48-011-1
- WJ232, '114/O', No.807 Sqn, HMS Ocean, Korea, 1952
- VW238, '107/O', No.802 Sqn, HMS Vengeance, 1948
- VW225, '117', No.817 Sqn, Royal Canadian Navy
- TG113, BC•K, No.803 Sqn, Royal Canadian Navy, 1948

1/48th #48-011-2 Hawker Sea Fury in Foreign Service
- '321', Iraqi Air Force, 1956
- UB-471, Burmese Air Force, 1959
- FAR 42, Cuban Revolutionary Air Force, 1963
- 27•6, No.860 Sqn, Royal Netherlands Navy, 1952
- L976, Pakistan Air Force, 1953

Tigerhead Decals
1/72nd #72015 Hawker Sea Fury (Overseas Operators)
- Iraqi Air Force
- Pakistan Air Force
- FAR-541
- FAEC '505'

1/72nd #72022 Hawker Sea Fury Part 2
- '221' No.7 Squadron, Iraqi Air Force, Moascar al-Raschid AB
- FAR-541
- TG117, ZZ•A, Winter Experimental Establishment, RCN, circa 1950

1/48th #48015 Hawker Sea Fury (Overseas Operators)
- Iraqi Air Force
- Pakistan Air Force
- FAR-541

Trust Decals
1/72nd #041
- N588, 'White 16'. During the 1965 air race season

Ventura
1/72nd #VA7207 RNZAF Kittyhawk, RCN Seafire and RAN Sea Furies
- WH589, No.115 Sqn, Royal Australian Navy Display Team
- WH676, '138/K', No.805 RAN, HMAS Sydney, Korea
- VX730, '109/K', No.805 RAN, HMAS Sydney, Korea

1/72nd #VA7209 Revised Seafire, Sea Fury & Harvard Inc.
- T Mk 20, VX280, '85'

Xtradecal
1/48th X48061 Sea Fury FB.11
- WZ632, '155', No.804 NAS, 1953
- WH587, '105', No.805 NAS, Royal Australian Navy, Nowra NSW, 1950
- VW225, '117', No.870 Sqn, Royal Canadian Navy, Dartmouth, 1950s
- VX688, AA•A, No.883 Sqn, RCN, Dartmouth, 1950s

1/72nd #X72074 Hawker Sea Fury FB.11
- WZ632, '155', No.804 NAS
- VX639, '136/CW', No.739 NAS, RNAS Culdrose
- TF991, '110/JR', No.805 NAS, Royal Australian Navy, RNAS Eglington, 1949
- WH589, '115/NW', No.724 NAS, Royal Australian Navy, Nowra NSW, 1961-2
- WH589, '105', No.805 NAS, Royal Australian Navy, Nowra NSW
- VX688, AA•A, No.803 Sqn, Royal Canadian Navy, Dartmouth, 1950
- VW225, '117', No.871 Sqn, RCN, Dartmouth, 1953
- 10•2, No.860 Sqn, Royal Netherlands Navy, 1947-48
- 6•31 No.860 Sqn, Royal Netherlands Navy, 1950

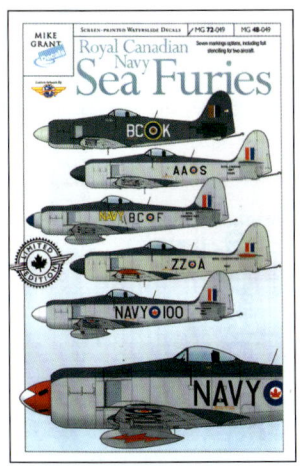

Mike Grant #MG 72-049

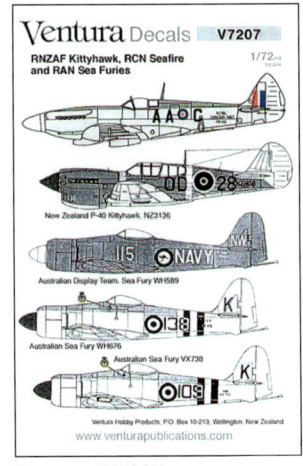

Ventura #V7207

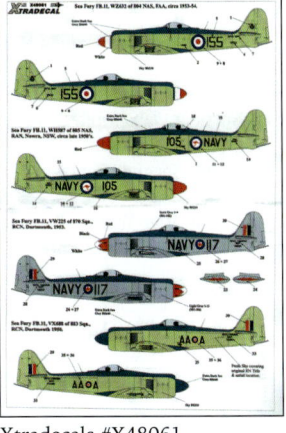

Xtradecals #X48061

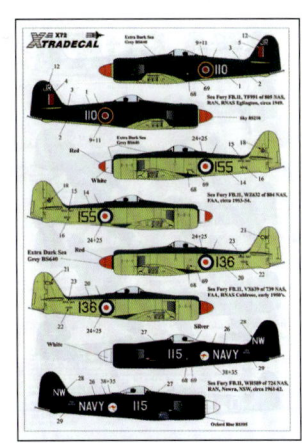

Xtradecals #X72074

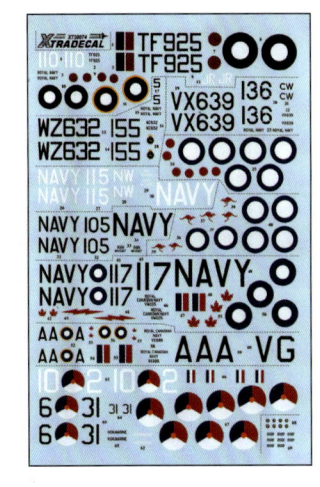

Fury & Sea Fury Bibliography
Appendix IV

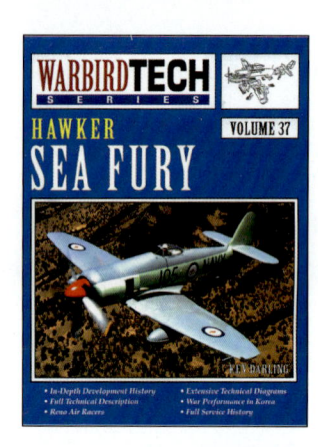

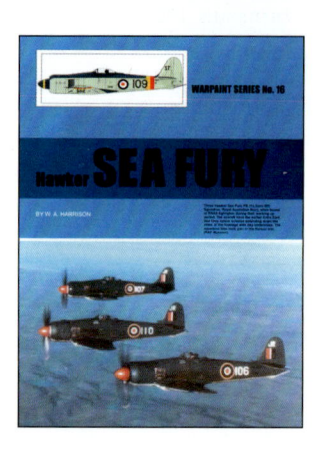

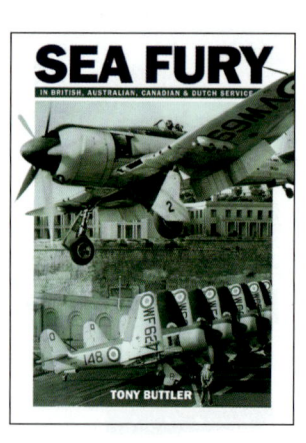

The list of Hawker Fury & Sea Fury related publications below is as comprehensive as possible, but there are bound to be omissions so if you have amendments or additions, please contact the author via the Valiant Wings Publishing address shown at the front of this title.

Official Documents
- Sea Fury FB Mk 10 – Air Publication 4018A
- Sea Fury FB Mk 11 – Air Publication 4018B
- Sea Fury T Mk 20 – Air Publication – 4018C
- Pilot's Notes Sea Fury 10 & 11 – Air Publication 4018A & B – P.N.

Publications
- Aircraft Archive – Fighters of World War Two Volume 2 [FB Mk 11 & T Mk 20] (Argus Books 1988 ISBN:0-85242-953-3)
- Air War over Korea: A Pictorial Record by L. Davis (Squadron/Signal Publications 1982 ISBN: 0-89747-137-7)
- Air War over Korea by J. Mesko (Squadron/Signal Publications 2000 ISBN: 0-89747-415-5)
- British Naval Aircraft since 1912 by O. Thetford (Putnam)
- Combat Aircraft Since 1945 by S. Wilson (Airlife, 2001)
- Fleet Air Arm Fixed Wing Aircraft since 1946 by R. Sturtivant, M. Burrow & L. Howard (Air-Britain (Historians) 2004)
- Hawker by D. Hannah, Flypast Reference Library (Key Publishing 1982 ISBN: 0-946219-01-X)
- Hawker Aircraft since 1920 by F.K. Mason (Putnam)
- Hawker Sea Fury by A. Pelletier (Quest France 1983)
- Hawker Sea Fury by F.K. Mason, Profile No. 126 (Profile Publications 1966)
- Hawker Sea Fury by Ron Mackay, In Action No.117 (Squadron/Signal Publications 1991, ISBN: 0-89747-267-5)
- Hawker Sea Fury by W.A. Harrison, Warpaint No.16 (Hall Park Books 1998 ISSN: 1363-0369) – Reprinted in 2004
- Hawker Sea Fury by N. Geldhof & L. Boerman, Dutch Profile No.2 (Dutch Profile Publications 2005)
- Hawker Sea Fury by Kevin Darling, WarBird Tech Volume 37 (Specialty Press, ISBN: 1-58007-063-9)
- RAF Fighters Part 2 by W. Green & G. Swanborough, WW2 Aircraft Fact Files (Jane's Publishing Co., Ltd 1979 ISBN: 0-354-01234-7)
- Sea Fury In British, Australian, Canadian & Dutch Service by T. Buttler (Dalrymple & Verdun Publishing 2008 ISBN: 978-1-905414-11-6)
- Sea Fury Special, Random Thoughts Vol.6 Nos.1 & 2 (IPMS/Canada)
- The Cold War Years: Flight Testing at Boscombe Down 1945-1975 by T. Mason (Hikoki Publications 2001 ISBN: 1-902109-11-2)
- The Hawker Sea Fury in the Royal Canadian Navy by L. Pettipas (1989)
- The History of the Fleet Air Arm by J.D.R. Rawlings (Ian Allan)
- The Secret Years: Flight Testing at Boscombe Down 1939-1945 by T. Mason (Hikoki Publications 1998 ISBN: 1-951899-9-5)

Periodicals & Part-works
- Aeroplane Monthly, March 1980, December 1985 & January, February, March & April 1986, August 1987 & August 1993
- Air International, February 1980
- Air Progress, May 1971
- Aviation News, Vol.7 No.8
- Flight, 31st January 1946
- Luftfahrt International No. 6 Nov-Dec 1974
- Model Airplane International Vol.1 Iss.10 (May 2006) & Vol.4 Iss.38 (September 2008)
- Model Airplane News, January & February 1963
- Random Thoughts, IPMS Canada, Sept 1972 & Jan/Feb 1973
- Replic No.191 (Jul 2007), No.192 (Aug 2007), No.228 (Aug 2010)
- Scale Aircraft Modelling Vol.7 No.4 January 1985 & Vol 11 No.6 March 1989
- Scale Models International Vol.14 No.168 October 1983 & Vol.18 No.209 March 1987
- Scale Models Warplane Special (Model & Allied Publications Ltd 1982)
- The Aeroplane, 28th January 1949

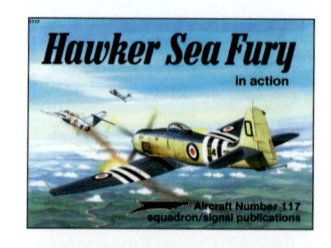

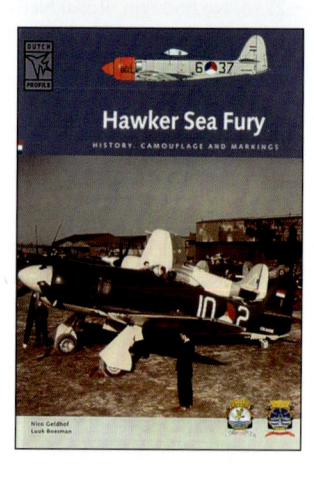

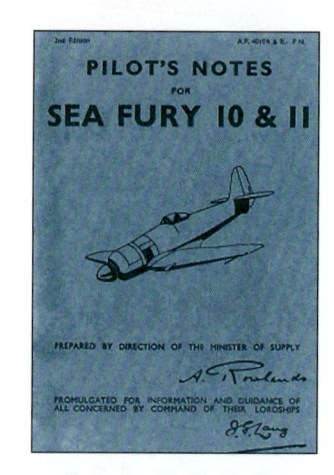